Student Learning

Student Learning

Research in Education and Cognitive Psychology

Edited by JOHN T. E. RICHARDSON,
MICHAEL W. EYSENCK AND DAVID WARREN PIPER

The Society for Research
into Higher Education
& Open University Press

Published by SRHE and
Open University Press
Open University Educational Enterprises Limited
12 Cofferidge Close
Stony Stratford
Milton Keynes MK11 1BY, England

and
242 Cherry Street, Philadelphia, PA 19106, USA

First published 1987

British Library Cataloguing in Publication Data

Student learning : research in education and
   cognitive psychology.
   1. Learning   2. Educational psychology
   I. Richardson, John T.E.   II. Eysenck, Michael W.
   III. Piper, David Warren
   370.15'23   LB1060

ISBN 0 335 15601 0

ISBN 0 335 15600 2 Pbk

Printed in Great Britain

To William and Mary Perry

Contents

Contributors

JAN J. BELIËN, Department of Educational Development and Research, Rijksuniversiteit Limburg, The Netherlands

DAVID BESWICK, Centre for the Study of Higher Education, University of Melbourne, Australia

N.C. BOREHAM, Centre for Adult and Higher Education, Department of Education, University of Manchester, UK

JOHN BOWDEN, Centre for the Study of Higher Education, University of Melbourne, Australia

SETH CHAIKLIN, Center for Children and Technology, Division of Research, Bank Street College of Education, New York, USA

RUFUS CLARKE, Department of Anatomy, University of Newcastle, Australia

YRJÖ ENGESTRÖM, Institute of Education, University of Helsinki, Finland

NOEL J. ENTWISTLE, Department of Education, University of Edinburgh, UK

MICHAEL W. EYSENCK, Department of Psychology, Birkbeck College, University of London, UK

WILLEM S. DE GRAVE, Department of Educational Development and Research, Rijksuniversiteit Limburg, The Netherlands

DAI HOUNSELL, Centre for Teaching, Learning and Assessment, University of Edinburgh, UK

MICHAEL J. A. HOWE, Department of Psychology, University of Exeter, UK

MARK KEANE, Department of Psychology, Trinity College, University of Dublin, Ireland

DIANA LAURILLARD, Institute of Educational Technology, Open University, UK

SARAH J. MANN, Centre for the Study of Management Learning, University of Lancaster, UK

ELAINE MARTIN, Faculty of Community and Social Studies, Newcastle upon Tyne Polytechnic, UK

JOS H. C. MOUST, Department of Educational Development and Research, Rijksunalia Limburg, The Netherlands

MICHAEL PROSSER, Centre for Teaching and Learning, University of Sydney, Australia

PAUL RAMSDEN, Centre for the Study of Higher Education, University of Melbourne, Australia

JOHN T. E. RICHARDSON, Department of Human Sciences, Brunel University, Uxbridge, UK

DESMOND RYAN, Edinburgh, UK

ROGER SÄLJÖ, Department of Communication Studies, University of Linköping, Sweden

HENK G. SCHMIDT, Department of Educational Development and Research, Rijksuniversiteit Limburg, The Netherlands

ROBERT J. STERNBERG, Department of Psychology, Yale University, New Haven, USA

MAURICE L. DE VOLDER, Department of Educational Development and Research, Rijksuniversiteit Limburg, The Netherlands

DAVID WARREN PIPER, Centre for Staff Development in Higher Education, University of London Institute of Education, UK

Preface

In July 1985, the Society for Research into Higher Education and the Cognitive Psychology Section of the British Psychological Society held an international conference at the University of Lancaster on 'Cognitive Processes in Student Learning'. It was a conference that brought together, possibly for the first time, a large number of prominent educational researchers and cognitive psychologists to share and elaborate upon their common interests in the patterns and mechanisms of student learning in higher education. Speakers were asked not only to evaluate and develop existing theoretical accounts of the nature of the learning process, but also to consider the practical implications of such research for teaching and learning in higher education.

This book contains a selection of the papers presented at the conference. We are most grateful for the advice and guidance of Dai Hounsell (representing the SRHE Publications Committee) in arriving at the final collection. The papers were chosen for the extent to which they made specific and timely contributions to our understanding of student learning in higher education. They include descriptions of empirical research as well as discussions of a purely conceptual or theoretical nature. They are structured around what we perceive to be the key issues in current research in this area, as they emerged at the conference.

At the end of the conference the participants were generally critical of the format that had been adopted (that is, a traditional scientific meeting based on formal presentations of prepared papers), but they were appreciative of the experience they had shared. As organizers, we were deeply grateful to the speakers for bringing their different perspectives to the event, and especially to Noel Entwistle, Dai Hounsell, Michael Howe, Diana Laurillard, Roger Säljö, Roger Schank, and Robert Sternberg. A special acknowledgement should be given to William Perry, whose remarkable four-hour presentation was for a great many participants the highlight of the proceedings.

We hope that the resulting book will be of value: to educational researchers as a source of sophisticated alternative models of the strategies and processes employed in student learning; to cognitive psychologists in providing a rich and qualitatively different body of evidence against which to evaluate theories of human learning and development; and to teachers and students alike in higher education in revealing interesting yet practical insights into the nature of the learning process and into the means for enhancing both the quality and the experience of student learning.

John T. E. Richardson
Michael W. Eysenck
David Warren Piper   *February 1986*

Part 1

Categories of Student Learning

1

Research in Education and Cognitive Psychology

John T.E. Richardson

The systematic investigation of student learning in higher education falls within the area of overlap between two different academic disciplines, but on the fringes of both. On the one hand, it develops and extends the theories and techniques of mainstream educational research to encompass the specific forms of learning which are to be found in colleges, polytechnics, and universities. On the other hand, it applies the models and procedures of cognitive psychology to a specific real-life activity involving complex intellectual feats.

For both disciplines, therefore, student learning in higher education is a topic which questions the validity and generalizability of a significant body of established research, and one which also provides the opportunity for importing new ideas from a cognate field of inquiry. On the latter point, it is sometimes suggested that the most exciting areas of theoretical development occur at the boundaries of scientific disciplines: this book provides good evidence for such a notion so far as cognitive psychology and education are concerned.

Nevertheless, readers from outside these disciplines may have some difficulty in appreciating the reasons why the investigation of student learning should have such significance for the two different fields of research. It will perhaps be useful to start, therefore, with a brief description of their characteristic features, as they bear upon the analysis of learning in higher education. It should become clear that the strengths and weaknesses of the two disciplines are essentially complementary, and the rationale of this book is the belief that our understanding of student learning would be considerably enhanced by exploiting and integrating their respective insights.

Research in Cognitive Psychology

According to Drever's (1964) *Dictionary of Psychology*, 'cognition' is 'a general term covering all the various modes of knowing – perceiving, remembering, imagining, conceiving, judging, reasoning' (p.42). The main task of 'cognitive psychology' is the scientific investigation of these faculties by means of systematic experimental procedures. As a rather crude generalization, one can say that mainstream cognitive psychology tends to be concerned with the study of the *processes* and *mechanisms* within individual human beings that are responsible for intelligent behaviour. This has a number of consequences for the sorts of theories which cognitive psychologists tend to develop, for the sorts of evidence which they collect, and for the applicability of their research in educational settings.

First of all, cognitive psychologists tend to develop theories about the processes and mechanisms that are *common* to all individuals. These theories are often based upon a considerable body of empirical evidence, and provide elaborate accounts of human intellectual capabilities. However, cognitive psychologists have typically had very little interest in studying *differences* between individuals in terms of underlying cognitive function. Moreover, they have also tended to ignore the possibility of development and change occurring *within* individuals over the course of time (Entwistle and Hounsell 1975).

The second point is that, following the established tradition within human experimental psychology, cognitive psychologists have been mainly interested in evidence of a *behavioural* nature. In other words, their models and theories of normal cognitive function are supposed to be tested against objectively verifiable performance. Moreover, it is normally expected that such evidence should be expressed in quantitative terms, so that it can be submitted to established techniques of statistical analysis. As a result, cognitive psychologists have had little interest in the experiential aspects of human cognition, which are notoriously difficult to quantify and to verify against objective behaviour.

A third and related point is that cognitive psychologists have usually been interested (at least in the first instance) in those aspects of human cognition which can be conceptualized and quantified in terms of specifiable experimental procedures. As a result, a familiar criticism of cognitive psychology is that it is fairly difficult to relate to practical, everyday situations. During the last ten years or so cognitive psychologists have made considerable attempts to deal with the problem of the poor 'ecological validity' of their methods and models. Unfortunately, it is still quite unclear whether the latter can be applied successfully to the specific situation of learning in higher education. Certainly, the procedures involved in the vast majority of laboratory experiments on human memory bear little resemblance to the learning tasks which confront students in courses of study in higher education (Richardson 1983a).

Finally, the experimental model has itself had unfortunate consequences for the way in which cognitive psychologists tend to think about learning and the scope for enhancing the efficacy of learning. In a psychological experiment, the researcher is expected to control the parameters of the testing situation and hence to manipulate the cognitive processes which experimental subjects are able to employ. Those few cognitive psychologists who have written about the relevance of experimental research to higher education have similarly emphasized the manipulation and control of the learning process on the part of the teacher, and have virtually ignored the possibility of individual differences and qualitative change among the students themselves (Bjork 1979; Broadbent 1975).

Research in Education

Making what is once again a somewhat crude generalization, one can say that educational research on human learning tends to be concerned with the differences that exist between individual learners in terms of the styles and strategies which they adopt, and with the implications of these differences for the educational system. It follows that research in education provides something in the way of a contrast with cognitive psychology on each of the points mentioned above.

First, the main focus of educational research on human learning (especially in so far as it concerns higher education) is precisely upon differences among individual learners. We are offered what are often extremely sophisticated taxonomies of different possible approaches to learning. Unfortunately, the obverse of this is that educational research has tended to be fairly weak in providing well articulated general theories of human learning. The taxonomies are descriptive rather than explanatory when it comes to the nature of learning itself, and we are told very little about what actually happens when a student learns. It is almost as though the student were a 'black box', subject to observable inputs and producing observable outputs, but having internal states and processes that must remain entirely mysterious.

Second, learning is a human capacity, and like all capacities is manifested directly in terms of observable behaviour. It is thus not surprising that educational research, like that of experimental psychology, is based primarily upon the systematic study of behaviour. Moreover, both disciplines were radically influenced by the American behaviourist movement, which disparaged the use of introspective accounts of cognitive processes. Nevertheless, an interest in styles and strategies of learning inevitably directs one's attention towards how the learner perceives and construes the learning situation. At least in recent years, therefore, educational research has been rather more sensitive to the experimental aspects of cognition, and more open to using personal, subjective evidence in its accounts of learning.

On the third point, it would of course be entirely reasonable to expect that research in the general field of education would find fairly direct and obvious application in the investigation of learning in *higher* education. But there has been a tendency for educational theorists to generalize their research in a somewhat uncritical manner. It has been too commonly assumed that the accepted accounts of learning in secondary education are equally valid when applied to higher education. The tendency has become much less pronounced in recent years with the development of research into higher education as a specific and separate area of theorizing and investigation. Indeed, some writers have argued explicitly that the investigation of student learning in higher education stands in need of its own concepts, methods, and procedures (Knowles 1978; Marton and Svensson 1979; Perry 1981).

Although there is a significant experimental tradition within educational research, the vast majority of work on learning in higher education is of a more naturalistic, descriptive nature and typically involves situations that are much more recognizable as being at least analogous to conventional academic learning. This means that there is normally much less difficulty in relating the results of such research to real-life educational settings for institutional policy and for teaching practice (though the task of identifying their specific implications may be far from straightforward). Moreover, because there is much less emphasis upon the notions of experimental manipulation and control, educational researchers tend to give more attention to the sorts of learning activities that are initiated by the learners themselves.

Nevertheless, the paucity of experimental investigations might go some way to explain why much educational research seems to be lacking in explanatory content. To take a simple analogy, one gains little idea of the constituent structure of rocks by observing them in their natural setting; rather, one has to subject them to the artificial and atypical environment of the laboratory. Similarly, it could be argued that formal experiments conducted under laboratory conditions (and thus quite possibly lacking many of the substantive features of real-life situations) are necessary to achieve any real understanding of the nature of the learning process. More generally, while the findings of educational research on student learning may well have major implications for both policy and practice in higher education, they still need to be interpreted within clearly articulated theories of the underlying cognitive processes.

Research into Higher Education

Against this background, it will be useful to consider the three main groups of researchers whose ideas have predominantly determined the nature of thinking about student learning in higher education during the last ten or fifteen years.

The first of these is associated with William Perry (1970), who proposed that students proceed through a sequence of developmental stages, moving from a simplistic or absolute stance on the fundamental nature of knowledge to a complex, pluralistic perspective:

> Position 1: The student sees the world in polar terms of we-right-good vs. other-wrong-bad. Right Answers for everything exist in the Absolute, known to Authority whose role is to mediate (teach) them. Knowledge and goodness are perceived as quantitative accretions of discrete rightnesses to be collected by hard work and obedience (paradigm: a spelling test).
>
> Position 2: The student perceives diversity of opinion, and uncertainty, and accounts for them as unwarranted confusion in poorly qualified Authorities or as mere exercises set by Authority 'so we can learn to find The Answer for ourselves'.
>
> Position 3: The student accepts diversity and uncertainty as legitimate but still *temporary* in areas where Authority 'hasn't found The Answer yet'. He supposes Authority grades him in these areas on 'good expression' but remains puzzled as to standards.
>
> Position 4: (a) The student perceives legitimate uncertainty (and therefore diversity of opinion) to be extensive and raises it to the status of an unstructured epistemological realm of its own in which 'anyone has a right to his own opinion', a realm which he sets over against

Authority's realm where right-wrong still prevails, or (b) the student discovers qualitative contextual reasoning as a special case of 'what They want' within Authority's realm.

Position 5: The student perceives all knowledge and values (including Authority's) as contextual and relativistic and subordinates dualistic right-wrong functions to the status of a special case, in context.

Position 6: The student apprehends the necessity of orienting himself in a relativistic world through some form of personal Commitment (as distinct from unquestioned or unconsidered commitment to simple belief in certainty).

Position 7: The student makes an initial Commitment in some area.

Position 8: The student experiences the implications of Commitment, and explores the subjective and stylistic issues of responsibility.

Position 9: The student experiences the affirmation of identity among multiple responsibilities and realizes Commitment as an ongoing, unfolding activity through which he expresses his life style. (pp. 9-10)

Perry summarized his scheme in the form of three main divisions: the period of dualism (Positions 1, 2, and 3); the period of relativism (Positions 4,5, and 6); and the period of commitment in relativism (Positions 7, 8, and 9). His work is based upon the analysis of unstructured interviews with students throughout their courses of study, and explicitly rejects both experimental and psychometric methods as being inappropriate for research into 'developmental phenomenology' (Perry 1981; for further discussion, see Richardson 1983b; Wilson 1981, pp.61-76).

The second line of research is that which was carried out by Gordon Pask. He claimed that there were two general categories of learning strategy which could be identified in cognitive tasks: 'Serialists learn, remember and recapitulate a body of information in terms of string-like cognitive structures where items are related by simple data links.... Holists, on the other hand, learn, remember and recapitulate as a whole' (Pask and Scott 1972, p.218). Subsequently, Pask (1976) suggested that holism and serialism were 'extreme manifestations of more fundamental processes':

Some students are disposed to act 'like holists' (*comprehension* learners) and others 'like serialists' (*operation* learners), with more or less success. There are also students able to act in either way, depending upon the subject matter, and if they excel in both pursuits, we refer to those students as *versatile*. It is these distinctions which can, more appropriately, be referred to as learning style. (p.133)

The distinctions are supposed to reflect qualitative differences among students in terms of their approaches to academic learning, differences that are to be identified from introspective reports concerning their learning processes. Further discussion of Pask's work is to be found in Holloway (1978), Richardson (1983a) and Wilson (1981, pp.119-134).

The third line of research is that of Ference Marton and his colleagues, which can be summarized as follows. First, the outcome of learning is to be studied by a careful, qualitative analysis of recall protocols which pays special attention to the content both of the original material to be learned and of each individual learner's attempt to recount or explain that material. Typically, attempts by students to recall a particular text appear to reflect around four qualitatively distinct, but hierarchically related levels of comprehension (Marton and Säljö 1976).

Secondly, the process of learning is to be studied by means of introspective, semi-structured interviews, either on a particular learning experience or on a student's general approach to academic study. This allows the description of qualitative differences in the nature of the learning process. Marton and Säljö (1976) distinguished two different approaches to learning:

> In the case of *surface-level processing* the student directs his attention towards learning the text itself (*the sign*), ie he has a 'reproductive' conception of learning which means that he is more or less forced to keep to a rote-learning strategy. In the case of *deep-level processing*, on the other hand, the student is directed towards the intentional content of the learning material (*what is signified*), ie he is directed towards comprehending what the author wants to say about, for instance, a certain scientific problem or principle. (pp.7-8)

Lennart Svensson (1977), another member of the same research group, arrived at a similar distinction between 'atomistic' and 'holistic' cognitive approaches:

> The *atomistic* approach was indicated when students described their activities as involving: focusing on specific comparisons, focusing on the parts of the text in sequence (rather than on the more important parts), memorising details and direct information indicating a lack of orientation towards the message as a whole. In contrast the *holistic* approach was characterised by students' attempts: to understand the overall meaning of the passage, to search for the author's intention, to relate the message to a wider context and/or to identify the main parts of the author's argument and supporting facts. (p.238)

Thirdly, the relationship between process and outcome is to be compared across individual subjects. In this context, the analysis of the content of learning and of the nature of student learning in terms of commensurable descriptive categories allows the expression of qualitative differences among different learners (Marton and Säljö 1976; Svensson 1977). Such differences are claimed to go beyond the nature of any particular instance of learning, and to apply to an individual student's very conception of what learning actually is, what is involved in being a learner, and how to respond to the demands of different learning situations (Säljö 1979).

The three groups of researchers have in common a concern with the qualitative and subjective aspects of student learning (see Marton, Hounsell, and Entwistle 1984). There is a general agreement that any serious analysis of the cognitive processes involved in student learning will demand a critical evaluation of the traditional conceptions of research to be found in mainstream education and cognitive psychology, and an exploration of alternative research methodologies (Elton and Laurillard 1979; Marton and Svensson 1979; Perry 1981). With that thought in mind, we will now review the contents of this book.

Categories of Student Learning

The remaining chapters in Part 1 originate within the traditional framework of educational research, as outlined above. All three offer extremely sophisticated taxonomies of approaches to learning in higher education, but in addition depict the outcome of the learning process as the result of a complex interrelationship between learning, teaching, and assessment.

Noel Entwistle considers the characteristics both of the learner and of the situation in which learning takes place, and his analysis has given rise to the idea of a computer simulation that he is currently developing with Phil Odor. Michael Prosser explores the interactive relationship between the learning strategies and the cognitive structures which individual students bring to the learning task. Finally, David Newble and Rufus Clarke consider the effects of variations in the curriculum and in the conduct of teaching and assessment upon students' approaches to learning.

Thinking and Problem Solving

In contrast, the chapters in Part 2 are concerned with some classical questions relating to human cognition, and originate within the traditional framework of cognitive psychology. However, each addresses issues that are not normally posed within that framework, issues of individual differences, experiential aspects of cognition, and the relevance of experimental research to academic settings.

First, Robert Sternberg applies an information-processing account of human intelligence to the analysis of individual differences in cognitive tasks. It is striking to note the parallels between the three aspects of intelligence which he identifies ('internal', 'experiential', and 'external') and the three general approaches to learning suggested by Noel Entwistle ('surface', 'deep', and 'strategic'). Mark Keane provides a cognitive theory of the construction and apprehension of analogies which falls within the same general class of componential models considered by Sternberg. Seth Chaiklin explicitly criticizes conventional cognitive accounts of problem solving; he directs our attention towards how students construe the problems with which they are presented, and therefore how they choose and evaluate possible lines of reasoning. Finally, and from a similar perspective, Nick Boreham considers the employment of abstract, high-level knowledge structures in problem solving.

Learning as Construing

Part 3 takes up the question of how individual learners actually conceive of the learning process. Roger Säljö considers variations and development in how students conceive of themselves in this respect, and explores the hidden assumptions behind the manner in which researchers, teachers, or students construe the nature and possibility of research into higher education. Both he and Dai Hounsell advocate a 'semi-anthropological', 'experiential', or 'phenomenographic' approach to research on student learning, and Dai Hounsell uses the specific task of essay writing to consider the general manner in which we conduct academic discourse. Finally, Yrjö Engeström considers the process whereby students construct their own individual perceptions of the discipline into which they are being initiated.

Improving Student Learning

The penultimate part explores the practical implications of research in education and cognitive psychology for the improvement of student learning. Michael Howe starts from a similar theoretical position to that adopted by Robert Sternberg, according to which human intelligence is based upon a modular organization of multi-purpose intellectual abilities; he offers some general guidelines for the practical business of teaching, with an emphasis upon the needs of individual students. Jos Moust and his colleagues provide a careful experimental analysis of the effectiveness of small group discussion, and suggest that it may well be of benefit even to the notorious student who fails to contribute to the proceedings.

Finally, the two chapters by Elaine Martin, Paul Ramsden, David Beswick, and John Bowden provide a timely evaluation of the currently fashionable interventions designed to enhance students' learning skills; they emphasize that such interventions need to be carefully linked both to the *content* of what is to be learned and to the *context* in which it is to be learned, but even then they are sceptical as to whether any significant development in the student's conception of learning or in the techniques of learning can actually be achieved in this manner.

Assumptions, Objectives, Applications

The dominant theme of Part 5, the final section of this book, is that current research on student learning in higher education poses more questions than it answers, not only about the nature of student learning but also about the nature of teaching and the nature of research itself. Taking up some of the issues raised by Roger Säljö, the concluding chapters argue that we need to consider not merely how students construe their learning but also how both researchers and teachers construe research on how students learn.

Sarah Mann introduces the theme by asking researchers to consider the conceptions of human nature and of human learning which are expressed through their own research practices, and the role and status which they ascribe to themselves in their investigations of student learning. In contrast, Desmond Ryan is concerned with the survival of the academic profession in a cold climate, and specifically with the question why academics show little enthusiasm for research into student learning, preferring instead to remain atheoretical and intuitive in their conceptions of how students learn. He argues that the 'hard-nosed phenomenography' which has been so successful in identifying the realities of student learning should now be addressed to all the counterpart activities of academic teaching.

The last two chapters take up some of the points made earlier in this opening chapter and try to identify the particular characteristics of research in education and cognitive psychology which have tended to inhibit a proper convergence of the two disciplines upon the nature of student learning. Diana Laurillard emphasizes the different explanatory goals and contexts of application of the two disciplines: she suggests that psychological theories explain why people do learn, in terms of their immediate and elaborated access to the 'natural' environment of the real world, while educational theories explain why people fail to learn, in terms of their tenuous and restricted access to the 'unnatural' world of academic ideas. She concludes that research into higher education should need cognitive psychology if it is to reconstruct academic environments so that they 'afford' learning.

In their closing commentary, Michael Eysenck and David Warren Piper tend to agree with Diana Laurillard's general conclusion, but they dispute many of the premises on which it is based. They emphasize the *un*naturalness of much laboratory research in cognitive psychology, and the molecular level at which learning tends to be studied in the experimental literature, but they suggest that cognitive psychology does contain important insights of potential relevance to both educational theory and practice. They suggest that the distinctive feature of most academic environments is not their 'unnaturalness' but their emphasis upon non-interactive forms of communication, such as books, examinations, and lectures. They also pursue some of Desmond Ryan's ideas in suggesting that academics have at present little reason to call upon the few insights that educational theory has so far yielded, and that in general educational systems serve a great many purposes, of which the effective teaching and learning of course content is only a small part. Their general conclusion is that improving student learning is but a small part of the task of improving the educational system.

In considering the wider implications of his scheme concerning the cognitive and ethical development of college students, William Perry (1981) suggested that a somewhat analogous process of growth was evident in the attempts of educational researchers and theorists to understand the intellectual development of college students. To be sure, it may occur to the reader that the deliberate confrontation of educational research and cognitive psychology which was the rationale of this book seems to have generated just those sorts of discrepancies and inconsistencies amongst the different authority figures which according to Perry's scheme should promote intellectual development. My co-editors and I hope that it may therefore stimulate to some small degree a qualitatively deeper approach in contemporary ways of thinking about the cognitive processes underlying student learning.

References

Bjork, R.A. (1979) Information-processing analysis of college teaching *Educational Psychologist* 14, 15-23

Broadbent, D.E. (1975) Cognitive psychology and education *British Journal of Educational Psychology* 45, 162-176

Drever, J. (1964) *A Dictionary of Psychology* (Revised edition) Harmondsworth: Penguin Books

Elton, L.R.B. and Laurillard, D. (1979) Trends in research on student learning *Studies in Higher Education* 4, 87-102

Entwistle, N.J. and Hounsell, D. (1975) How students learn: Implications for teaching in higher education. In Entwistle, N.J. and Hounsell, D. (Eds) *How Students Learn* 175-199. Lancaster : Institute for Research and Development in Post-Compulsory Education, University of Lancester

Holloway, C. (1978) Learning and instruction. In *Cognitive Psychology, Block 4: Learning and Problem Solving (Part 1)* Milton Keynes : Open University Press

Knowles, M. (1978) *The Adult Learner: A Neglected Species* (2nd edition) Houston, Texas : Gulf Publishing

Marton, F., Hounsell, D. and Entwistle, N.J. (1984) *The Experience of Learning* Edinburgh : Scottish Academic Press

Marton, F. and Säljö, R. (1976) On qualitative differences in learning: I. Outcome and process *British Journal of Educational Psychology* 46, 4-11

Marton, F. and Svensson, L. (1979) Conceptions of research in student learning *Higher Education* 8, 471-486

Pask, G. (1976) Styles and strategies of learning *British Journal of Educational Psychology* 46, 128-148

Pask, G. and Scott, B.C.E. (1972) Learning strategies and individual competence *International Journal of Man-Machine Studies* 4, 217-253

Perry, W.G., Jr. (1970)*Forms of Intellectual and Ethical Development in the College Years: A Scheme* New York : Holt, Rinehart and Winston

Perry, W.G., Jr. (1981) Cognitive and ethical growth: The making of meaning. In Chickering, A.W. and Associates *The Modern American College: Responding to the New Realities of Diverse Students and a Changing Society* 76-116. San Francisco : Jossey-Bass

Richardson, J.T.E. (1983a) Student learning in higher education *Educational Psychology* 3, 305-331

Richardson, J.T.E. (1983b) The intellectual development of students in higher education *Psychology Teaching* August, 6-13

Säljö, R. (1979) Learning about learning *Higher Education* 8, 443-451

Svensson, L. (1977) On qualitative differences in learning: III. Study skill and learning *British Journal of Educational Psychology* 47, 233-243

Wilson, J.D. (1981) *Student Learning in Higher Education* London : Croom Helm

2

A Model of the Teaching-Learning Process

Noel Entwistle

This paper summarizes the results of two five-year research programmes carried out at Lancaster between 1968 and 1981, together with more recent work at Edinburgh and elsewhere. The findings are used to develop a heuristic model of the teaching-learning process that emphasizes a three-way interaction between student, teacher, and institutional procedures. The model appears at the end of the paper as an integrative summary of the research findings discussed in the previous sections, but could be used as an 'advance organizer' if required (Fig. 2, p.23). It is intended to allow both researchers and practitioners to consider students' cognitive processes and study strategies in relation to the strong environmental pressures created by both teaching and assessment structures and procedures.

A distinctive feature of the research programmes at Lancaster was an emphasis on the interplay between qualitative and quantitative methodologies. Initially interviews ran separately and parallel to psychometric analyses, but increasingly the two sources of data were brought together to build a more complete and convincing description of student learning and its individual and contextual influences.

Identifying the Characteristics of Successful Students

The first research programme at Lancaster sought to identify the factors associated with academic success and failure at university. It explored the contributions made by school attainment, verbal and mathematical aptitudes, personality, motivation, work habits and study methods, using multivariate analyses of psychometric measures and examination grades. Factor analysis produced a dimension describing the distinction between arts and science in terms mainly of verbal and numerical abilities. The other two main factors combined aspects of motivation, work habits, study methods, and personality in the way indicated in Figure 1 (Entwistle and Wilson 1977, p.120).

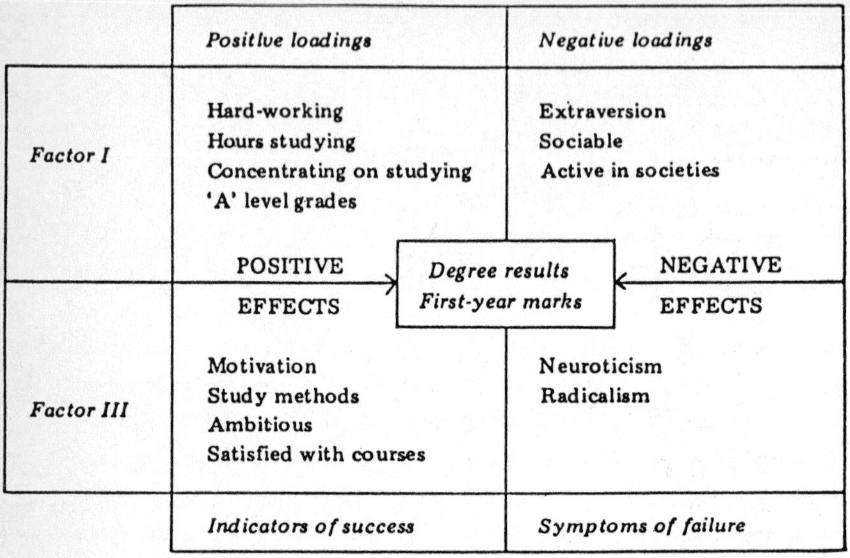

	Positive loadings	Negative loadings
Factor I	Hard-working Hours studying Concentrating on studying 'A' level grades	Extraversion Sociable Active in societies
	POSITIVE EFFECTS →	*Degree results* *First-year marks*	← NEGATIVE EFFECTS
Factor III	Motivation Study methods Ambitious Satisfied with courses	Neuroticism Radicalism
	Indicators of success	*Symptoms of failure*

Figure 1

The correlational and factor analyses produced, however, an unrealistic stereotype of the academically successful student as a paragon of all virtues, combining intellectual ability with high motivation and conscientiousness. Cluster analysis markedly changed the picture by identifying three distinctive patterns of characteristics, all of which were, to some extent, associated with academic success (Table 1).

One group of students did seem rather like the correlational stereotype, but also appeared to be competitive, unemotional, and asocial. The second group was almost the antithesis of the first, being afflicted by self-doubt and fear of failure, yet these students reached above average levels of attainment apparently through working long hours and sticking very closely to the course requirements (syllabus-bound). The final group also worked very hard, but along more idiosyncratic lines; in addition, they showed aesthetic interests and radical attitudes.

Interviews were used to explore the reality of the patterns of characteristics suggested by the cluster analysis (Thompson 1981). The distinction between the competitive, self-confident students characterized by 'hope for success' and the apprehensive but very hard-working students dominated by 'fear of failure' was very clear in the interviews, particularly in comments on examinations:

Variable	Cluster		
	1	2	3
	(n=47)	(n=52)	(n=52)
Degree result	10	1	4
'A' level grades	9		
Verbal aptitude			4
Maths aptitude	8	−7	−5
Academic achievement motivation	8	−9	6
Organized study methods	6		5
Hours worked independently		5	9
Syllabus-freedom		−6	6
Extraversion		−6	
Neuroticism	−6	8	
Self-confidence		−5	
Aesthetic interest	−4		7
Radicalism	−5		6

Note This table is based on three of the most distinctive cluster groupings reported in Entwistle and Wilson (1977, Tables 10.1 and C9). An average score would be represented by 0, while a full standard deviation above or below the mean would be shown by 10, values below 4 are, however, omitted. The selection from the 29 defining variables shown here represents the main defining features of these clusters.

Table 1
Standard mean scores of three distinctive student groups.

I *enjoy* doing exams. I can do them. In fact, I find the atmosphere rather stimulating. It gingers me up, keeps me on my toes. I think it's just the *challenge*. You've got three or four hours and, somehow or other, you've got to get out of yourself enough of a pattern to knit something up, to knit three or four different garments out of a tangle of wool. It's fun sometimes – when you know enough to *make* it fun. (p.511)

For myself, just the thought of Finals now makes me feel weak! I don't know what I'll be like in June. But they're like a big 'Thing' hanging over you all the time you're here. People tell you, you can't fail, but you know it's at the back of your mind. (p.514)

The students' own comments not only confirmed the existence of distinctive types of student, they also suggested that the differing groups not only tackled their academic work in contrasting ways, but had very different perceptions of the university as an academic and social environment (Entwistle et al. 1974).

Neither the interviews nor the psychometric analyses, however, examined the strategies or processes used in carrying out everyday academic work. This became the main focus of the second five-year programme.

Approaches to Learning in Natural Settings

The stimulus for the change in direction in the second programme was the work of Ference Marton's research group in Gothenburg, and of Gordon Pask and his colleagues then in Richmond. The challenge was, on the one hand, to operationalize and investigate the correlates of deep and surface approaches to learning (Marton 1975; Marton and Säljö 1984) and operation and comprehension learning styles (Pask 1976), and, on the other hand, to explore the contextual influences on students' approaches to learning experienced in their everyday academic tasks. The quantitative and qualitive research ran in parallel, but with important interchanges of ideas, findings, and perspectives.

The main findings have been discussed in detail elsewhere (Entwistle 1981; Ramsden 1981; Ramsden and Entwistle 1981; Entwistle and Ramsden 1983). Here it is sufficient to point up some of the main conclusions. Marton's original idea of approach to learning was derived from a specific naturalistic experiment on students reading an academic text. The Lancaster work extended the definitions of the deep and surface categories so that they could be applied to students' work on a range of academic tasks in their natural setting (Table 2). It was shown that the meaning of a deep approach, in particular, had to some extent to be interpreted anew within each separate academic discipline, given the varying academic demands made on students.

DEEP APPROACH
- Intention to understand
- Vigorous interaction with content
- Relate new ideas to previous knowledge   } Comprehension
- Relate concepts to everyday experience   } learning
- Relate evidence to conclusions   } Operation
- Examine the logic of the argument   } learning

SURFACE APPROACH
- Intention to complete task requirements
- Memorize information needed for assessments
- Failure to distinguish principles from examples
- Treat task as an external imposition
- Focus on discrete elements without integration
- Unreflectiveness about purpose or strategies

STRATEGIC APPROACH
- Intention to obtain highest possible grades
- Organize time and distribute effort to greatest effect
- Ensure conditions and materials for studying appropriate
- Use previous exam papers to predict questions
- Be alert to cues about marking schemes

Table 2
Defining features of approaches to learning.

The research also suggested that the intention to adopt a deep approach did not necessarily imply that it would be carried out fully or effectively. Particularly in science, a deep approach depended on having adequate prior knowledge of the topic involved, and there was some indication that it might also depend on general intellectual ability. Students also appeared to differ stylistically in the ways they set about seeking understanding. Some seemed to rely more on previous knowledge and concentrated on the most relevant facts and details (operation learning), while others appeared to be more concerned with personalizing their understanding by relating ideas to other topic areas and everyday experience (comprehension learning) (Entwistle et al. 1979). This distinction brings together approach and style, suggesting that a fully deep approach demands the interplay of comprehension and operation learning in building up understanding (Entwistle 1981). Preference for starting a deep approach using serialist or holist strategies, combined with a lack of time, would leave students exhibiting the incomplete learning characterized by Pask's pathologies of improvidence or globetrotting. They would present facts without an overview (improvidence), or a personal conclusion without evidence (globetrotting).

Besides broadening Marton's two main categories, the research at Lancaster introduced a third – a strategic approach. The deep approach is defined by an intention to seek *understanding*. The surface approach depends on *reproducing* what is thought to be required by the lecturer. The strategic approach involves the intention to *maximize grades*, partly by systematic management of time, effort, and study conditions, but also by manipulation of the assessment system to the student's own advantage (Table 2). This idea can be traced to the interview study of Miller and Parlett (1974). They discovered that students varied markedly in their perceptions of assessment procedures. Some considered the lecturers' judgements of their achievements to be largely objective: they could influence the outcome only by their own knowledge and effort. Others had an entirely different view. They believed that being alert to cues about marking systems or likely examination questions and creating a good impression on the lecturer would all affect their grading. As one student summed it up:

> I play the examination game. The examiners play it, so we play it too....
> The technique involves knowing what's going to be in the exam and how
> it's going to be marked. You can acquire these techniques from sitting in a
> lecturer's class, getting ideas from his point of view, the form of his notes,
> and the books he has written – and this is separate to picking up the actual
> work content. (Miller and Parlett 1974)

Another main finding from this research was that approaches to studying could be viewed as relatively consistent individual differences. The original Gothenburg work tended to stress that an approach was a reaction to particular content in a specific context, but even in that research indications of consistency were found (Svensson 1977). Interviews showed that, across a range of everyday academic tasks and across departments, most students showed enough consistency to justify describing approaches characteristic of individuals. Thus the operationalization of approaches to learning and learning styles through inventories measuring general strategies and processes could be justified. The Approaches to Studying Inventory was designed to assess sixteen sub-scales across four domains and has typically produced four main factors, which, most recently, have been described as deep, surface, organized, and strategic (Entwistle and Waterston 1985). The deep and surface factors contain among their component items the defining features derived from the qualitative research, while the other two factors are less stable and represent the two main facets of the strategic approach. It is interesting to note the close parallel between the defining features of the three main approaches to learning and the distinctive clusters identified in the previous research programme.

Measures of Ability, Cognitive Style & Personality	Approaches and Styles							
	DA	RI	UE	CL	OL	SA	OS	ST
		(n=60)						
Verbal reasoning			23	23			28	−15
Abstract generalizing					−28		16	−25
Field independence	−21	−15	23					
Reflectiveness	20	15			23			
Verbal fluency	24	17		16				
Thinking introversion	48	36		52	−23	−31		
Social extraversion	18							28
Anxiety		19	16	22		17	22	
Impulse expression	28	21		30			23	15
Aestheticism	31	33		43	−30			
Autonomy		26		17	−16	−22		
Complexity	27	27	−16	33	−37	−18		
Theoretical outlook	38	28	15	39		−26		20
Practical outlook			20	−23	39	38		37

Note Decimal points and correlations less than 0.15 are omitted. Correlations > 0.22 are significant at 5% level

Key to Approaches and Styles

DA	=	Deep Approach	OL	=	Operation Learning
RI	=	Relating Ideas	SA	=	Surface Approach
UE	=	Use of Evidence	OS	=	Organized Studying
CL	=	Comprehension Learning	ST	=	Strategic Approach

Tests Used Moray House Advanced Verbal Reasoning; Peel's Abstract Generalizing; Witkin's Embedded Figures; Kogan's Matching Familiar Figures; Guilford's Uses of Objects; the Omnibus Personality Inventory

Table 3
Correlates of approaches and styles.

Following up the description of approaches and styles as individual differences, the Lancaster research sought to relate them to psychometric measures of ability, cognitive style, and personality. A summary of the main correlations is shown in Table 3 (from Entwistle and Ramsden 1983, p.235). The conclusion drawn from correlational and factor analyses was that there are underlying personality traits associated with the tendency to prefer comprehension or operation styles of learning. It also appears that a deep (approach) involves, at least to some extent, the abilities to think both logically and flexibly, combined with the personality characteristics described as sceptical intellectual autonomy. (Entwistle and Ramsden 1983, p.79)

However, perhaps the most consistent and salient correlates of approaches to learning are the contrasting forms of motivation. The earlier study had already pointed up how 'hope for success' and 'fear of failure' were associated with different ways of studying. In the second study the inventory also provided measures of intrinsic motivation (learning out of interest) and extrinsic motivation (learning geared to vocational qualifications). Table 4 shows the clear pattern of correlations between approaches to learning and contrasting forms of motivation. Interest facilitates both deep and organized approaches, while fear of failure and narrowly vocational concerns are associated with a surface approach. Hope for success is related to a deep approach, but is more strongly associated with being strategic in studying.

Contrasting Forms of Motivation	Approaches to Learning			
	Deep	Surface	Organized	Strategic
	(n=2208)			
Intrinsic	47	−20	22	17
Fear of failure	−05	32	−22	03
Extrinsic	−12	28	−07	16
Hope for success	19	11	10	25

Note Decimal points omitted. Correlations > 0.06 ar significant at the 5% level

Table 4
Relationships between approaches to learning and contrasting forms of motivation.

Interactions with other individual difference variables have been reported by other researchers. Biggs (in press) has shown that below a certain level of ability the factor structure describing the three main approaches disintegrates. He has also shown a similar effect among students who make external attributions of the cause of their academic performance. Prosser (see Chapter 3) has found an interaction between indices of conceptual organization and approaches to learning. Without a fairly high level of initial conceptual organization, a deep approach has little or no effect on the outcome of learning. Conversely, better organized study methods influence the outcome only for students with initially low levels of conceptual organization.

Interactions have also been found with personality and study methods. Stable introverts have better organized study methods, work longer hours, and obtain better degree results on average than unstable extroverts. But extraverts who do have well-organized study methods and high achievement motivation are just as successful academically as the stable introverts (Entwistle and Wilson 1977, Tables C6 and 6.8).

The Influence of Learning Context

The findings presented so far have been selected for their evidence of stability in approaches to learning and styles of learning and to show their correlations with conventional measures of individual differences. But the evidence can also be interpreted to demonstrate the marked effects of the academic context on the quality of student learning. Constructs describing student learning strategies and processes have a certain stability over time and across situations, but they also have more important variability. Diana Laurillard (1984) has stressed how students' problem solving depends just as much on the perceived assessment demands as on the content of the task itself. Fransson (1977) demonstrated in a naturalistic experiment that students who perceived a learning situation as threatening tended to adopt surface approaches. But it is important to bear in mind that it is the *perception* of the situation, rather than the context itself, which influences study behaviour. As Magnusson (1984) argues:

> When we describe ... current behaviour in terms of person-situation interaction processes ..., the problem is not how the person and the situation as two separate parts ... interact. It is, rather, ... how individuals by their perceptions, thoughts, and feelings function in relation to the environment ... (including their) conceptions of the external world ... (and their) self-conceptions. (p.231)

The perception of a learning context can thus be viewed as another individual difference, but if the perceptions of a whole class are averaged they provide a useful indicator of learning context, and one which can be relatively easily investigated.

Teaching Characteristics

In the second Lancaster programme the effects of lecturers and of departmental characteristics were investigated both qualitatively and quantitatively in terms of the students' perceptions. Ramsden (1981) showed from a Course Perceptions Questionnaire that students in departments perceived as having 'good teaching' also showed higher scores on deep approach to learning and intrinsic motivation. His 'good teaching' scale indicates 'how much help is given with study problems, (and) how competent and well-prepared staff are perceived to be' (Ramsden 1984, p.160). The interviews with students enabled this description of good teaching to be expanded. The most frequent descriptions included comments on a lecturer's ability to pitch material at the right level, maintain an appropriate pace, and provide a clear stucture. Relationships with students were also seen as important, particularly in anticipating potential difficulties, and in providing sympathetic and ready feedback on submitted work or help with problems. But above all students remarked on the effects of striking explanations and enthusiam. For example, a physics student recounted how:

Recently we were doing Fourier analysis, and the lecturer mentioned in passing that it was something which they used when they transmit moon pictures back to earth ... Another example he quoted was about how when you bang a drum you get lots of different sounds rather than when you, say, play a violin you just get one note ... he said, if you look at this you can see why – and he was right, you can see why; it did make sense. (Ramsden 1984, p.145)

Striking illustrations seem to help students both to share the lecturer's enthusiasm and, in some instances, to shift both conceptions and approaches to learning. A detailed study of students' experiences of lectures led Hodgson (1984) to conclude:

Vicarious experience of relevance can ... be viewed as providing a bridge between extrinsic experience or a surface approach and intrinsic experience or a deep approach ... to go beyond the outward demands of a learning situation and make connections between the content of the lecture and their understanding of the world around them. (p.102)

Lecturers thus play a crucial role, not just in transmitting information efficiently, but also in transforming ways of learning which would otherwise prevent personal understanding being attempted, let alone being achieved.

What students perceive as 'good teaching' will, of course, depend on their own conceptions of learning. Students who are intent on seeking understanding will appreciate lecturers who emphasize personal meaning:

Firstly I learn to broaden my outlook: secondly to eventually be able to do work I consider meaningful.... (So, for me) good teaching links up with things you come across yourself in your own life: you see the meaning of what you're engaged in. (van Rossum and Deijkers, in press p.14)

But students who have a reproductive conception of learning are more likely to emphasize the importance of efficient transfer of knowledge in simple language, without major intellectual demands. Van Rossum and Deijkers have, in fact, demonstrated a 91 per cent agreement between categories describing reproductive versus meaningful conceptions and directedness versus openness in preferred teaching methods.

Departmental Characteristics

The influence of other aspects of departmental organization can be seen most strongly in assessment procedures. Ramsden (1984) quotes a psychology student on the effects of repeated short-answer tests:

I hate to say it, but what you've got to do is to have a list of the 'facts', you write down ten important points and memorize those, then you'll do all right in the test ... if you can give a bit of factual information – so and so did that, and concluded that – for two sides of writing, then you'll get a good mark. (p.144)

And that student did – consistently. He finished with what seems to have been a strategic 'First' (Class Honours degree) by being prepared to sacrifice his preference for a deep approach to the perceived demands of the assessment procedures.

In another study Newble and Jaeger (1983) found that a change from an oral clinical examination to ward ratings resulted in students spending less time on the wards and more time in the library. Apparently they soon realized that the ward ratings were almost without exception above the pass level, while the theory examinations produced failures. Reintroducing a clinical examination, though in a more reliable form, shifted the balance of the students' activities back to the wards, as the lecturers required.

Academic staff also do not seem to realize how their comments on the assessment procedures affect their students' learning strategies. For example, Gibbs (1981) describes how he was invited to advise a psychology department on improving students' reading skills. The students were simply not covering the necessary background reading. Interviews with the students indicated that they were spending most of their time writing up practical reports, which they had been led to believe would substantially affect their end-of-year marks. Correcting this misapprehension immediately provided reading time. Students marshalled limited time to produce the greatest perceived 'pay-off'.

Related to assessment procedures is the quality of feedback on a student's learning – particularly the comments they receive from lecturers on their coursework (Hounsell 1984). And the quality of the feedback may well, in turn, be a function of the lecturers' interest in teaching and empathy with the students.

The type of learning materials provided may also influence approaches to learning. It is generally assumed that detailed handouts, or supplementary audio-tutorials, will help students to learn. In quantitive terms this may well be true; students may obtain higher marks. But detailed handouts may also foster dependency: students come to believe that all that is required of them is to reproduce the information in the form provided by the lecturer. They then cease to think things out for themselves and they adopt passive surface approaches to learning (Mahmoud 1985). The side-effects of support become clear only from a detailed qualitative study. In principle, of course, handouts could encourage a deep approach by encouraging wider reading, and by stimulating a critical and questioning attitude in learning, but these effects have not been demonstrated empirically within the present studies.

The importance of independence in learning, however, has been demonstrated. One of Ramsden's questionnaire scales described 'freedom in learning' or 'how much discretion students have over the choice of content and methods of studying' (Ramsden 1984, p.160). Lack of such freedom, particularly if combined with a heavy workload, appeared to induce a surface approach to studying. Its existence seems to influence learning partly through a self-matching of learning style to selected task, and partly through the increased level of interest.

Some institutions are now providing study skills courses, workshops or clinics. Traditional courses have emphasized the rudimentary skills of note-taking, speed reading, and so on – and have had little lasting influence. But where such courses try to help students reflect on purposes and strategies – to become more aware or metacognitive about their approaches to learning – and where the students themselves are well motivated there is evidence that academic performance markedly improves (Biggs, in press). Training procedures emphasizing the elaborative skills essential to a deep approach have also been shown to influence the quality of learning (Weinstein and Underwood 1985). But we should not expect such courses to have a uniform effect. Students who already have effective, but idio-syncratic, study methods will not find such training helpful (Selmes 1985), indeed it may be dysfunctional (Snow and Lohman 1984).

A Heuristic Model

The above research findings have provided the components for a heuristic model of the teaching-learning process. The precise relationships between these components cannot yet be articulated, let alone the complex interactions which may be anticipated. But the model (Figure 2) does provide both a summary of the research findings and a starting point for lecturers wishing to consider the likely effects of their teaching or departmental policies on students with differing sets of characteristics.

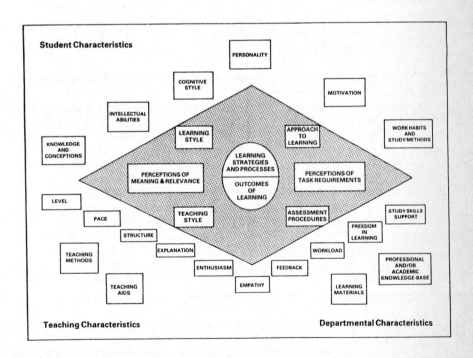

Figure 2
A heuristic model of the teaching-learning process in higher education.

The central core of the model contains the learning strategies and processes which lead to the wide variations in learning outcomes which are observed. Approaches to learning and styles of learning are concepts closely related to those strategies, processes, and outcomes. Learning style can be considered to be an expression, in the academic context, of more fundamental, and relatively stable, components of cognitive style and personality. Approaches to learning draw attention to the crucial importance of intentionality in academic learning – and so also to the influence of personal motives for studying not just on the degree of effort exerted but also on the direction and quality of that effort (Taylor 1983). Previous knowledge and conceptualization clearly have an important influence on approaches and outcomes, as do the balance and level of intellectual abilities, but the research described here, by its methodology and focus, has de-emphasized this whole area.

The model is intended to suggest that the effects of teaching characteristics are filtered through the students' idiosyncratic perceptions of meaning and relevence, while perceived task requirements embody many of the features of departmental characteristics. These perceptions are, of course, a product of the student's previous academic and personal history, as well as of intellectual and personality chacteristics.

Teaching style is chosen as the variable most directly influencing learning style. The implication is that the differing teaching methods and teaching aids can be utilized in widely different ways, reflecting the preferences of the individual teacher. But the term 'teaching style' is perhaps misleading as the components identified in the model are in fact competencies – aspects of what the students perceived as 'good teaching'.

The positions of the components of the model have been chosen to indicate the closeness of relationships between concepts, and this is true both within and, to some extent, between the three domains. In particular, the components of teaching style have been chosen to parallel elements of student chacteristics, with implied connections between knowledge/conceptions and level, intellectual abilities and pace, and cognitive style and both structure and explanation. Connections can also be seen between personality and both enthusiasm and empathy. Of course, these particular connections canot yet be supported with detailed empirical evidence, but research is beginning to explore the personal reactions of students to the styles and to the implied ideological frameworks of the teaching they experience (van Rossum and Deijkers, in press; Meyer, personal communication).

Finally, one controlling feature of the way teaching and assessment is organized within a department is the nature of the discipline or of the profession. Clearly there are strong traditions about the ways in which the content of the curriculum is chosen and presented to students, about the types of task set, and about what evidence of competence is required. Schwab (1964) has, in fact, sought to classify disciplines in terms of four components – their subject matter, the competencies they require, their methods and modes of inquiry, and the kinds of knowledge or other outcomes at which they aim. Major differences of this kind make it extremely hazardous to present general principles for teaching and learning in higher education. However, one advantage of our heuristic model is that it encourages and guides specific analyses of the three-way interactions between students, teachers, and departments within each distinctive discipline.

Conclusions

The model can at the moment be little more than a heuristic device guiding the direction of future research and helping departments to consider the likely effects of change in their procedures. The repercussive effects of innovation cannot be predicted in detail from the model, but when linked to the developing techniques of 'soft' systems thinking (Checkland 1981) it could lead to considerably more control over both desirable and undesirable outcomes. By a careful analysis of educational aims in relation to the interactions implied by the model, it ought to be possible to obtain more effective quality control of the product – student learning.

Although examination of the total set of interactions suggested by the model is currently a formidable, even an impossible, task, it might be possible to investigate the interactions of a sub-set of the components by implementing them within an interactive computer simulation. Such an attempt is currently under way at Edinburgh (Entwistle and Odor 1984). It will produce a simulation based as closely as possible on real-life experiences of learning and studying, but will also have important implications for the development of computer-assisted learning materials in general. The program will be partly expert system and partly game, with the interactions designed to help students explore in a variety of problem situations the likely outcomes of different strategies in relation to the system's representation of their current psychological and academic status. This representation would be based partly on test scores and partly on the developing history of the individual's interaction with the model.

This simulation will make formidable demands on the programmer. It is currently envisaged to contain a 'theatre' in which the simulations of events and consequences are played out, a set of inferential rules derived from the models determining the predicted outcome of each simulation episode, a guided pattern-seeker deducing current psychological and academic status from the accumulating history of episodes and outcomes, and a further set of inferential rules controlling the guidance provided to the student (Odor et al. 1985).

Students will be able to move backwards and forwards between game and reality, being able to utilize, on demand, materials to encourage developments in their own levels of metacognition and study skills. They will also be able to call for explanations of the predictions made from the model, which will require yet another set of rule-based responses within the system. The students will have the opportunity to comment on the adequacy of the model both in general terms and in relation to specific incidents or predicted outcomes. As a result, the model itself will develop towards a more effective mapping of 'recognizable reality'.

It would seem appropriate that this type of model, and this simulation, should be taken seriously by cognitive psychologists. If cognitive theory is to have more useful educational applications, the gulf which currently exists between theories of cognitive processes (based on controlled decontextualized experiments and simplified learning materials) and the complex interactions of learning in academic contexts will have to be bridged.

On the basis of the research reported here, there would be considerable advantage in extending work in cognitive psychology to naturalistic experiments which systematically mimic aspects of real-life learning situations. It would be necessary, in parallel, to explore the salient characteristics of varying learning contexts and identify their most influential components.

Magnusson (1984) has stressed the importance of developing a taxonomy of situations to parallel the impressive catalogue of constructs describing individual differences. Cronbach (1982) has indicated the value to be gained from recording qualitative differences in, for example, the implementation of educational innovations. In the research reported here it has been repeatedly demonstrated how quantitative analysis and decontextualized experiment may, on their own, seriously misrepresent the processes and outcomes of student learning. Qualitative analysis, on its own, may lack precision and conviction.

By a careful combination of qualitative and quantitative investigations of learning settings, backed up by systematic naturalistic experiments and computer simulations, it should be possible to develop a range of models representing the interactions between individual characteristics, cognitive processes, and environmental influences. Just as Cronbach (1957) launched studies of aptitude-treatment interactions with a demand to capitalize on the methodologies and conceptualizations of both experimental and survey research, so now the path forward should surely lead to the interplay between the established quantitative approaches and the developing qualitative methods developed in examining student learning in its natural context (Marton et al. 1984).

Acknowledgements

The research summarized here has been supported by grants from the Joseph Rowntree Memorial Trust, the SSRC, and the Leverhulme Trust. I am grateful for the comments of Phil Odor and Michael Prosser.

References

Biggs, J.B. (in press) The role of metalearning in study processes *British Journal of Educational Psychology*

Checkland, P. (1981) *Systems Thinking, Systems Practice* London: Wiley

Cronbach, L.J. (1957) The two disciplines of scientific psychology *American Journal of Psychology* 12, 671-684

Cronbach, L.J. (1982) *Designing Evaluations of Educational and Social Programs* San Francisco: Jossey Bass

Entwistle, N.J. (1981) *Styles of Learning and Teaching* London: Wiley

Entwistle, N.J., Hanley, M., and Ratcliffe, G. (1979) Approaches to learning and levels of understanding *British Educational Research Journal* 5, 99-114

Entwistle, N.J. and Odor, P. (1984) *The Interactive Simulation of Student Learning* Project proposal, Department of Education, University of Edinburgh

Entwistle, N.J. and Ramsden, P. (1983) *Understanding Student Learning* London: Croom Helm

Entwistle, N.J., Thompson, J.B., and Wilson, J.D. (1974) Motivation and study habits *Higher Education* 3, 379-396

Entwistle, N.J., and Waterston, S. (1985) *Approaches to Studying and Levels of Processing: A Comparison of inventories derived from contrasting theoretical bases* Paper presented to the International Conference on Cognitive Processes in Student Learning, Lancaster University, July 18-21, 1985

Entwistle, N.J. and Wilson, J.D. (1977) *Degrees of Excellence: The academic achievement game* London: Hodder and Stoughton

Fransson, A. (1977) On qualitative differences in learning. IV – Effects of motivation and test anxiety on process and outcome *British Journal of Educational Psychology* 47, 244-257

Gibbs, G. (1981) *Teaching Students to Learn* Milton Keynes: Open University Press

Hodgson, V. (1984) Learning from lectures. In Marton et al. (1984)

Hounsell, D.J. (1984) Learning and essay-writing. In Marton et al. (1984)

Laurillard, D. (1984) Learning from problem-solving. In Marton et al. (1984)

Magnusson, D. (1984) The situation in an interactional paradigm of personality research. In V. Sarris and A. Parducci (Eds) *Perspectives in Psychological Experimentation: Towards the Year 2000* Hillsdale, NJ: Erlbaum

Mahmoud, M.M. (1985) *Contrasting Perceptions of an Innovation in Teaching Civil Engineering* Unpublished PhD thesis, University of Edinburgh (in preparation)

Marton, F. (1975) What does it take to learn? In N.J. Entwistle (Ed.) *Strategies for Research and Development in Higher Education* Amsterdam: Swets and Zeitlinger

Marton, F., Hounsell, D.J. and Entwistle, N.J. (1984) (Eds) *The Experience of Learning* Edinburgh: Scottish Academic Press

Marton, F. and Säljö, R. (1976) On qualitative differences in learning. II – Outcome as a function of the learner's conception of the task *British Journal of Educational Psychology* 46, 115-127

Marton, F. and Säljö, R. (1984) Approaches to learning. In Marton et al. (1984)

Miller, C.M. and Parlett, M.R. (1974) *Up to the Mark: A study of the examination game* Guildford:SRHE

Newble, D.I. and Jaeger, K. (1983) The effect of assessments and examinations on the learning of medical students *Medical Education* 17, 25-31

Odor, J.P., Entwistle, N.J. and Anderson, C.D.B. (1985) *The Interactive Simulation of Student Learning. Working Paper 1: The development of a systems representation of the simulation* Department of Education, University of Edinburgh

Pask, G. (1976) Styles and strategies of learning *British Journal of Educational Psychology* 46, 128-148

Ramsden, P. (1981) *A Study of the Relationship between Student Learning and its Academic Context* Unpublished PhD thesis, University of Lancaster

Ramsden, D and Entwistle, N.J. (1981) Effects of academic departments on students' approaches to studying *British Journal of Educational Psychology* 51, 368-383

Schwab, J.J. (1964) Structure of the disciplines: meanings and significances. In A.W. Ford and L. Pugno (Eds) *The Structure of Knowledge and the Curriculum* Chicago: Rand McNally

Selmes, I.P. (1985) *Approaches to Learning at Secondary School: Their identification and facilitation* Unpublished PhD thesis, University of Edinburgh

Snow, R.E. and Lohman, D.F. (1984) Toward a theory of cognitive aptitude for learning from instruction *Journal of Educational Psychology* 76, 347-376

Svensson, L. (1977) On qualitative differences in learning. III – Study skill and learning *British Journal of Educational Psychology* 47, 233-243

Taylor, E. (1983) *Orientations to Study: A longitudinal interview investigation of students on two human studies degree courses at Surrey University* Unpublished PhD thesis, University of Surrey

Thompson, J.B. (1981) *An Interview Study of the Attitudes, Expectations, and Motivations of 124 Students in Higher Education* Unpublished PhD thesis, University of Lancaster

van Rossum, E.J. and Deijkers, R. (in press) Students' conceptions of learning and good teaching *Higher Education*

Weinstein, C.E. and Underwood, V.L. (1985) Learning strategies: the 'how' of learning. In J.W. Segal, et al. (Eds) *Thinking and Learning Skills* Hillsdale, NJ: Erlbaum

3

The Effects of Cognitive Structure and Learning Strategy on Student Achievement

Michael Prosser

The origins of this paper lie in an evaluation of the use of television lectures in a first-year physics course for life science students at the University of Sydney. The aim of that review was to provide the School of Physics with information and views that would assist in determining its immediate and future policy on the use of TV lectures. The review (1) described the production process and subsequent use of TV lectures, (2) collected the views of the various participants on the development and use of TV lectures, (3) described the use of TV lectures in the context of the course in general. Details of the review can be found in Prosser (1984). Because of time restraints it was not possible to study in any detail students' understanding of the subject matter. That is the focus of the present study.

Recently there has been a shift by a number of science education researchers from an empiricist view of the nature of knowledge (ie one in which knowledge is built up from objective impartial sensory data and in which incorrect knowledge is replaced and new knowledge added) to a constructivist view (ie one in which the concepts that are held by an individual play an important role in what is perceived by the senses and in which new knowledge is integrated into the existing knowledge structure with subsequent changes to that structure) (Strike and Posner, in press; Novak and Gowin 1984). This change in epistemology has led to theories of learning which focus on meaningful learning, ie the incorporation of new concepts to old concepts in terms of the proposition which connects them. Meaningful learning is contrasted to rote learning in which new concepts are arbitrarily added to cognitive structure.

A number of theories are presently being used to explain meaningful learning, among them Ausubel's learning theory (Ausubel, Novak and Hanesian 1978) and conceptual change theory (Posner 1983). These theories distinguish between two types of changes in cognitive structure – assimilation and accommodation. Assimilation is when new concepts are integrated into the existing conceptual framework with only small changes to the structure (for example, the integration of the concept of momentum into an existing Newtonian conceptual structure). On the other hand, accommodation occurs when the concept structure in an area of knowledge needs to be substantially revised (for example in going from a pre-Newtonian or impetus view of motion to a Newtonian view).

How in practice might such assimilation and accommodation be accomplished? Some researchers are focusing on teaching techniques, as yet with little success (Posner 1983). Others are focusing on learning techniques with seemingly greater success. For example, Novak is teaching students concept mapping techniques as meaningful learning strategies (Novak 1984).

At the same time, researchers in Europe and Australia have been focusing their attention on student learning strategies and motives (for example Entwistle and Ramsden 1983; Biggs 1979). They are showing that the learning strategies students adopt play an important role in what students learn.

Their focus is, among other things, on learning strategies. But whereas Novak is experimentally testing prescriptive strategies, Entwistle and Biggs have been investigating the strategies students adopt in their everyday courses. Biggs has shown that students adopt to a greater or lesser extent (1) rote learning strategies aimed at passing the course, (2) meaningful learning strategies aimed at understanding the material, and (3) study skills and organizational strategies aimed at high achievement in the course (Entwistle and Ramsden 1983). Interestingly, the meaningful learning strategies described by Biggs have aims similar to those of the interventionist strategies developed by Novak.

What do these developments mean for the study of student understanding of the subject matter in a course? The design of the course outlined earlier is based on an empiricist view of knowledge, one in which incorrect knowledge can be replaced and correct knowledge added to the present store of knowledge in a student's cognitive structure without any reference to what the student already knows. Students are selected on the basis of prior general academic ability, they are taught and then assessed according to the following model:

$$\left.\begin{array}{l}\text{Prior}\\\text{Academic}\\\text{Ability}\end{array}\right\} \quad \left.\begin{array}{l}\text{Teaching}\\\text{Strategies}\end{array}\right\} \qquad \begin{array}{l}\text{Subsequent}\\\text{Assessment}\end{array}$$

No account is taken of the existing cognitive structure and how the concepts to be taught in the course are to be assimilated into the cognitive structure or how these new concepts interact with the existing cognitive structure. Nor is any account taken of the learning strategies adopted by the students. I believe a more appropriate model for the course may be:

$$\left.\begin{array}{l}\text{Prior}\\\text{Academic}\\\text{Ability}\\\text{(PAA)}\end{array}\right\} \left.\begin{array}{l}\text{Prior}\\\text{Cognitive}\\\text{Structure}\\\text{(CS)}\end{array}\right\} \left.\begin{array}{l}\text{Teaching}\\\text{Strategies}\\[1em]\text{Learning}\\\text{Strategies}\\\text{(LS)}\end{array}\right\} \begin{array}{l}\text{Subsequent}\\\text{Assessment}\end{array}$$

The research and theories so far outlined suggest that this model may be more appropriate and it is being applied to the evaluation of the course described here.

Methodology

In order to study the applicability of the above model to the course in question it is necessary to obtain indicators or measures of the various components of the model. Indicators of each of the components used in this study are given below.

The indicator of Prior Academic Ability was the rank order score used to select students into the university (PAA). The score is based upon external subject matter examination of students at the end of grade 12 high school.

Indicators of prior cognitive structure were obtained from a conceptual analysis of propositions generated by students in a tree construction, concept-mapping task before studying the topic 'Electricity'. (While information is stored in many ways in cognitive structure, eg images, personal experience, etc., in this paper I am concentrating on the propositional concept structure of cognitive structure.) The task was suggested in a series of articles by Stewart (1979, 1980). The students were presented with a list of the central concepts included in the course that had been identified from a content analysis of the curricular materials and subsequently verified by the academics who developed the materials. The students were asked to select the two concepts most closely related, write them down on a piece of paper, connect them with a line and number the line. They were then asked to select the concept most closely related to either of the two already mapped and add it to the structure. Once all concepts were mapped in this way, the students were asked to add any biology concepts they thought appropriate. The physics concepts will be referred to as internal concepts and the related propositions as internal propositions. The biology concepts will be referred to as external concepts and the related propositions as external propositions. An example of such a map is shown in Figure 1. The students were then asked to write a sentence or two describing the relationship between each pair of concepts mapped (see Figure 2).

The propositions and not the maps were subsequently scored on several dimensions. The scoring was suggested by White and Gunstone (1980). The dimensions used were:

1 The total number of internal propositions correct and included in the curriculum materials, CS1.
2 The total number of internal propositions correct but not included in the curriculum materials, CS2.
3 The total number of internal propositions incorrect, CS3.
4 The total number of external propositions correct and included in the curriculum materials, CS4.
5 The total number of external propositions correct and not included in the curriculum materials, CS5.
6 The total number of external propositions incorrect, CS6.

PHYSICS CONCEPT LABELS

Electrolysis
Nernst equilibrium
Electric charge
Electrochemical reversibility
Capacitance

Electric current
Electric field
Electric potential
Resistance
Ion diffusion

CONCEPT TREE

(Now draw your concept tree in the space provided, carefully following steps 1 to 4, placing your first two concepts in the middle of the space provided).

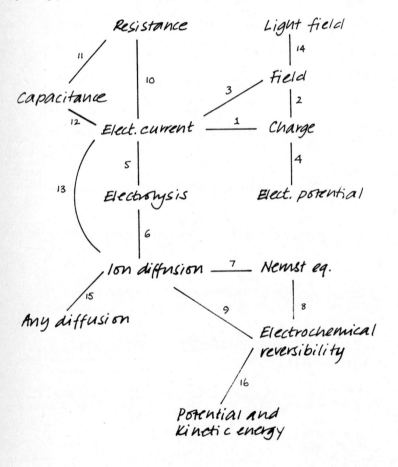

Figure 1
Example of a concept map.

CONCEPT RELATIONS
Step 6.
In column one below is a number for each of the connecting lines in your concept tree. For each of these connecting lines, please explain in column two why the two concepts are related. Write one sentence for each connecting line making sure to include the two concepts that line connects.

Column 1 (connecting lines)	Column 2 (connecting line explanation)
1	V=IR - Charge and current are connected
2	Charge determines strength of elect. field
3	Current likewise affects field
4	The charge in a source affects the potential it has
5	A current is passed thru water to perform electrolysis
6	Seemed like a good idea
7	Diffusion forms an equilibrium
8	Equilibrium can often be reversed
9	Ions can react or go back seemingly against equilibrium
10	V = IR - Related by formula
11	Can't remember why - but know they are
12	Capacitors store electricity

Figure 2
Example of propositions for concept map in Figure 1.

These dimensions were suggested from the ideas for meaningful incorporation of concepts into cognitive structure as detailed in Ausubel's learning theory. For example, if, prior to studying a topic, a student's propositions connecting the internal concepts were consistent with those presented in the course, it would be expected that integration would occur more easily than if the propositions were correct but not consistent with those presented in the course.

The indicators of student learning strategies were obtained from the results of the Biggs (1979) questionnaire on learning strategies referred to previously. The dimensions on which the questionnaire was scored were:

1   Rote-learning strategy, LS1.
2   Meaningful learning strategy, LS2.
3   Study skills and organization strategy, LS3.

Finally, the indicator of subsequent achievement was the mark obtained by the student in the normal examination for the topic, E1. The examination consisted of nine questions, each taking about ten minutes to complete. They would probably be classified at the comprehension or application level of Bloom's taxonomy.

Multiple regression analysis was used to analyse the results. Because it was thought the learning strategies might interact with cognitive structure, multiplicative interaction terms were included in the regression analysis. For example, one might expect that attempts by students to integrate concepts meaningfully into a well developed cognitive structure might have a different result from attempts to integrate into a less well developed structure.

Full sets of data were obtained from eighty-two students studying the topic. The analysis which follows is descriptive rather then inferential. In this context deviations from normality of some of the measures are not as troublesome as they would be if attempting inferential analysis. In any event, Spearman rank order correlation coefficients were used as the basis of subsequent analysis. There seems to be some consensus among those working in the area of cognitive research in science education that the area is not well developed and that explanatory studies aimed at identifying and documenting phenomena for further investigation are more appropriate than confirmatory studies aimed at obtaining population characteristics. In this context the effect sizes of the phenomena under study are probably more appropriate than the level of statistical significance. In the rest of the paper I have used criteria developed by Cohen (1977) for judging the effect size. Cohen has argued that even small effect sizes may be significant in research in which the measures are not well developed.

The strategy adopted for the analysis was as follows (note that tests of statistical significance were used as the criterion to delete variables from the model; they are not used for inferential purposes):

1   Test for significance of the model as a whole. (The explained variance is significant at the 0.05 level.)
2   Test for significance of the multiplicative interactions as a set. (The set added significantly to explained variance at the 0.05 level when all main effects were included.)

3 If the multiplicative interactions as a set were significant, test for the significance of the individual multiplicative interactions. (The multiplicative interaction added significantly to explained variance at the 0.05 level when all main effects and other multiplicative interactions were included.)

4 Test for the significance of the individual main effects. (The individual main effect added significantly to explained variance at the 0.05 level when all other main effects and significant multiplicative interactions were included.)

5 As the interpretation of multiplicative interactions is problematic, analyse interactions separately if they are significant.

This strategy was adopted so that (1) any overlapping variance due to correlations between the variables was not counted twice, (2) the variance due to the main effects was included before that due to the multiplicative interactions.

Results

The model tested was:

E1=f(Prior Academic Ability; Concept Structure; Learning Strategy; Prior Academic Ability x Concept Structure; Prior Academic Ability x Learning Strategies; Concept Structure x Learning Strategies)

Table 1 shows the intercorrelation matrix for the criterion and main effects predictor variables. While it also shows inferential statistics, the effect sizes shown are probably more appropriate. The table shows that achievement correlates positively with PAA (prior academic ability), CS1 (number of correct internal propositions which were included in the curriculum materials), CS4 (number of correct external propositions which were included in the materials) and LS2 (meaningful learning strategies). It correlated negatively with CS3 (number of incorrect internal propositions) and CS6 (number of incorrect external propositions). The correlation with LS1 is almost zero. These correlations are as would be expected, and show that the propositions and not just the connections are important.

Of the other correlations, it may be of interest to note that CS3 (number of incorrect internal propositions) correlates negatively with LS2 (meaningful learning strategy) and LS3 (study skills and organizational learning strategy) but positively with LS1 (rote learning strategy). Also, CS1 (number of correct internal positions which were included in the curriculum materials) correlates very positively ($r=0.43$) with LS2 (meaningful learning strategy). But with LS3 (study skills and organizational learning strategy) the correlation is much smaller and with LS1 (rote learning strategy) the correlation is negative.

The full model was significant and the effect size was large ($F = 3.43;\text{d.f.}=35,46; p <0.01; \hat{R}^2 = 0.51$). The set of multiplicative interactions was also significant, with a medium to large effect size ($F = 1.74;\text{d.f.}=25,46; p <0.05; \hat{R}^2 = 0.21$). (Note: $\hat{R}^2$ is an R^2 statistic adjusted for the number of independent variables and sample size.)

The individual main effect and multiplicative interactions which were not

	Variable Name									
	PAA	CS1	CS2	CS3	CS4	CS5	CS6	LS1	LS2	LS3
E1	0.59	0.28	0.04	−0.30	0.11	0.11	−0.14	0.01	0.17	0.05
PAA		0.44	−0.25	−0.21	0.41	−0.03	−0.12	−0.07	0.26	−0.03
CS1			−0.16	−0.65	0.26	0.18	−0.29	−0.10	0.43	0.12
CS2				−0.19	−0.06	−0.11	−0.05	0.01	−0.03	0.00
CS3					−0.04	−0.22	0.20	0.19	−0.21	−0.19
CS4						−0.13	−0.23	−0.06	0.24	−0.05
CS5							−0.17	−0.32	0.20	0.11
CS6								−0.09	−0.17	−0.02
LS1									0.10	0.03
LS2										0.39
LS3										

Notes $p < 0.05$ if $r > 0.19$ or $r < −0.19$
     $p < 0.01$ if $r > 0.26$ or $r < −0.26$

Effect size   small $r = 0.1$
          medium $r = 0.3$
          large $r = 0.5$

Table 1
Intercorrelational matrix for criterion and predictor variables.

significant were deleted from the model. This reduced model was significant with a large effect size ($F = 8.75$; d.f.$= 13,68$; $p < 0.01$; $\hat{R}^2 = 0.55$).

It can be argued that the cognitive structure, learning strategy and multiplicative interaction variables should be considered to be the interaction. In this case the interaction was significant with a large effect size ($F = 4.11$; d.f.$= 12,68$; $p < 0.01$; partial $R^2 = 0.32$). The increments in R^2 and $\hat{R}^2$ are 0.28 and 0.20 respectively. If only the multiplicative interactions are considered to be the interaction then it is again significant with a large effect size ($F = 6.45$; d.f.$= 5,68$; $p < 0.01$; partial $R^2 = 0.27$). The increments in R^2 and $\hat{R}^2$ are respectively 0.18 and 0.16.

It seems that the interaction of concept structure and learning strategy indicators does add substantially to the explanation of achievement variance in the sample studied, and that the more complex model described earlier in this paper is applicable to the sample. This result is reinforced by the fact that some of the concept structure and learning strategy variance would have been included in the indicator of prior academic ability (PAA).

As the interpretation of multiplicative interactions is problematic they were analysed separately. To simplify the analysis of the interpretation, two concept structure variables were formed from the six used in the previous analysis. CS1 and CS2 were added to form a single variable CSI, and CS4 and CS5 were added to form a single variable CSE. The following interactions were then tested by simple regression analysis (using Pearson correlation coefficients):

E1=CSIxLS1, CSIxLS2, CSIxLS3, CSExLS2, CSExLS3

The first three interactions were tested by selecting the top sixteen and bottom sixteen students on the basis of their CSI scores, and then for both of these samples simple regressions were conducted between E1 and LS1, LS2, LS3; similarly for the CSE indicators. Three interactions were considered to be substantial. The first of these, E1=CSIxLS2, showed that for students that had a poorly developed internal concept structure before starting the course, attempting to use meaningful learning strategies had little effect on final result; but for students with a well developed internal concept structure before starting, attempting to use meaningful learning had a positive effect. The second of these interactions, E1=CSIxLS3, showed that for students with a well developed internal concept structure before starting, attempting to use study skill and organizational strategies had little or no effect on final result; but for students with a less developed internal concept structure, the use of such strategies did have a positive affect. The final substantial interaction, E1=CSExLS3, showed that students with a less developed external concept structure were better served by a study skills and organizational learning strategy than those with a better developed concept structure.

These interactions are readily explained by Ausubel's learning theory. One would expect that attempts to integrate concepts meaningfully into concept structure would be substantially more successful for students with a well developed concept structure than for those with a less developed sturcture. It would then be predicted that the former students would have a higher subsequent achievement. But for the latter, conceptual integration would be less successful, and study skills and organizational strategies more successful. The interactions are consistent with these expectations.

Conclusion

The study described here used multiple regression analysis and recent research on student learning and learning strategy to describe student achievement in terms of the interaction between concept structure and learning strategies in a first-year physics course. For the sample studied, the interaction of concept structure and learning strategy indicators explains a substantial amount of variance. The interactions were interpretable by a well developed and accepted learning theory which suggests that the results are not spurious or sample dependent. It does seem that the more complex model discussed earlier in the paper, which incorporates prior concept structure and learning strategies, is supported by the results.

The study shows tentatively that the course planners and teachers in this first-year physics course need to take account of prior concept structure and learning strategies when revising the structure of the course and the teaching methods used. A major issue arises if such a conclusion can be accepted. Should course planners and teachers attempt to maximize achievement results or meaningful learning? That is, for those students with poorly developed concept structure should we recommend study skills and organizational strategies aimed at maximizing their marks, or attempt to improve their concept structure and recommend meaningful learning strategies? It seems to me that the former option is a band-aid option, one often used in tertiary institutions, and is the basis of many study skills programmes. While the latter is likely to have substantially better long-term benefits, the means of pursuing it remains problematic.

Note

This paper was written while the author was a Visiting Fellow in the Department of Education, Cornell University.

References

Ausubel, D., Novak, J. and Hanesian, H. (1978) *Educational Psychology: A Cognitive View* New York: Holt, Rinehart and Winston

Biggs, J. (1979) Individual differences in study processes and the quality of learning outcomes *Higher Education* 8, 381-394

Cohen, J. (1977) *Statistical Power Analysis* New York: Academic Press

Entwistle, N. and Ramsden, P. (1983) *Understanding Student Learning* Beckenham: Croom Helm

Novak, J. and Gowin, D. (1984) *Learning How to Learn* New York: Cambridge University Press

Posner, G. (1983) A model of conceptual change: Present status and future prospect *Proceedings of the International Seminar on Misconceptions in Science Education* Ithaca: Department of Education, Cornell University

Prosser, M. (1984) Towards more effective evaluation studies of educational media *British Journal of Educational Technology* 15(1) 33-42

Stewart, J. (1979) Content and cognitive structure: Critique of assessment and representation techniques used by science education researchers *Science Education* 63 (3) 223-235

Stewart, J. (1980) Techniques for assessing and representing information in cognitive structure *Science Education* 64(3) 223-235

Strike, K. and Posner, G. (In press) A conceptual change view of learning and understanding In L.West and A. Pines (Eds) *Cognitive Structure and Conceptual Change* New York:Academic Press

White. R. T. and Gunstone, R. F. (1980) Converting memory protocols to scores on several dimensions. In I. D. Smith (Ed.) *Papers Presented at the 1980 Annual Conference of the Australian Association for Research in Education* (Part B). Sydney: Australian Association for Research in Education

4

Approaches to Learning in a Traditional and an Innovative Medical School

David Newble and Rufus Clarke

In a recent article we reported a longitudinal study which demonstrated the marked effect that assessments and examinations have on the learning of medical students (Newble and Jaeger 1983). In addition, we showed that a deliberate change in the format and content of the examinations, designed to match the assessment more closely to the objectives of the course, was successful in redirecting student learning along more 'desirable' lines. The impact of the change was so great as to indicate that examinations might be the major factor influencing student learning in a medical school with a traditional curriculum. However, the educational literature suggests that other factors may play a significant role.

One such factor which is exciting a good deal of attention at present arises from studies of the cognitive processes used by students. Unfortunately, the literature on the subject is complex and confusing. This seems to be partly because the basic work arises from within different disciplines and partly because of an apparent selective blindness of researchers who publish predominantly either in North America or in Europe. One issue which still remains unclear is the relative importance of learning style and educational context in determining the approach to studying that students adopt. We therefore decided to investigate the approaches to learning of medical students in schools with different curricula.

Medical Schools and their Curricula

Medical schools can broadly be classified into two types which have been called 'traditional' and 'innovative'. Within each type there is, of course, considerable variation. The key curriculum strategies which characterize different schools have recently been described by Harden et al. (1984). They defined six dimensions along which the approach taken by a medical school could be placed:

Student centred	....	Teacher centred
Problem based	....	Information gathering
Integrated	....	Discipline based
Community based	....	Hospital based
Electives	....	Standard programmes
Systematic	....	Apprenticeship based/ Opportunistic

The traditional school would usually have a profile towards the right end of each of these dimensions while the innovative schools would largely be placed towards the left end.

One notable omission from this list is the assessment strategy which, as we have said, can have a profound effect on the curriculum and in many cases is responsible for the production of the 'hidden curriculum' described by Snyder (1971). In general, traditional schools have come to rely heavily on objective-type tests. Innovative schools are more variable, with some relying almost entirely on informal continuing assessment and most using a wider variety of assessments aimed at measuring skills such as problem solving, in preference to concentrating on the testing of factual knowledge. In fact, one of the features of the philosophy of the innovative schools is a greater concern with the process by which students learn to solve clinical problems than with the quantity of information they acquire.

This is not the time to explore the philosophies and principles underlying the two educational approaches used by medical schools. However, it must be pointed out that only a small minority fit into the innovative category and few, if any, of the established medical schools have changed their approach from the traditional to the innovative approach. This may seem strange to educationalists when the features of the innovative school seem to be more likely to produce graduates with the characteristics most institutions would vigorously espouse in their aims. Though some of the reason for this may lie in the difficulty faced by most institutions in introducing any substantial change in their educational and administrative structures, it must also be admitted that many see little necessity to change. As yet, no convincing evidence has emerged that graduates from innovative schools are superior to or even different from those from traditional schools. This is hardly surprising, because comparative studies have been few and far between and have usually used criteria and methods which are inappropriate, such as performance on national licensing examinations. The use of the students' approach to learning as a criterion provides a new dimension on which a comparison could be made.

Approaches to Learning

It is not our intention to review the literature on this subject as this has been done elsewhere in several recent publications (Entwistle 1981; Marton et al. 1984; Newble and Entwistle, in press). Suffice to say, it now appears that individual students have a preferred learning style probably related to their personality traits. They also have distinctive approaches to learning which are influenced by an array of characteristics of the department and of the teaching to which they are exposed. The result is that students can be observed to use one of three broad approaches to learning which are now generally called 'surface', 'deep' and 'strategic' (or 'achieving'). Each is characterized by features relating to the students' motivation and intention towards the subject being studied (Newble and Entwistle, in press; see also Chapter 2).

The attributes which we would desire in a university graduate are very much those embodied in the deep approach. Disturbingly, the little evidence we have suggests that not only are these attributes unlikely to be achieved by some students but also that students might be actively inhibited from achieving them by our curriculum structures and our teaching and examining methods.

In order to explore further the relationship between educational context and approaches to learning we have conducted a study which compared the approaches to learning by medical students in the University of Adelaide and the University of Newcastle (NSW) (Newble and Clarke, in press). The former is a traditional school admitting most students directly from school on the basis of matriculation results. It has a six-year curriculum divided into a preclinical and a clinical component (Cox 1971). The teaching is, as might be expected in such a school, heavily dependent on lecturers and supported by tutorials and ward work in the clinical years. Assessment is largely based on end-of-course examinations with a predominance of objective-type tests. Clinical assessment includes ward ratings and an objective structured clinical examination (Newble and Elmslie 1981).

In contrast, the University of Newcastle is an innovative school (Engel and Clarke 1979). Students may be admitted by two routes. The first is previous academic achievement based on school matriculation scores or a tertiary equivalent. The second is by multiple criteria whereby a lower level of academic achievement is a threshold criterion and selection within this group is based on written tests and a structured interview designed to assess appropriate intellectual and personal attributes. About half Newcastle entrants are admitted straight from school. The rest have had some post-secondary life experience or education, or may be graduates. The school has a five-year problem-based curriculum in which students learn by confronting selected clinical problems which require them to acquire the relevant basic and clinical skills. Students work predominantly in small groups and much time is spent in individual study. Achievement is assessed annually, using a range of instruments. Prominent is the so-called 'Modified Essay Question' which is used to measure diagnostic and/or management skills and to test the ability to apply the underpinning basic sciences (Feletti et al. 1983). Clinical skills are assessed by observation of patient interviews and examinations, and clinical problem-solving skills by oral examination. The ability to evaluate research papers is also tested annually.

On the basis of the literature we have briefly reviewed it might be expected that the Adelaide curriculum would tend to support or induce a surface approach or, at best, a strategic one. On the other hand, the curriculum, teaching methods and forms of assessment at Newcastle would be expected to encourage the deep approach. As the educational strategy used at Newcastle is largely designed to remedy the problems perceived in conventional medical schools, a failure to demonstrate a significant difference between the two institutions would seriously undermine the philosophical and educational justification of the innovative problem-based approach.

Methods

As yet, no instrument has been specifically designed to measure the approaches to learning of medical students. However, we have chosen to use the Lancaster 'Approaches to Studying Inventory' (LI) which is a general inventory derived from the work of Entwistle and his group (Entwistle and Ramsden 1983).

The LI is a 64-item self-report questionnaire. The items are grouped into sixteen sub-scales which are themselves combined to form three major factors: reproducing orientation, meaning orientation and strategic orientation. The questionnaire also includes a grouping of sub-scales related to styles and pathologies of learning. The reproducing orientation factor includes the features we have described as the surface approach. The meaning orientation factor contains features which are almost identical to those we have called the deep approach. The strategic orientation factor includes the features we have described as the strategic approach. It is important to remember that there is a possibility of confusing the terminology we have used for the approaches with the terminology of some of the orientation sub-scales. The concepts we have described as surface, deep and strategic are more comprehensive than those described for the sub-scales of the same name in the LI. On the other hand, the concepts we have described are not exactly represented by the reproducing, meaning and strategic orientations. Nevertheless, for the purposes of this study, we shall assume that the concepts of surface, deep and strategic approach are broadly represented in the inventory by the reproducing, meaning and strategic orientations respectively.

The LI was administered in Adelaide and Newcastle to first, third and final-year (Adelaide, 6th year; Newcastle, 5th year) students approximately two-thirds of the way through each year. It was also administered to another cohort of third-year Adelaide students approximately half-way through the year, a few weeks prior to their final preclinical examinations.

Comparisons were made between equivalent Adelaide and Newcastle student groups using Student's t-test.

Results

In Adelaide the LI was completed by 87 per cent of first-year students (n=97), 89 per cent of pre-examination third-year students (n=94), 98 per cent of clinical third-year students (n=104) and 91 per cent of the final-year group (n=43). The relative smallness of the final-year group is due to the fact that the investigators had access to only that half of the class which, at the time, was undertaking student internships in medicine and surgery. However, the results represent a 91 per cent return from a unselected sample. In

Newcastle, the LI was completed by 95 per cent of the first-year students (n=63), 81 per cent of third-year students (n=46) and 76 per cent of final-year students (n=44).

The results and comparisons made between the Adelaide and Newcastle students are shown in Tables 1 and 2. Table 2 also contains comparisons between Newcastle first-year students admitted without previous tertiary experience and Adelaide first-year students.

	Year 1		Year 3			Final Year	
	A	N	A1	A2	N	A	N
	(n=97)	(n=63)	(n=94)	(n=104)	(n=46)	(n=43)	(n=44)
MEANING ORIENTATION	38.1±8.4	44.2±8.5	38.6±8.7	40.3±9.2	46.4±9.3	42.5±9.5	45.8±8.4
Deep approach	10.8±2.7	11.7±2.7	11.2±2.8	11.1±2.9	12.5±2.6	11.4±3.1	11.8±2.5
Interrelating ideas	10.0±2.9	11.5±2.8	9.5±2.9	10.7±2.7	12.2±2.7	11.6±2.4	12.0±2.3
Use of evidence	9.1±2.8	10.5±2.7	9.7±2.6	10.0±2.7	10.8±3.0	11.0±3.2	11.4±2.5
Intrinsic motivation	8.2±2.9	10.4±2.7	8.3±3.1	8.5±3.3	10.9±3.3	8.4±3.4	10.6±3.6
REPRODUCING ORIENTATION	33.4±8.2	26.8±8.2	35.2±7.5	30.5±7.8	26.1±7.3	32.2±7.3	25.7±9.6
Surface Approach	13.9±3.8	12.0±4.0	15.1±3.2	13.9±3.8	11.5±3.9	14.7±4.1	11.6±4.6
Syllabus-boundness	8.9±2.1	7.0±2.8	9.2±2.1	7.8±2.3	6.2±2.9	8.0±2.5	5.2±2.8
Fear of failure	5.5±3.1	5.2±2.8	6.3±2.9	5.5±3.0	6.0±3.0	6.3±3.0	6.1±2.9
Extrinsic motivation	5.1±3.5	2.4±2.4	4.6±3.6	3.3±2.7	2.5±2.6	3.4±3.1	2.8±3.0
ACHIEVING ORIENTATION	37.5±8.3	38.7±8.5	37.1±9.3	38.3±9.1	36.8±9.1	36.0±11.0	34.8±8.9
Strategic approach	11.3±2.8	10.4±4.1	11.8±2.5	11.5±2.3	10.8±2.4	11.6±3.0	10.1±2.6
Disorganized study methods	9.5±4.2	8.4±4.1	8.4±4.3	7.7±4.4	8.0±4.6	9.5±4.9	7.0±4.3
Negative attitudes	5.4±3.5	3.6±2.7	6.8±3.9	5.7±3.7	6.1±4.2	6.5±3.9	6.4±4.1
Achievement motivation	9.1±3.5	8.2±3.5	8.5±3.6	8.1±3.7	7.7±3.7	8.0±4.0	6.6±3.9
STYLES AND PATHOLOGIES	–	–	–	–	–	–	–
Comprehension learning	8.1±3.2	9.0±3.6	7.3±3.4	8.7±3.1	9.2±3.9	8.3±3.8	9.4±3.7
Globetrotting	7.5±2.5	7.5±3.1	6.8±2.8	8.2±2.5	6.9±3.6	7.5±2.6	8.0±3.4
Operation learning	11.2±2.6	9.8±3.1	10.7±2.7	10.6±2.5	9.4±2.7	10.6±2.5	9.3±3.0
Improvidence	7.4±2.8	6.4±3.2	7.7±3.0	7.4±3.0	5.9±2.9	6.6±2.6	5.6±2.5

A = Adelaide   N = Newcastle   1 = Pre-exam   2 = Post-exam

Table 1

Means and standard deviations on the Lancaster Inventory.

Newcastle students rate themselves higher on meaning orientation than Adelaide students in all years, these differences being highly significantly different in Years 1 and 3. The scores for the two final-year groups are not significantly different. The scores for Adelaide students rise for each year and the changes between first, third and sixth-year groups were significant when tested with a one-way analysis of variance followed by Duncan's post-hoc multiple-range tests. Newcastle students scored consistently higher on all four sub-scales contributing to meaning orientation, with significant differences in most sub-scales between first and third-year groups.

Similar results, but in the opposite direction, were found for reproducing orientation. Adelaide students scored themselves higher in all years than

	Year 1 All students		Year 1 Direct entrants		Year 3		Year 5/6	
	t	p	t	p	t	p	t	p
MEANING ORIENTATION	4.45	0.001	2.67	0.01	4.35	0.001	1.35	NS
Deep approach	2.05	0.05	2.36	0.02	3.21	0.01	0.67	NS
Interrelating ideas	3.23	0.01	2.38	0.02	3.43	0.001	0.80	NS
Use of evidence	3.57	0.001	1.40	0.05	2.26	0.05	0.64	NS
Intrinsic motivation	4.79	0.001	2.93	0.01	4.63	0.001	2.60	0.05
REPRODUCING ORIENTATION	5.03	0.001	3.60	0.001	3.20	0.01	2.70	0.01
Surface Approach	3.06	0.01	2.25	0.05	3.43	0.001	2.49	0.02
Syllabus-boundness	4.87	0.001	3.03	0.01	4.10	0.001	4.36	0.001
Fear of failure	0.62	NS	0.74	NS	1.13	NS	0.31	NS
Extrinsic motivation	5.33	0.001	3.88	0.001	1.89	NS	0.59	NS
ACHIEVING ORIENTATION	0.88	NS	0.24	NS	0.92	NS	0.57	NS
Strategic Approach	1.95	NS	1.58	NS	1.69	NS	2.43	0.02
Disorganized study methods	1.63	NS	0.87	NS	0.63	NS	2.19	0.05
Negative attitudes	3.45	0.001	1.90	NS	0.43	NS	0.23	NS
Achievement motivation	1.58	NS	0.76	NS	0.61	NS	1.98	0.05
STYLES AND PATHOLOGIES	–	–	–	–	–	–	–	–
Comprehension learning	1.65	NS	1.54	NS	1.02	NS	1.07	NS
Globetrotting	0.00	NS	0.94	NS	2.04	0.05	0.59	NS
Operation learning	3.02	0.01	3.48	0.001	3.12	0.01	2.17	0.05
Improvidence	2.08	0.05	1.00	NS	2.84	0.01	1.92	NS

Table 2

Comparisons of Adelaide and Newcastle students.

Newcastle students and these differences were significant. It is interesting to note that the highest score was found in the pre-examination third-year Adelaide group. The group tested a few weeks after this examination, at the time when they had just started their clinical course and when there was no immediate threat of examinations, produced a score which was the lowest of all Adelaide groups. The sub-scales contributing most to these differences were surface approach and syllabus-boundness. Fear of failure sub-scales were almost identical in all years, with a rising trend with seniority. Extrinsic motivation was significantly higher in Adelaide first-year students but later years showed no significant difference.

In achievement orientation there were no significant differences between Adelaide students and their Newcastle counterparts. There was a downward trend in scores in both schools in progressive years. Among the sub-scales in this orientation, only negative attitude to studying stands out as a highly significant discriminator and only in the first year. In both schools there is an upward trend in this sub-scale with seniority.

The group of sub-scales dealing with styles and pathologies showed that Adelaide students rated themselves significantly higher than Newcastle students on operation learning, and to a lesser extent on the associated pathology of improvidence.

Because of the possibility that first-year differences might have been due to the variation in selection criteria, a comparison between direct entrants in both schools was made. This showed results that were almost identical to those obtained from the total group.

Discussion

The results of this study show a marked difference between the responses of students in the two schools. Whilst it must be pointed out that the results are based on a self-report questionnaire, which asks students to reflect on their approaches to studying and is not a direct measure of the approaches they actually use, it would be impossible to explain away the findings simply in terms of the nature of the instrument. Overall, it is clear that the approaches to learning apparently used by Newcastle students are very much those which would be thought desirable by all medical schools. They are very high on deep approach and very low on surface approach. These desirable attributes, as expressed both in the main orientations and in the sub-scales of the LI, are more evident than in Adelaide medical students and indeed than in any other group of students tested previously in other institutions. The same attributes were seen in students who had been admitted using the same criteria as those used to admit students of the Adelaide school so the selection process itself is unlikely to have contributed significantly to the observed differences. Adelaide students, on the other hand, have less desirable attributes. They rate themselves highly on surface approach. While initially scoring low on deep approach there is an increase in scores in later years. Whether this is due to a positive effect of the institution or a maturational and developmental effect cannot be determined.

As these results have been replicated in a similar European study (Coles 1985) it appears that the observed differences in approaches to learning are most likely to reflect contrasts in the educational environment. It is impossible to say which components of the environment are the most influential as there are substantial differences between the innovative and conventional schools in the areas of curriculum, teaching methods, assessment and staff/student relationships, and all are likely to contribute in some way.

The study also provides one of the first pieces of evidence of a difference between students at a traditional school and an innovative problem-based school. It also shows that the students in the problem-based school appear to have an approach to studying that closely approximates to the aims of most medical schools. On the other hand, the approach adopted by students at the conventional school are far from the ideal. The results provide strong support for the philosophies and educational strategies of the problem-based schools. In addition, the idea of investigating the way in which students approach their learning is providing fundamental and new insights into a hitherto ignored component of the educational equation.

References

Coles, C. (1985) *Undergraduate Medical Curricula and the Learning they Generate*

Paper presented at ASME annual meeting, 1984. Abstract *Medical Education* 19, 85

Cox, L.W. (1971) New medical course in Adelaide *Medical Journal of Australia* 53, 720

Engel, C.E. and Clarke, R.M. (1979) Medical education with a difference *Programmed Learning and Educational Technology* 16, 72

Entwistle, N.J. (1981) *Styles of Learning and Teaching* Chichester: Wiley

Entwistle, N.J. and Ramsden, P. (1983) *Understanding Student Learning* London: Croom Helm

Feletti, G.I., Saunders, N.A. and Smith, A.J. (1983) Comprehensive assessment of final year student performance based on undergraduate programme objectives *Lancet* 2, 34

Harden, R.M., Sowden, S. and Dunn, W.R. (1984) Some educational strategies in curriculum development: the SPICES model *Medical Education* 18, 284

Marton, F., Hounsell, D.J. and Entwistle, N.J. (Eds) (1984) *The Experience of Learning* Edinburgh: Scottish Academic Press

Newble, D.I. and Clarke, R.M. (In press) The approaches to learning of students in a traditional and in an innovative problem-based medical school *Medical Education*

Newble, D.I. and Elmslie, R.G. (1981) A new approach to the final examination in medicine and surgery *Lancet* 2, 517

Newble, D.I. and Entwistle, N.J. (In press) Learning styles and approaches: implications for medical education *Medical Education*

Newble, D.I. and Jaeger, K. (1983) The effect of assessments and examinations on the learning of medical students *Medical Education* 17, 165

Snyder, B.R. (1971) *The Hidden Curriculum* New York: Knopf

Part 2

Thinking and Problem Solving

5

The Triarchic Theory of Human Intelligence

Robert J. Sternberg

Investigators of intelligence are doing in the 1980s what perhaps they should have done many decades ago: attempting reflectively and self-consciously to define the domain of intelligence. In order to understand why psychologists have been so slow to arrive at what is, arguably, the most basic possible question about intelligence, it is necessary to examine some of the past history of the field.

The 'traditional' or psychometric account of intelligence sought to understand intelligence as a functional map of the mind. Various theories proposed different maps. For example, Spearman (1927) proposed that a single factor – 'g' or general intelligence – is the most important functional region in the 'land of intelligence' and that other, specific factors are much less important. Thurstone (1938) proposed that the lie of the land is best understood in terms of a set of about seven overlapping regions, or primary mental abilities, such as verbal comprehension, spatial relations, inductive reasoning, memory, and the like. Hierarchical theorists such as Vernon (1971) showed that theories such as Spearman's and Thurstone's need not be viewed as incompatible; rather, they can be viewed as dealing with separate levels of a single hierarchy. Thus, one could conceive of a hierarchical structure of intelligence in which 'g' is at the top, and the primary mental abilities at some lower level. Perhaps the most elegant of the hierarchical theories is one recently proposed by Gustafsson (1984), who used confirmatory factor analysis to propose a fairly detailed model.

Whereas the psychometric approach to intelligence dominated up to the 1960s, the cognitive, or information-processing approach dominated in the 1970s. A primary motivation for this approach was the concern on the part of cognitive psychologists that static, 'map-based' theories had very little to say about the mental processes that underlie intelligence. For example, just what does it mean, in terms of mental processes, for a subject to be relatively higher or lower in reasoning ability?

Cognitive psychologists have sought to understand the mental processes that they believe underlie the factors of intelligence. Although most would indeed view the mental processes as, in some sense, underlying the factors, the question of depth of analysis is by no means resolved. It is possible that the factors generate the processes, rather than the reverse.

An array of cognitive theories of intelligence has been proposed. A major distinguishing feature of these is the complexity of information processing at which they seek to isolate the loci of intelligence. At the simple end, Jensen (1979) has sought to understand individual differences in intelligence in terms of differences in mental speed of information processing in choice reaction-time tasks. Hunt (1978) has used slightly more complex tasks, suggesting that speed of retrieval for lexical information in long-term memory can serve as a basis for individual differences in verbal intelligence. Sternberg (1979) has sought to understand individual differences in intelligence in terms of the information-processing components of reasoning tasks, and Simon (1976) has studied individual differences in complex problem solving.

In retrospect, the information-processing 'revolution' seems to have been less of a revolution than its instigators had thought. On the one hand, the methods of task analysis certainly have differed from those of psychometricians. In particular, the information-processing psychologists have concentrated upon analysing task rather than person sources of variation. On the other hand, the tasks that they have studied have borne some of the same problematical aspects as the tasks studied by the psychometricians.

Psychometric tasks can be and have been criticized for their lack of an a priori psychological rationale. Psychometricians seem to have chosen the tasks to some extent because their forebears used them, and these forebears in turn appear to have used the tasks because their forebears used them. There has been no solid theoretical rationale for choosing some tasks rather than others (Sternberg 1979). Unfortunately, the situation for cognitive psychologists does not appear to be much different from the situation for psychometricians. The tasks cognitive psychologists have studied have, for the most part, been borrowed either from the psychometric repertoire or from that of other cognitive psychologists. The rationales have, in effect, been borrowed from the work of others. There is even a certain circularity in this work (Neisser 1983), in that cognitive psychologists have used standard psychometric tests as a standard against which to validate their tasks and task models.

With increasing awareness of the failure of both psychometricians and cognitive psychologists to define the domain of intelligence adequately prior to their selection of tasks, investigators of intelligence in the 1980s have become increasingly concerned with going back to basics and defining the scope that theories of intelligence should provide.

Three recent theories of intelligence particularly well represent this new concern – those of Baron (1985), Gardner (1983), and Sternberg (1985). Baron seeks to understand intelligence in terms of rational thinking, and chooses tasks that measure the ability of an individual to think accordingly. Gardner proposes that there is no one thing that appropriately should be called intelligence at all. Rather, there exist multiple intelligences, such as linguistic intelligence, mathematical/logical intelligence, musical intelligence, and the like, each of which is posited to be independent of the others. Finally, Sternberg has proposed a triarchic theory of intelligence that seeks to understand intelligence in terms of three distinct but interrelated aspects: the internal world of the individual, the external world of the individual, and the experience of the individual. The remainder of this chapter will be devoted to an explication of the triarchic theory and its implications for understanding, investigating, testing, and training intelligence. Each of these four aspects of the theory and its implications will be considered in turn.

Understanding Intelligence

The triarchic theory of human intelligence deals with three aspects of intelligence – its relation to the internal world of the individual, its relation to the external world of the individual, and its relation to the experience of the individual (see Sternberg 1984, 1985). Consider first the motivation for the theory, and then each of these three aspects of the theory, or sub-theories, in turn.

Motivation for the Triarchic Theory

A given theory can be motivated in multiple ways. Two such motivations will be presented here, one of which is metatheoretical and the other of which is wholly practical.

Consider first the metatheoretical motivation. There exist a large number of theories of intelligence, which are usually viewed as competing. It is possible to view these as largely complementary, however, rather than as competing. Sternberg (1985) classified them in terms of a taxonomy of the domains to which they apply, and found that extant theories of intelligence could be classified in terms of the same set of aspects of intelligence that generate the triarchic theory: as relating to the internal world, the external world, and experience. Psychometric and cognitive theories, as well as biologically-based theories, tend to focus upon the relation of intelligence to the internal world of the individual. Contextual theories, often from cross-cultural psychology, tend to focus upon the relation of intelligence to the external world of the individual. Developmental theories tend to focus upon the relation of intelligence to experience and to its complement, maturation. A few theories cross these boundaries – for example, Piaget's (1972) theory considers both the internal world and experience – but for the most part, the theories concentrate each on a single aspect of the three possible relations for intelligence.

From one point of view, then, the triarchic theory can be viewed not as an attempt to compete with past theories, but as an attempt to subsume these theories under a single, more nearly complete theory, one that deals with all three aspects of intelligence. The triarchic theory is certainly not the only possible one that could deal with all three aspects. But it represents one viable attempt to be somewhat more comprehensive.

Consider second the practical motivation. During the late 1970s, I, like many other investigators of intelligence, was busily involved in the information-processing analysis of intelligence-test items. To this day, a portion of my research continues in this tradition. But as the 1970s wore on, I became increasingly concerned about an assumption underlying this analysis, namely, that such items provide a reasonably comprehensive index of intelligence. My own experience with graduate students seemed to belie this view. Consider three such students, whom I shall call Alice, Barbara, and Celia.

Alice was the admissions officer's dream. She came to Yale with high test scores, high grades, excellent letters of recommendation, and overall, pretty close to a perfect record. Alice proved to be, more or less, what her record promised. She had excellent critical, analytical abilities, and these abilities helped her earn outstanding grades in her course work during her first two years at Yale. But after the first two years, Alice no longer looked quite so outstanding. The reason is that the demands of the programme shifted from emphasis on critical, analytical abilities to emphasis on creative, synthetic abilities, and Alice's synthetic abilities were far inferior to her analytic ones. Thus, Alice was 'IQ-test' smart, but she was not equally intelligent in all senses of the word, and in particular, not in the synthetic side of intelligence.

Barbara was the admissions officer's nightmare. She came to Yale with very low test scores and grades that, although good, did not compare to Alice's. What she had going for her was an already impressive list of research accomplishments, which her referees assured us were a sign of her own ability to generate and follow through on good ideas, not just a sign of the abilities of her advisors. Barbara, too, proved true to her record. She received good grades in her classes, although her grades were not at the same level as Alice's. Where Barbara excelled was in her research. When the demands of the graduate programme shifted from an emphasis on analytical abilities to an emphasis on synthetic abilities, Barbara was ready: indeed, she was in her element. Barbara did not have Alice's analytical abilities, but she greatly surpassed Alice in synthetic abilities.

Celia, on paper, appeared to be somewhere between Alice and Barbara in terms of suitability for admission. She was good on almost every measure of potential success, but not great on any of them. We admitted her, expecting her to come out near the middle of the class. This did not happen. Celia has proved to be outstanding, although in a way that is quite different from Alice or Barbara. Celia's expertise is in figuring out and in adapting to the demands of the environment. She knows what she needs to do to get ahead, and does it. In conventional parlance, Celia is 'street-smart'.

From the standpoint of the triarchic theory, Alice is someone who excels in the internal aspect of intelligence, Barbara someone who excels in the experiential aspect, and Celia someone who excels in the external aspect. All three are intelligent, but in different ways. Just what are these ways? This question is considered and addressed below.

Intelligence and the Internal World of the Individual

The first, or componential sub-theory of the triarchic theory of human intelligence, specifies the kinds and identities of mental processes involved in intelligent thought. Thus, according to the theory, the selection of tasks that measure intelligence should be guided, in part, by the extent to which the tasks measure the proposed information-processing components of intelligence.

The theory posits three different kinds of components, although this taxonomy is proposed as one of convenience rather than one that reveals some fundamental property of mind. The three kinds of components are metacomponents, performance components, and knowledge-acquisition components.

Metacomponents are higher order or executive processes used to plan what one is going to do, to monitor it while it is being done, and to evaluate it after it is done. Some examples of metacomponents are (a) recognizing that a problem exists, (b) defining the nature of a problem, (c) choosing a set of steps for solving a problem, (d) combining these steps into an overall strategy, and (e) allocating one's mental and physical resources in problem solving. For example, in solving an algebra-word problem, the very first steps to solution would require one to define exactly what type of problem one is confronting (eg, a time-rate-distance problem), to figure out what steps will be needed to solve the problem, to figure out the order in which the steps should be executed, and so on. These steps would have to precede actual application of any algorithm to the solution of the problem.

Performance components are the mental processes that execute the instructions of the metacomponents. Examples of such components are (a) encoding the terms of a problem, (b) inferring relations between terms of a problem, (c) applying a formula or rule, (d) comparing alternative possible answers to a problem for plausibility, and so on. In the time-rate-distance algebra problem, for example, reading the terms of the problem and applying the $D=RxT$ formula would involve performance components.

Knowledge-acquisition components are the processes used in learning how to solve a problem (acquisition of procedural knowledge) or in learning new facts or concepts (acquisition of declarative knowledge). We have isolated three mental processes that appear to be critical in the acquisition of new knowledge: (a) selective encoding, (b) selective combination, and (c) selective comparison. Selective encoding is used to determine what new information is potentially relevant for one's purposes in learning. Selective combination is used to integrate the potentially relevant information once it is isolated. Selective comparison is used to relate new to old information. For example, consider how one might go about learning the meaning of a new word presented in context. First, one would have to determine what information in the text is potentially relevant for figuring out the meaning of the word. Second, one would have to put together this information in order to form a plausible definition. Finally, one would have to relate the new information to old information so as to integrate the meaning of the new word into existing cognitive structures.

Metacomponents, performance components, and knowledge-acquisition components work together, not in isolation, but in interaction in intelligent cognition. Their interactivity can make them difficult to isolate experimentally. In particular, metacomponents activate performance and knowledge-acquisition components, which in turn provide feedback to the metacomponents. This interaction has implications both for testing and for training. The critical implication is that the various kinds of components can be viewed as forming a chain in a sequence of information processing, and the chain can be no stronger than its weakest link.

Intelligence and the External World of the Individual

Whereas psychometric and cognitive psychologists have tended to concentrate on the relation of intelligence to the internal world of the individual, contextualist psychologists, and especially those specializing in cross-cultural psychology, have tended to concentrate on the relation of intelligence to the external world of the individual. Their concentration upon the external world derives from their recognition that, on the one hand, the environment in which we live shapes our notions of intelligence, and, on the other hand, our notions of intelligence shape what we do – and what we teach others to do – in the environment.

For example, cultures and subcultures differ in the relative extent to which they emphasize memory versus reasoning in their notions of intelligence. In some cultures, the 'intelligent' child is one who can memorize perfectly those texts that are believed to be important in the education of the child. In other cultures, rote memorization is more or less frowned upon, and the 'intelligent' child is viewed as the one who can reason well. This difference can be found subculturally as well as cross-culturally. Heath (1983), for example, found that different subcultures within the United States differ with respect to their relative emphasis on memory versus reasoning as bases of intelligence. Parents 'socialize' their children in terms of what and how they believe an intelligent child should learn.

The contextual sub-theory specifies the functions the components of intelligence should serve when applied to the everyday world. According to the sub-theory, there are three such functions: (a) adaptation, (b) selection, and (c) shaping.

Adaptation refers to modifications individuals make in themselves in order better to fit into the surrounding environment. For example, in learning how to adjust to a new job, one must adapt. The notion of intelligence as adaptation is, by itself, inadequate. The reason for this inadequacy is that there are times when it is, in effect, maladaptive to adapt. There can be any number of reasons for this phenomenon. Consider, for example, starting a new job. One may find that one's level or pattern of abilities does not fit the job; for example, that it requires conceptualizing or typing or packing widgets at a rate or level that exceeds one's capacity. Or, one may find that the requirements of the job are inconsistent with one's values. For example, one might go to work for a computer company in the hope of applying one's logical abilities, and end up in the industrial espionage section, employing instead one's ability to spy. One simply may not believe in spying as a way of life, whether or not one is good at it. Or, one might find that a given job is unsuitable for one's pattern of interests – in a word, that the job is boring,. The point to be made, quite simply, is that there are times when, at a higher level, adaptation can be maladaptive.

In cases in which adaptation does not work, a second option is that of the environmental selection: one leaves the environment in which one finds oneself and moves to a different environment. The environmental transfer might be a physical one, as in changing jobs, or it might be a conceptual one, as in changing, for example, research problems. In this latter case, one might decide that one has milked a problem for what it is worth, and that the time has come to consider a new one.

Although environmental selection provides an alternative to environmental adaptation, it does not always provide an ideal alternative. There are times when the desirable course of action is neither to adapt nor to select. For example, if a couple has its first major dispute while on a honeymoon, a partner might not want simply to adapt, but would probably not be well advised to select a new environment, say through divorce, right away. Similarly, if one is unhappy with a new job after a few weeks, one does not necessarily immediately seek a new job. A third option is that of shaping.

Shaping involves modification of the environment so as to make it a better fit for oneself. Thus, whereas adaptation involves changing the self to suit the environment, shaping involves changing the environment to suit the self. One may attempt to shape the interpersonal relations in a marriage, or to shape the kinds of tasks one does in a job. Shaping represents an especially viable alternative to adaptation when leaving a given environment is impossible, as, for example, when one's religious beliefs preclude leaving a marriage, or when the laws of a country severely restrict emigration from it.

Adaptation, selection, and shaping operate interactively, and often hierarchically. One first attempts to adapt to an environment, and when adaptation does not work, or when it becomes a non-optimal strategy, one may then attempt selection and then shaping, or shaping and then selection.

These three strategies for operating upon the interaction between the self and the environment are not distinct from, but rather bound to, the components of intelligence. Adaptation, selection, and shaping are not themselves components of intelligence, but rather, *functions* that components can serve when they operate upon the environment. For example, one might define a problem (a metacomponent) as one of shaping the environment (a function of the metacomponent). Thus, the contextual sub-theory cannot be viewed in isolation from the componential sub-theory. Rather, components are always applied in contexts, and they can serve at least three different functions in these contexts.

Intelligence and the Experience of the Individual

Components are applied to contexts at varying levels of experience, whether the contexts are conceived in terms of tasks, situations, or interactions between tasks and situations. According to the experiential sub-theory, there are two regions of experience, or facets of intelligence, that are particularly relevant to the measurement of intelligence: coping with relative novelty and automatization of information processing.

Coping with relative novelty requires one to understand and act expeditiously upon tasks and situations that are largely, but not wholly, unfamiliar. The exclusion of wholly unfamiliar tasks and situations is motivated by the fact that such instances cannot measure intelligence, because if they are truly totally unfamiliar we have no mental wherewithal to bring to bear upon them. Thus, calculus problems would scarcely provide suitable measures of intelligence among pre-school children. On the other hand, problems that are largely familiar do not provide discriminative measures of intelligence: tying shoelaces, for example, would scarcely provide a suitable measure of intelligence among normal adults.

Automatization of information processing refers to the transition between conscious, serial, and effortful information processing, on the one hand, and subconscious, parallel, and effortless processing, on the other. For example, when we learn to read, to drive, or to speak a foreign language, we usually transit from controlled to automatic information processing. The ability to automatize processing in tasks like these is essential for their efficacious performance.

Coping with novelty and automatization of information processing represent regions near, but not at, opposite ends of the continuum from total unfamiliarity to total familiarity with tasks and situations. The two regions of the experiential continuum, and the abilities underlying them, are intimately interrelated. Superior ability to deal with novelty enables one to move more rapidly and effectively along the experiential continuum toward automization. At the same time, superior automatization ability frees more mental resources for dealing with novelty. The more aspects of a task or situation that one has automatized, the more one is able to turn one's attention to the novel aspects of the task or situation. Thus, each ability potentially facilitates the operation of the other.

These two facets of intelligence operate in interaction not only with each other, but with the other aspects of the triarchy of intelligence. The components of intelligence adapt, select, and shape environments at varying levels of familiarity with tasks and situations. Thus, the ability to cope with novelty is not distinct from the components of intelligence, but rather represents the application of these components at a specific region of the experiential continuum. Similarly, automatization is of components of information processing; it is not some separate entity that can be understood in isolation from the components. In sum, the three aspects of the triarchic theory must be understood in interaction with, not in isolation from, each other.

Investigating Intelligence

What kinds of evidence are available to support the various claims of the triarchic theory? Although it would not be feasible to review here the full array of empirical documentation (see Sternberg (1985) for such a review), it is possible to say something about the kinds of evidence that have been adduced.

The Componential Sub-Theory

By far the largest amount of data has been collected to test the internal, or componential sub-theory. For the most part, experiments have involved isolating distinct components of intellectual information processing. Consider examples of experiments isolating each of the three kinds of processing components.

Sternberg (1981) sought to isolate two metacomponents of information processing: global strategy planning and local strategy planning. Global strategy planning is the planning one does for a set of things that need to be accomplished. The 'things' might be test problems in a sub-test, a set of homework problems, a set of activities one might hope to accomplish during a day, and so on. Local planning is the planning one does for one of the things in the set – a single test problem, one of a set of homework problems, or one of the activities one seeks to accomplish during the day. Each of these kinds of strategy planning is needed in our everyday activities, both academic and practical.

Subjects in the experiment – Yale College students – received complex multiple-choice analogies in which either one, two, or three terms might be replaced with multiple-choice options, and in which the locations of the missing terms could vary from one problem to another. For example, particular pairs of terms that might be replaced by answer options in the analogy, A:B::C:D, might be A and B, A and C, B and C, and so on. Items were presented, within-subjects, in either mixed or blocked format. In the mixed format, items in various formats were intermixed. In the blocked format, items in a single format all appeared together. The purpose of this manipulation was to permit isolation of the global-processing metacomponent. Only the blocked condition enabled one to formulate a global strategy. The mixed format required strategy shifting on successive items, and thus precluded formulation of a global strategy. Local strategy planning was isolated as a metacomponent by estimating the amount of disruption in information processing caused by the presence of multiple answer options, with amount of disruption estimated on the basis of information processing as specified by Sternberg's (1977) componential theory of analogical reasoning.

The critical result in this experiment was an interaction between amount of time spent on each kind of planning and reasoning skill. Better reasoners were found to spend relatively more time on global planning than poorer reasoners, but to spend relatively less time on local planning than poorer reasoners. If one were to examine only the overall correlation of response latency with inductive reasoning skill, one would conclude simply that better reasoners were faster information processors. The componential decomposition shows that better reasoners are sometimes faster, but sometimes slower, than poorer reasoners. The better reasoners are best characterized as superior resource and time allocaters who know when to be fast and when to be slow in their information processing.

Consider now a second study, comprising a series of experiments on inductive reasoning. The global purpose of this series of experiments was to address a potentially serious objection to performance-componential accounts of intelligence, namely, that the number of performance components in a theory of intelligence, like the number of factors in such a theory, can keep on increasing indefinitely. Just as the number of factors in factor theories seemed pretty much to keep increasing over time, so the number of performance components could keep on showing such an increase over time.

In our experiments, a single set of Yale College subjects received schematic-picture, verbal, and geometric analogies, series completions, and classifications (Sternberg and Gardner 1983). Because tasks and contents were crossed, subjects received items in a total of nine conditions in all. Order of conditions was counterbalanced, but all subjects ultimately received the same test items. Our basic theoretical question was whether a single theory of inductive reasoning, originally proposed just for analogies, could be extended to other kinds of induction problems without increasing the number of performance components posited. In other words, would the number of components keep rising as the number of tasks increased, as suggested by critics of componential analysis (eg Neisser 1983)?

The results were quite clear-cut: a single theory could in fact account for performance across tasks and task contents. This theory posited just seven distinct performance components: (a) encoding stimulus terms, (b) inferring relations between stimulus terms, (c) mapping higher order relations between relations, (d) applying previously inferred relations to a new domain, (e) comparing answer options, (f) justifying a particular answer option as superior to alternative answer options, even if it is non-ideal, and (g) responding to the problem. The components, with slight variation in the strategy by which they were applied and exactly which components were used for each kind of problem, well characterized information-processing performance. There were substantial individual differences in skill of using the various performance components, but not in the strategies into which the components were combined. Thus, psychometric 'g' seems to be characterizable in large part in terms of individual differences in the seven performance components that characterize the core of intellectual information processing.

Finally, consider a third set of studies focusing on knowledge-acquisition components. Our particular concern in these studies was with why it is that vocabulary proves to be pretty much the best single predictor of overall intelligence test scores (Matarazzo 1972). The underlying theory was that vocabulary provides such superior measurement of intelligence because tests of it indirectly measure people's ability to learn from context. If this is indeed the case, then an even better measure of intelligence should be a test of the student's ability to learn meanings of words in context. Such learning, according to our proposed theory of verbal comprehension, involves three elements (Sternberg 1986b; Sternberg and Powell 1983):

1. Knowledge-acquisition components: selective encoding, selective combination, and selective comparison, as described earlier.
2. Context cues to which the knowledge-acquisition components are applied: functional cues, spatial cues, temporal cues, class membership cues, etc.
3. Mediating variables that affect how well the knowledge-acquisition components can be applied to the context cues: number of repetitions of the unknown word, placement of cues regarding the meaning of the unknown word, variability of contexts in which the unknown word is presented, etc.

We found that the elements of our theory of verbal comprehension provided good prediction of the relative difficulty of figuring out the meanings of the various unknown words. Thus, whether or not a word was relatively easy or hard to learn from context did depend on the theory variables. Moreover, the elements of the theory of verbal comprehension are moderately highly related to conventionally-measured verbal intelligence. The results, taken as a whole, suggest that knowledge-acquisition components provide an important basis for the kinds of intelligent learning we need in our everyday lives, whether in school or outside it.

We have conducted a large number of experiments, only a few of which have been summarized here, to test the componential sub-theory of human intelligence, and to investigate the implications of the sub-theory. The results have generally supported the tenets of the sub-theory, and have demonstrated the importance of components in understanding individual differences in intelligence.

The Experiential Sub-Theory

The experiential sub-theory deals with two facets of the relation of intelligence to experience, although our research to date has focused upon the novelty facet. Consider one of our sets of experiments that sought to understand the relation of coping with novelty to intelligence.

The experiments (Davidson and Sternberg 1984; Sternberg and Davidson 1983) were made in an attempt to understand the nature of insight and its relation to intelligence. We proposed that scientists had considerable difficulty in understanding the nature of insight because they believed insight to be a single entity. According to our theory, however, there are three distinct kinds of insights, which correspond to the processes of knowledge acquisition described earlier: selective encoding, selective combination, and selective comparison.

An insight of selective encoding involves separating relevant from irrelevant information. For example, Fleming's discovery of penicillin was via an insight of selective encoding: Fleming noticed that an experiment that failed with respect to the original purpose for which it was conceived succeeded with respect to wholly different and new purposes. The typical scientist would not have selected out as relevant this new information, which was not even originally being sought. Similarly, a detective engages in an insight of selective encoding when recognizing which of the multitudinous pieces of information at the scene of a crime constitutes a clue. A doctor engages in such a use of selective encoding when deciding which of the myriad tests that might be conducted is relevant for diagnosing plausible diseases.

An insight of selective combination occurs when an individual puts together diverse sources of data in a novel and consequential way. For example, Darwin's formulation of the theory of natural selection was based, in part, upon one or more insights of selective combination. The information needed to formulate the insight was available to large numbers of individuals. What Darwin was able to see was how to put this information together. Similarly, a detective engages in insightful selective combination when putting together a set of clues in order to arrive at a hypothesis regarding a possible suspect in a crime. A doctor engages in selective combination when combining the results of multiple tests in order to arrive at a diagnosis.

An insight of selective comparison results when one relates new to old information in a novel and consequential way. For example, Kekule's interpretation of a particular dream constituted an insight of selective comparison. Kekule had been seeking the structure of the benzene ring, but without success. Then, one night, he allegedly had a dream in which he imagined a snake dancing around and biting its tail. When he woke up, Kekule realized that the snake dancing around and biting its tail formed a visual metaphor for the structure of the benzene ring.

In our experiments we sought to isolate each of the three processes of insight described above. Obviously, we could not involve subjects in insights of the profundity or impact of those of Fleming, Darwin, and Kekule. Rather, we used relatively straightforward mathematic/logical insight problems, such as the following:

> You have black socks and brown socks in a drawer, mixed in a ratio of 4 to 5. How many socks do you have to take out of the drawer to be assured of having a pair of socks of the same colour?

Perhaps the most critical features of this problem are (a) that it cannot be solved via routine application of a standard algorithm and (b) that subjects who answer the problem incorrectly tend to focus upon the ratio information which, alluring as it may be, is irrelevant to solution of the problem. In other words, errors tend to be associated with subjects' failure to have proper insights of selective encoding.

We performed separate experiments with children in grades four through six to isolate each of the three kinds of insights. Our experimental manipulation in each experiment involved presenting the insight problems either in unmodified form or with pre-cueing that essentially provided the subjects with the insight. Using this technique, we were able to isolate that increment in performance in each kind of problem that was due to subjects' having the requisite insight. Moreover, we found that what seemed best to separate children identified (in advance) as gifted from those not so identified was their set of insight skills. Hence, insight skills appeared to be critical in distinguishing the gifted from the non-gifted children. This aspect of coping with novelty is truly a central aspect of intelligence.

The Contextual Sub-theory

It proves to be easier to talk about intelligence in context than to measure it. However, we have sought to measure it, as it is manifested in real-world contexts (Wagner and Sternberg 1985).

We started by investigating the intelligence manifested in two occupational contexts: business management and academic psychology. We interviewed highly successful business executives and university professors of psychology in order to find out just what it is that makes for practical intelligence in their spheres.

Our respondents agreed on three things. First, that whatever practical intelligence is, it is not what is measured by IQ tests. Indeed, the most practically intelligent individuals in both fields were usually not perceived to be those with the highest IQs, and the least practically intelligent were not perceived to be those with the lowest IQs. Second, much of what one learns in higher education has little to do with the development of practical intelligence and much of the rest quickly becomes irrelevant, or dated. Third, what does seem to matter is tacit knowledge, or knowledge of what it is that counts in real-world environments. Such knowledge is not explicitly taught but is critical for adaptive success. In effect, tacit knowledge is the product of the various kinds of components, and especially of the knowledge-acquisition components, as they are applied to learning in everyday contexts.

On the basis of these interviews, past literature and our own intuitions, we constructed tests of tacit knowledge for business executives and for academic psychologists. We measured tacit knowledge about managing oneself, others, and one's career. We asked the business executives questions about how they should allocate their time, what kinds of advice they should and should not give junior executives, what kinds of considerations they should take into account when selecting projects on which to work, and so on. On the psychologists' questionnaire, we asked similar questions, though slanting them towards psychology. We also asked questions that would apply to psychologists but not to business executives (and vice versa), such as how to weigh various considerations in deciding to what journal to submit an article.

We sent the business questionnaire to senior and junior level executives both in major companies (near the top of the Fortune 500) and in minor companies (not listed in the Fortune 500), to business graduate students in highly rated business schools and in those that were not highly rated, and to Yale undergraduates. We sent the psychology questionnaire to senior (full) and junior (assistant) professors in highly and modestly rated psychology departments, to graduate students in these same departments, and to Yale undergraduates.

We scaled and selected our final test items on the basis of their ability to discriminate among the responses of the groups at the various levels of expertise. We then scored the questionnaires, and correlated scores on them with two basic kinds of criteria: (a) a test of verbal intelligence, and (b) real-world criteria of success. For the business executives the latter included level of company, merit salary increases, performance ratings, and number of employees supervised; for the psychologists, they included citation rates, productivity, number of professional papers presented at meetings, and quality rating of university department.

Two major findings emerged from the study. First, verbal intelligence test scores were uncorrelated with tacit-knowledge scores, at least for the undergraduates, who were the only ones whom we could realistically test in this way. Second, scores on the tacit-knowledge measures were moderately correlated with the real-world criteria of success (generally at about the 0.4 level). We concluded that tacit knowledge does appear to be an important aspect of practical intelligence, and that practical intelligence, for whatever it may be, is not merely IQ as measured by standard intelligence tests. Intelligence tests are poor measures of people's abilities to adapt to real-world environments.

To conclude, the predictions of the various aspects of the triarchic theory appear to be empirically testable, at least to some extent. The empirical tests that have been done to date have been supportive of the triarchic theory. In the next section, I will describe the plans that are now being made for development of a standardized test that will measure the profile of abilities specified by the triarchic theory.

Testing Intelligence

Because the triarchic test of intelligence is still in the planning stage, it is possible to describe at this point only the tentative specifications for it.

The test, to be published by The Psychological Corporation, a subsidiary of Harcourt, Brace, Jovanovich, will be group-administered and will probably consist of nine levels, ranging in age suitability from four years to adulthood. It will be usable both as a standard intelligence test, and for the special purpose of screening for gifted programmes. There will be two parallel forms, rendering it suitable not only for standard re-testing purposes, but as a pre-test post-test sequence for intellectual-skills training programmes.

Each level will consist of 60 to 80 items measuring three aspects of the triarchic theory – components (academic intellectual skills), one facet (coping with novelty), and functions (practical or contextual intelligence) – through three content vehicles – verbal, numerical, and figural (non-verbal).

Test items will be of the kinds that have been used in the development and validation of the triarchic theory: for example, complex analogies, learning from context, insight problems, tacit knowledge, and so on. Sub-scores will be available for each of the three aspects of the triarchic theory, and for each of the three content vehicles, yielding six sub-scores in all. However, separate sub-scores will not be available for the three different kinds of components, or for the crossing of aspects by contents (eg, coping with novelty via the numeric content vehicle).

Current plans call for linkage of the test to one or both of the two major achievement tests published by The Psychological Corporation – the Stanford Achievement Test and the Metropolitan Achievement Test – and for a variety of score formats, such as percentiles, stanines, and standard scores (converted to a mean of 100 and a standard deviation of 16).

The test is expected to be published in the summer of 1989.

Training Intelligence

The triarchic theory of intelligence has been embodied in a programme for training intellectual skills, *Intelligence Applied: Understanding and Increasing Your Intellectual Skills*, to be published by Harcourt, Brace, Jovanovich late in 1985 (Sternberg 1986a). The programme is suitable for high school students of at least average ability, and for college students at varying levels. It is best suited to a year-long course, although it can be used in abbreviated form in a semester course as well.

The programme consists of two basic elements: the student text and a teacher's guide. The student text is divided into five parts. Part I provides background information regarding past views on the nature of intelligence, past attempts to train intelligence, and the triarchic theory of human intelligence. Chapters in Part I set the stage for the training material to come later, but they should also be viewed as a part of the training itself. They help the student understand why they are pursuing the programme in the first place, and how it can be useful to them. (The teacher's guide also contains materials that help the students apply to the introductory material the same analytical and synthetic skills that the remainder of the programme will develop.) Part II explicates and develops the component skills that emanate from the componential sub-theory of intelligence, with chapters on metacomponents, performance components, and knowledge-acquisition components. Part III emanates from the experiential sub-theory of intelligence, with chapters on coping with novelty and on automatization. Part IV contains a single chapter emanating from the contextual sub-theory – on practical intelligence. Part V also contains a single chapter, on emotional and motivational blocks to the utilization of one's intelligence.

The teacher's guide has chapters each containing eight elements: (a) purpose of the chapter, (b) chapter outline, (c) main ideas, (d) questions for class discussion, (e) suggested paper topics, (f) supplementary activities, (g) suggested readings, and (h) suggested time allocation.

The programme has several features that maximize its value, and that distinguish it from many similar programmes.

First, it contains problems that range in content from highly abstract to highly concrete. The idea is to encourage students to use their intellectual skills in a wide range of problems.

Second, the problems range widely over content areas, so that students can instantiate the mental processes in many domains.

Third, the problems range from the academic to the practical, so that students will use the mental skills taught in the programme both in their school work and in everyday life.

Fourth, the programme includes problems that range from well-structured and soluble by systematic algorithms to ill-structured and soluble only by heuristics or insights. In this way students are encouraged to apply their intelligence not only in 'hard-core' problem solving, but in intuitive problem solving as well.

Fifth, the programme contains a wide variety of kinds of activities in order to reinforce the intellectual skills through a variety of vehicles. These include reading text, individual problem solving, writing papers, class discussions, and individual and group projects.

Sixth, the programme contains a variety of motivational aids. Students are informed of how and why the programme can help them, so that they are not going into it 'blind'. Many concrete, real-world examples are provided, and students are encouraged in a variety of ways throughout the text to apply intellectual skills to their own lives.

Seventh, there is a whole chapter on motivational and emotional blocks to the utilization of intelligence, so that students will be in a position to understand and possibly overcome the non-intellective factors that impede intellectual performance.

Finally, the programme is based on an empirically-validated theory that has been shown to be of at least some value in understanding the nature of intelligence. It trains intelligence as defined in a broad way, in a way that is likely to involve a wide array of domains of thought in which students must engage.

To conclude, *Intelligence Applied* is a new programme for developing intellectual skills, based on the triarchic theory of human intelligence. It has not yet been evaluated as a whole, but evaluations of aspects of it have been very encouraging (Davidson and Sternberg 1984; Sternberg 1986b). The programme, used in conjunction with the pre-test and post-test, seems capable of providing an important element in the training of intellectual skills.

I have described in this chapter a triarchic theory on the basis of which my collaborators and I have sought to understand, investigate, test, and train intelligence. Although the theory is still evolving, the evolutionary process is far enough along to allow the theory to be tested and applied. Obviously, the triarchic theory is only one of the many alternative theories of intelligence that are available. However, to date, it has stood up well to empirical tests, and seems to deal with many of those aspects of intelligence that are critical for theory, for research, and for application.

Note

Preparation of this chapter was supported by Contract N0001483K0013 from the Office of Naval Research and Army Research Institute.

References

Baron, J. (1985) *Intelligence and Rationality* New York: Cambridge University Press

Cattell, R.B. (1971) *Abilities: Their structure, growth, and action* Boston: Houghton-Mifflin

Davidson, J.E. and Sternberg, R.J. (1984) The role of insight in intellectual giftedness *Gifted Child Quarterly* 28, 58-64

Gardner, H. (1983) *Frames of Mind: The theory of multiple intelligences* New York: Basic Books

Gustafsson, J.-E. (1984) A unifying model for the structure of intellectual abilities *Intelligence* 8, 179-203

Heath, S.B. (1983) *Ways with Words* New York: Cambridge University Press

Hunt, E.B. (1978) Mechanics of verbal ability *Psychological Review* 85, 109-130

Jensen, A.R. (1979) 'g': Outmoded theory or unconquered frontier? *Creative Science and Technology* 2, 16-29

Matarazzo, J.D. (1972) *Wechsler's Measurement and Appraisal of Adult Intelligence* Baltimore: Williams and Wilkins

Neisser, U. (1983) Components of intelligence or steps in routine procedures? *Cognition* 15, 189-197

Piaget, J. (1972) *The Psychology of Intelligence* Totowa, NJ: Littlefield, Adams

Simon, H.A. (1976) Identifying basic abilities underlying intelligent performance of complex tasks. In L.B. Resnick (Ed.) *The Nature of Intelligence* Hillsdale, NJ: Erlbaum

Spearman, C. (1927) *The Abilities of Man* New York: Macmillan

Sternberg, R.J. (1977) *Intelligence, Information Processing, and Analogical Reasoning: The componential analysis of human abilities* Hillsdale, NJ: Erlbaum

Sternberg, R.J. (1979) The nature of mental abilities *American Psychologist* 34, 214-230

Sternberg, R.J. (1981) Intelligence and nonentrenchment *Journal of Educational Psychology* 73, 1-16

Sternberg, R.J. (1984) Toward a triarchic theory of human intelligence *Behavioral and Brain Sciences* 7, 269-287

Sternberg, R.J. (1985) *Beyond IQ: A triarchic theory of human intelligence* New York: Cambridge University Press

Sternberg, R.J. (1986a) *Intelligence Applied: Understanding and increasing your intellectual skills* San Diego: Harcourt, Brace, Jovanovich

Sternberg, R.J. (1986b) The psychology of verbal comprehension. In R. Glaser (Ed.) *Advances in Instructional Psychology* (Vol. 3) Hillsdale, NJ: Erlbaum

Sternberg, R.J. and Davidson, J.E. (1983) Insight in the gifted *Educational Psychologist* 18, 52-58

Sternberg, R.J. and Gardner, M.K. (1983) Unities in inductive reasoning *Journal of Experimental Psychology: General* 112, 80-116

Sternberg, R.J. and Powell, J.S. (1983) Comprehending verbal comprehension *American Psychologist* 38, 878-893

Thurstone, L.L. (1938) *Primary Mental Abilities* Chicago: University of Chicago Press

Vernon, P.E. (1971) *The Structure of Human Abilities* London: Methuen

Wagner, R.K. and Sternberg, R.J. (1985) Practical intelligence in real-world pursuits: The role of tacit knowledge *Journal of Personality and Social Psychology* 49, 436-458.

6

Cognitive Theory of Analogy

Mark Keane

Students entering higher education are typically faced with unfamiliar subject-matter to learn. Since analogies are able to provide an immediate understanding of an unfamiliar topic by relating it to prior knowledge, it is clear that they should have an important role to play in this context. However, while the use of analogies has long been recognized by educators, it has wrongly been assumed that their construction is a straightforward and unproblematic matter.

Lecturers and the writers of introductory texts have given little consideration to the possibility that the analogies they use may have negative, as well as positive, consequences on what a student learns. Yet such negative consequences are not unusual. For example, Gentner and Gentner (1983) have shown that the frequently-used 'flowing waters' analogy for understanding the domain of electricity leads subjects to make systematic errors in certain types of circuit problems. Furthermore, it can be argued that the failure of some investigators (Ausubel and Blake 1958; Ausubel and Fitzgerald 1961; Dowell 1968; Drugge 1976; Hayes and Tierney 1982) and success of others (Royer and Cable 1975, 1976; Mayer and Bromage 1980) in finding evidence for the facilitating effects of analogy on learning can be attributed, in part, to the poorness of the analogies used in the former studies. It is thus clear that how an educator intends an analogy to be used may not be how it is actually used by the student. In short, the construction of effective instructional analogies is a non-trivial matter.

The present paper aims to specify guidelines for the construction of effective instructional analogies.[1] In the first section the guidelines, together with the research and theory on which they are based, are presented quite abstractly, in order to preserve the generality of the proposals; in the following section they are applied to a specific example.

Guidelines for Constructing Effective Analogies

The guidelines divide into a single general guideline and a number of specific ones. The general guideline sets up a broad constraint on the domain of knowledge from which such analogies should be drawn, while the specific guidelines suggest the steps to be gone through in constucting an effective analogy.

A General Guideline

An analogy can be said to involve the understanding of an unfamiliar *target domain* in terms of a familiar *base domain*. For example, when one says that 'the atom is like a miniature solar system', the atom (target domain) is understood in terms of the solar system (base domain). An important general guideline is that, when constructing an analogy, base domains should be drawn from the more general domain of one's everyday knowledge of concrete, physical objects and the interactions between them. For example, the billiard-ball analogy for gases involves a base domain which agrees with this guideline.

There are a number of reasons for the above suggestion. Firstly, it is important to be certain that the base domain used is wholly *familiar* to the student. Since we are all familiar with the properties of and interactions between concrete, physical objects from our everyday lives, this guideline will guarantee that the base domain is familiar to the student. Secondly, base domains drawn from this general domain can be *imagined*. Paivio (1983), in arguing for the role of imagery in analogy, has maintained that images (a) can be transformed or manipulated, (b) play a role in memory organization, in the sense that 'one should be able to remember relatively more information in an imagistic form because an image takes up less storage-space than words containing the same amount of information' (Paivio 1983, p.9), and (c) serve as good 'conceptual pegs' for retrieving associated information.

Specific Guidelines

Since most of the specific guidelines for the construction of effective analogies are based on detailed aspects of propositional theories of analogy (Gentner 1980, 1982, 1983; Gick and Holyoak 1980; Keane 1985; Winston 1980), it is necessary to consider such theories in some detail.

In general, propositional theories of analogy model the conceptual structure of the base and target domains as networks of predicates and object/concept nodes (see Gentner 1983). An analogy is thus viewed as a structure-mapping from base to target domain, in which *relations* (ie, multi-place predicates, like HIT [X,Y]) of the concept/objects (X and Y) are carried over, while the *attributes* (one-place predicates, like RED [X]) are not. In this sense, the theory is a more precise statement of the traditional literary notion that analogy asserts a similarity/identity of relations between domains involving dissimilar objects. For example, in the solar system/atom analogy, planets REVOLVE AROUND the sun just as electrons REVOLVE AROUND the nucleus, and one does not expect the attributes of the sun (YELLOWNESS, LARGE MASS) to be applicable to the nucleus. Furthermore, these 'lower-order relations' (like REVOLVES AROUND) are constrained by 'higher-order relations' (like CAUSE, ENABLE; see Schank and Abelson 1977). According to Gentner's *systematicity principle*, lower-order relations in a base domain which are not interconnected by higher-order relations will fail to be carried across to the target domain. For example, the sun is HOTTER THAN the planets but this relation will not be mapped into the atom domain because it is not casually-connected by higher-order relations to other lower-order relations which are relevant in the solar system (see Gentner 1983 for a detailed treatment).

Finally, Keane (1985) has pointed out that there is a stage prior to the mapping of relations during which the objects of a target domain (eg, the nucleus and electrons), corresponding to those in the base domain (ie, the sun and the planets), must be identified. At this stage, it is clear that if the target objects share certain attributes with their corresponding base objects then the process of drawing the analogy should be facilitated. One class of attributes which seems particularly important is that of *functionally-relevant attributes* (FRAs). FRAs are those attributes which become salient when an object is predicated by a relation (and which essentially allows the predication to be meaningful and non-anomalous). For example, as Anderson and Ortony (1975) have shown, when one talks of lifting a piano the FRA 'weight' becomes salient, while in talking of tuning a piano 'musicality' is its FRA, and this differential salience is incorporated into the person's mental representation of the event.

As well as the general guideline mentioned earlier, three specific guidelines, based on the above theories, can be applied in a sequential manner in order to construct a base domain which is an effective analogue to a chosen target domain.

Firstly, object parallelism – it must be ensured that there is a one-to-one correspondence between objects in the base and target domains, otherwise there may be difficulties in mapping relations (see Gentner 1982). Having set up such a correspondence, one must be sure that it can be easily recognized by the student.

Secondly, functionally-relevant attributes – one way to help the student recognize the correspondence between the objects is to point them out (as Gentner and Gentner 1983 do), although a more effective way is to make sure the base objects manifest the FRAs of their partner objects in the target domain. While these attributes may be intuitively discernible, when they are not then one useful rule of thumb is to check whether the objects may be appropriately predicated by the lower-order relations which one wishes to be established, by the student, in the target domain. The facilitating effect of FRAs in drawing analogies has been demonstrated in a problem-solving task, by Keane (1985). In Keane's experiment, subjects in two conditions received one of the two analogous solutions to a problem. The only difference between the two solutions was that the critical object/concepts of one had the same FRAs as those in the target domain, while those of the other did not. As predicted, significantly more subjects receiving the former analogous solution solved the problem than those receiving the latter.

Thirdly, checking higher-order relations – one of the reasons why analogy is so powerful is its *generativity* (Collins and Gentner 1982); that is, an analogy permits students to 'generate' their own predictions within the target domain. However, from an educator's viewpoint, most of the difficulties arise in attempting to control students' predictions. Since, in propositional terms, generativity is a function of mapping higher-order relations from the base domain, it is clearly important to check relations.

In particular, assuming one has found suitable parallel objects which may be predicated by the essential lower-order relations, one needs to check whether the appropriate higher-order relations may predicate the propositions. Higher-order relations must be accurate and complete. They must be *accurate* in the sense that the higher-order relations asserted to hold in the base domain must be those which one requires the student to apply in the target domain. Gentner and Gentner (1983) have demonstrated the importance of this point by teaching subjects about electricity using either a 'flowing waters' or a 'teeming crowds' analogy. Since neither analogy was wholly accurate, subjects made predicted mistakes on certain electric-circuit problems. The relations must be *complete* because of the systematicity principle mentioned earlier. Otherwise, potentially important lower-order relations will not be mapped into the target domain.

Another pertinent reason for checking higher-order relations is to ensure that anomalous predictions cannot be made. While one can never be wholly certain of excluding all anomalous predictions, since every student will encode the base domain in a slightly idiosyncratic way (because of the uniqueness of past experience), there are a number of ways of minimizing them. The best method is to test the base domain as an analogous 'explanation' for important phenomena in the target domain. If an anomaly is found, one can either explicitly inform the student that a certain prediction should not be made or one can modify the base domain to rule out the anomalous prediction.

These are the main guidelines for the construction of effective instructional analogies. Since the account has been relatively abstract, in the next section a specific example is considered.

Application of the Guidelines

The target domain chosen for the sample construction is that of water conduction and transpiration in plants, from biology. While this is not necessarily the best example of a wholly unfamiliar topic, it is useful for illustrative purposes.

What happens in the target domain is that water, taken in by the roots, is conducted upwards in the xylem (conductive tissue) to the leaves, a distance which, for example in large trees, may be over 100 feet. There are two main mechanisms behind this water transportation: root pressure and transpiration tension. Under certain conditions the roots will actively take in water from the soil and by forcing it into the conductive tissue will cause it to rise in the xylem. This is, however, only a minor factor in water transportation. More importantly, when water is lost from the leaves, as a result of photosynthesis and evaporation through the stomata (on the leaf's underside), there is a corresponding loss of water in the leaf cells, which transmits a strain to adjacent cells, and eventually to the water columns in the xylem. Since water molecules cohere in the xylem (because of electrostatic forces) this strain (transpiration tension) causes the upward movement of the water columns in the xylem (see Cronquist 1973).

In constructing an analogous base domain one needs, firstly, to select unambiguous parallel objects. Concentrating on the xylem and the water, the *parallel objects* which will be chosen here are wax-paper straws filled with very tiny balloons (note the overlapping FRAs between the xylem and the straws in their tube-like properties).[2]

Secondly, can the required *lower-order relations* be asserted of these objects ? Many can obviously be asserted (eg, STRAWS CONTAIN BALLOONS), but what of the cohere relation between the balloons ? The balloons can be plausibly predicated with this relation because under certain conditions (when rubbed vigorously), they cohere, due to similar electrostatic forces. If, say, billiard balls had been chosen initially, this relation could not have been convincingly predicated of them (because of their attributes) and some other object would have had to have been chosen.

Thirdly, the required *higher-order relations* also need to be asserted. Well, the loss of balloons from the top of the straw will CAUSE the column to rise BECAUSE the balloons cohere (thus explaining transpiration tension) and adding baloons to the bottom of the straw will CAUSE the column of balloons to rise (root pressure). So the critical predictions plausibly follow. But what of anomalous predictions ?

One way of checking for anomalies is testing the analogy against phenomena in the target domain. One such phenomenon is 'wilting'. Certain plants (like nettles) rely on hydrostatic pressure to remain upright and if the level of water in the conductive tissue drops the plants will wilt and collapse because of the weight of the leaves on the upper part of the plant. Similarly, if there is considerable weight on the top of the straw and the number of balloons decreases in it, its rigidity should be lost, causing it to collapse. Another phenomenon concerns the effects of cutting slips from plants. If plant slips are not cut under water the transpiration stream is broken and the slip may not recover from this. Similarly, it is implicit in the base domain that the balloons will only cohere if they are touching, so if the column is broken the balloons cannot attract other balloons across a wide vertical gap. One possible anomaly, which follows from this test, is that since balloons are light they will rise of their own accord. To exclude this anomalous prediction, one might add the extra information that the balloons are filled with a relatively heavy gas (though not heavy enough to overcome the cohesive forces between balloons if a vertical gap opens beneath them).

In summary, this analogy, with some minor modification, seems fairly resistant to any anomalous predictions although it clearly needs extension: that is, parallel objects need to be posited for the leaves, leaf cells and stomata, and the details of evaporation need to be plausibly modelled.

Conclusion

The implications of the present guidelines for student learning in higher education are clear. The use of analogies will significantly facilitate the learning of unfamiliar topics and sound construction of analogies will allow a greater control over the learning outcome. Furthermore, while these proposals may be used by individual educators, it is clearly preferable that they be applied systematically. Such an application would entail identifying target topics which students have difficulty in learning, constructing effective analogies to explicate these topics and applying these analogies as a standard part of the educational process.

Finally, in a more speculative vein, it can be argued that the potential of analogy has yet to be appreciated. Recent theories of learning (eg, Rumelhart and Norman 1978, 1981; Rumelhart and Ortony 1977; Schank 1982) all give a central emphasis to what are essentially analogical processes. If these theories are correct then the use of analogy, constructed in the manner prescribed here, may prove to tap processes which are fundamental to human learning.

Notes

1 It will be clear that the proposals outlined are best limited to the learning of scientific or technical subjects.
2 Ideally, it is best to find an existing domain (eg, the solar system for the atom) but since such domains seem scarce, the domain will usually have to be constructed.

References

Anderson, R.C. and Ortony, A. (1975) On putting apples in bottles: A problem of polysemy *Cognitive Psychology* 7, 167-180

Ausubel, D. and Blake, E. (1958) Proactive inhibition in the forgetting of meaningful school material *Journal of Educational Research* 52(4) 145-149

Ausubel, D. and Fitzgerald, D. (1961) The role of discriminability in meaningful verbal learning and retention *Journal of Educational Psychology* 56(6) 266-274

Collins, A. and Gentner, D. (1982) Constructing runnable mental models *Proceedings of the Fourth Annual Conference of the Cognitive Science Society* Michigan: Ann Arbor

Cronquist, A. (1973) *Basic Botany* New York: Harper Row

Dowell, R. (1968) *The Relation between the Use of Analogies and their Effects on Student Achievement in Teaching a Selected Concept in High School Biology* Unpublished PhD dissertation, Indiana University

Drugge, N.L. (1976) *The Facilitating Effect of Selected Analogies on Understanding Scientific Explanations* Unpublished PhD dissertation, University of Alberta

Gentner, D. (1980 *The Structure of Analogical Models in Science* BBN Report No. 4451

Gentner, D. (1982) Are scientific analogies metaphors ? In D. Miall (Ed.) *Metaphor: Problems and Perspectives* Sussex: Harvester Press

Gentner, D. (1983) Structure-mapping: A theoretical framework for analogy *Cognitive Science* 7, 155-170

Gentner, D. and Gentner, D.R. (1983) Flowing waters and teeming crowds: Mental models of electricity. In D. Gentner and A. Stevens (Eds) *Mental Models* Hillsdale, NJ: Erlbaum

Gick, M.L. and Holyoak, K.J. (1980) Analogical problem solving *Cognitive Psychology* 12, 306-355

Hayes, D. and Tierney, R. (1982) Developing readers' knowledge through analogy *Reading Research Quarterly* 17(2) 256-280

Keane, M. (1985) On drawing analogies when solving problems: A theory and test of solution generation in an analogical problem solving task *British Journal of Psychology* 76(4)

Mayer, R.E. and Bromage, B. (1980) Different recall protocols for technical texts due to advance organizers *Journal of Educational Psychology* 72, 209-225

Paivio, A. (1983) The mind's eye in arts and science *Poetics* 12(1) 1-18

Royer, J and Cable, G. (1975) Facilitated learning in connected discourse *Journal of Educational Psychology* 67(1) 116-123

Royer, J and Cable, G. (1976) Illustrations, analogies and facilitative transfer in prose learning *Journal of Educational Psychology* 68(2) 205-209

Rumelhart, D.E. and Norman, D.A. (1978) Accretion, tuning and restructuring: Three modes of learning. In J.W. Cotton and R. Klatzky (Eds) *Semantic Factors in Cognition* Hillsdale, NJ: Erlbaum

Rumelhart, D.E. and Norman, D.A. (1981) Analogical processes in learning. In J.R. Anderson (Ed.) *Cognitive Skills and Their Acquisition* Hillsdale, NJ: Erlbaum

Rumelhart, D.E. and Ortony, A. (1977) The representation of knowledge in memory. In R.C. Anderson, R.J. Spiro and W.E. Montague (Eds) *Schooling and the Acquisition of Knowledge* Hillsdale, NJ: Erlbaum

Schank, R. (1982) *Dynamic Memory: A theory of reminding and learning in computers and people* Cambridge: Cambridge University Press

Schank, R. and Abelson, R. (1977) *Scripts, Plans, Goals and Understanding* Hillsdale, NJ: Erlbaum

Winston, P.H. (1980) Learning and reasoning by analogy *CACM: Artificial Intelligence and Language Processing* 23(12) 689-703

7

Beyond Inferencing: Student Reasoning in Physical Science

Seth Chaiklin

Models of problem solving and learning play a critical role in instructional research, design, and practice (Bruner 1985; Sternberg 1985). Presumably, all attempts to address instructional questions contain at least an implicit model of thinking and learning. If educational researchers are dissatisfied with instructional applications and their outcomes, then one obvious response, among several, is to try to develop better models. This paper examines a contemporary class of cognitive models that have become predominant in educational research and instructional design. A central criticism is that these fail to include certain processes that are clearly part of student reasoning. Two such processes are described here, in the context of physical-science concept reasoning, and substantive implications are considered for models of reasoning, learning, and instruction.

The cognitive approach describes human thinking as the active processing of information structures. Within that purview, the cognitive psychology of problem solving has focused primarily on the knowledge that people use to perform specific tasks, and the knowledge necessary or sufficient for a person to perform a specific task successfully. Analyses are often presented as models that describe information structures such as schemata, and inferential processes such as production (if-then) rules that operate on the information structures (Greeno and Simon in press). Thus, the models focus on patterns of information, actions enabled by those patterns, and plans that organize the sequence of actions to accomplish a particular goal. I designate such models as *step-by-step*, to characterize their main thrust: to describe the informational inputs and outputs that yield the sequence of steps a person follows in using a particular information structure to answer a question.

Step-by-step models have been useful for addressing instructional problems because they provide a promising technology for (a) identifying and characterizing the content and structure of inferences that people make in solving mathematics and science problems at a school-age level, (b) noting critical differences in the information structures and inferential processes applied to the same task by people with different levels of skill (Chi, Feltovich and Glaser 1981; Larkin, McDermott, Simon and Simon 1980), (c) analysing what is required intellectually to perform a task successfully (Champagne and Rogalska-Saz 1984; Resnick 1976), and (d) accounting for observed errors of reasoning by identifying incorrect beliefs or missing knowledge (Brown and Burton 1978; Sleeman 1984).

An important issue for a comprehensive theory of problem solving is the *direction* of reasoning. In general, the question of direction is concerned with accounting for why particular actions occur among a variety of possible actions in a given situation. Two levels of analysis can be distinguished. The microscopic level is the particular sequence of actions carried out in solving a problem. The macroscopic level is the general approach used to solve a problem. Step-by-step models address the microscopic aspect, mainly as a consequence of presupposing an initial problem representation. Given a problem representation, the microscopic direction of reasoning is accounted for by the process of selecting productions (ie, by determining which production's application conditions are satisfied by the information accepted as true about the problem). This process yields the sequence of actions that reflects direction of reasoning.

Step-by-step models have little to say about the macroscopic level. This paper discusses two processes that affect the macroscopic direction of reasoning – selection of approach (or selection for short) and evaluation. The selection process corresponds to the following observed scenario. A problem-solver has several solution methods available. Some methods are easier to apply to a particular problem than others, yet the solver does not always select the easiest method. How does a solver select a method to apply ? What factors affect the process ? The step-by-step model does not address this question directly because the information pattern of the givens might be adequate to match several approaches.

Several investigators have recognized the selection problem, but ruled it outside their immediate concern or existing cognitive theory (Kintsch and Greeno 1985; Resnick and Neches 1983). Other investigators have noted that subjects can have more than one approach to a problem, and exhibit a preference, which they call *priority*, for one of these approaches (diSessa 1983; Larkin 1978). However, this is a redescription of the phenomenon, not an account. Still other investigators have tried to account for the phenomenon by using levels of activation for particular productions (Anderson 1983) or associative strength (Siegler and Shrager 1984) as a means for selecting an approach.

Evidence is presented for three factors that sometimes affect which approach is selected. They are: (a) the givens in the problem, (b) subject specifications of objects in the problem, and (c) recently solved problems (Einstellung). These factors are consistent with the Hayes and Simon (1977) observation that people focus on superficial features in the problem statement, and that this affects the representation of the states and operators used in problem solving. Selection of initial representation is critical because it is intimately related to the solution method used (Chi et al. 1981; Newell and Simon 1972).

The evaluation process determines the acceptance of generated solutions, which involves the evaluation of the propositions and inference rules used to generate solutions. Two kinds of scenario typically involve the evaluation process. In one scenario, a subject generates an answer to a question (ie, satisfies the goal), but then decides not to trust the generated answer, and attempts to produce another. In the other, two different answers are generated to the same question, and the subject must decide which one to accept. The evaluation process stands beyond the matching of patterns of information in the content of the subject matter. It influences the macroscopic direction of reasoning.

Selection and evaluation processes both influence the macroscopic direction of reasoning in problem solving because they affect the general orientation of the beliefs that are deployed in answering any particular question. The analysis of selection and evaluation presented here is grounded on a study of reasoning with the concept of density. Thinking-aloud protocols were analysed to determine the cognitive structures – schemata and declarative propositions – that subjects used to answer questions involving the concept of density. The protocols were also used to support a step-by-step model of density reasoning that applied these cognitive structures to solve density problems. The model provides a specific point of reference against which to describe the selection and evaluation processes. Subjects used two strategies to evaluate their solutions. One was to assess the truth of a density component or a particular application of the component. The other strategy was to assess how well the applied component has taken the given information into account.

The reasoning model has a blackboard control structure that attempts to apply density components (see below) to answer density questions (Chaiklin 1985a). The model is a typical cognitive process model, having the step-by-step characteristic. Four layers of control are needed to account for the non-linear character (in the sense of switching among goals) of the observed reasoning performance (Stefik 1981). The first layer sets general *intentions* such as to *answer question*. The next layer contains *strategies* to realize general intentions, such as *recall answer* or *construct solution*. The latter was the most common strategy for the questions used in this study. The next two layers involve *general* and *content-specific tactics* to realize strategies. Construct-solution can be realized by four general tactics: select a schema, fill its slots, execute the schema, and evaluate the result. Evaluation here is simply checking that the result produced by the schema matches the goal of the question. This is necessary, for example, with comparative density questions in which a person could compute numerical density for one material, but still would not have an answer until computing the numerical density for the other material. Some computer-simulation models, programmed by Ernest Rees, used the construct-answer strategy to solve density problems. These models help to validate the computational feasibility of both the density components and the processes involved in their application.

Method

The data for the analyses were problem-solving protocols obtained from individual interviews. Four undergraduates who had taken one or more semesters of university chemistry (B.G., M.F., Z.M., and D.B.) and a first-year biochemistry graduate student (S.A.) were asked to think aloud while they answered fifty-four questions involving the concept of density.

The questions were restricted to two classes: How does the density of material A compare with material B, with more or less information given about these materials, and how does the density of material A compare before and after some physical transformation is performed? An example of a comparison question was: How does the density of copper compare with aluminium? An example of a transformation question was: How does the density of a sliver of redwood compare with the density of the whole trunk of the tree?

The question set was designed thoroughly to assess subject beliefs about the concept of density. Four important design criteria were to (a) cover the major issues in a scientific analysis of the situations covered in the two classes of questions, (b) provide questions that raise issues about possible boundary conditions in the subject matter, (c) elicit a representative sample of solution methods that were used several times, and (d) provide questions that might be problematic for the kinds of conceptions about density held by the subjects. The complete set of questions, a discussion of their construction, and details of the procedure can be found in Chaiklin (1984).

Specific Density Beliefs

The observed structures that embodied specific beliefs about density will be referred to as *density components* (see Table 1). Each density component was self-contained: subjects did not need to apply two density components to produce an answer to the questions asked in the study. Questions about the relative densities of two materials could be answered by applying one of these components, providing its application conditions were met. Some subjects provided evidence for only a sub-set of these components, but each subject had several components that could be applied to the two classes of questions. Therefore, selection is an issue. Finally, the density components in Table 1 were stable, in the sense that subjects used them several times while working

---

COMPLEX DENSITY SCHEMATA
  – Numerical central schema
  – Ordinal central schema
  – Verbal central schema
  – Kinesthetic central schema
  – Floating schemata
  – Particle schema

SINGLE STEP SCHEMATA
  – Heaviness
  – Solid-liquid-gas
  – Harder
  – X is X
  – Equal-volume, different masses

DECLARATIVE PROPOSITIONS
  – eg Diamond is the densest of all materials
  – eg Water is most dense at 4°C

Table 1
Summary of observed density components.

through the problem set. Details about these components and supporting evidence are discussed in Chaiklin (1985a). They are summarized here for reference in the examples.

The first six schemata in Table 1 each had two or more associated inference procedures that handled a variety of problems. The first four are called *central* schemata because they are based directly on the formal definition of density as mass per unit volume. They are differentiated because their application depends on the availability of input data that are appropriate to their *data type*. For example, the numerical central schema uses real numbers; so a greater numerical value in the ratio of mass to volume implies a greater density. The ordinal central schema uses relative quantities of *more* and *less* mass and volume; and so forth.

Two forms of the floating schema were observed. The solid-liquid floating schema holds that a solid is more dense than a liquid if it sinks in that liquid, and less dense if it floats. The solid-solid floating schema holds that a solid that sinks is more dense than a solid that floats, and is indeterminate if both sink or both float. The particle schema holds that greater density means closer particles. This schema is valid only when the masses of the particles are identical. Subjects did not obey this constraint and also applied the schema to compare materials with different particle masses.

The next five schemata in Table 1 involved a single inferential step. Only the last two are scientifically correct. The heaviness schema took two forms. One form referred to materials as class entities. Thus lead is heavy and aluminium is light. The heavier material is denser. Another form referred to the weight of specific objects. Hence the heavier object is denser. The solid-liquid-gas schema holds that solids are denser than liquids which are denser than gases. The hardness schema holds that the harder a material, the greater its density. The X is X schema holds that a material has a chacteristic density regardless of its volume. The name comes from subjects saying things like 'water is water' to argue that the density of two different volumes of water is the same. The equal-volume, different-masses schema holds that if two samples have the same volume, then the sample with the greater mass has a greater density.

Some examples of declarative propositions used by subjects include: diamond is the densest of all materials, mercury is very dense, and water at 4°C is in its most dense state. The proposition about diamond is false.

Selection of Components

Subjects have several density components available, and, most times, more than one component is appropriate for a given problem. In other words, there is no one-to-one mapping between a problem and a component that can solve it. In their problem-solving protocols, subjects do not seem to consider every potentially applicable component. This raises a question about what determines which density component is selected.

Selection of a component was one of the four general tactics in the construct-solution strategy in the density reasoning model. The model of this strategy described the informational requirements that enable a density component to be applied, but not when or why one component would be selected over other viable candidates. In other words, there is no account of contingencies that affect the likelihood of selection and application of a density component for a particular question.

In another paper, I argued for two hypotheses that help to specify an approach to the selection question (Chaiklin 1985b). The *selection* hypothesis holds that density components are selected only if the information needed for pattern matching is active in current memory. The *informational access* hypothesis claims that subjects do not have access to the implications of a density component except when the component is applied in response to a goal. An important implication of these two hypotheses is that the contents of a component are not available for inspection unless it has been selected and applied, and this is affected by the information in current memory. I now discuss three factors – problem givens, subject specifications, and Einstellung – that influence the selection of a density component. In each case, these factors influence the contents of current memory, and hence the particular density component that is selected.

As well as showing the effect of givens, the first example shows that a subject can know that a particular solution method is incorrect, yet still pursue it. B.G. seemed to be influenced by the volume or weight of two objects. There was plenty of evidence that B.G. knew that volume or weight alone is not sufficient to determine density, and he had asserted, for several different problems, that weight or volume alone does not matter. Despite all this evidence, there were instances in which B.G. focused on weight in a way that seemed to affect his selection of a density component. When he compared the density of a 300-lb block of granite and a brass key, he mentioned that one should not think in terms of large and small. However, in his solution, he first seemed to be swayed by the volume using the heaviness of the two materials as a guide. He commented at the end that it was hard to compare brass and granite because he did not think of granite as ever being in small objects or brass being in large objects.

Close inspection of this case suggests the following. The givens in the problem, granite and brass, did not provide obvious cues to the floating schemata, nor was any information given that was obviously sufficient for the central schemata. Moreover, the givens emphasized both a volume and weight difference between the two materials. This alone would interfere with selecting the equal-volume, different-masses schema (which was eventually used) because, given the subject's beliefs about the volume of a key and a 300-lb rock, a direct representation of the givens would contradict the equal-volumes requirement. The emphasis on the volume difference and his comment about it being hard to think otherwise leaves the heaviness schema as a strong candidate. He knew that he should not but he seemed to do so anyway. I take this example to illustrate how the givens in a problem can affect the initial representation of the problem and hence the density component selected.

A second and related example arose when B.G. was asked to compare the density of three objects he could physically handle: a plastic block, an aluminium block and a wood block. Only three questions before this one, he had stated that one should ignore size when comparing a hand-size aluminium block with the trunk of a redwood tree, yet he focused on the weight of the large wood block and the weight of the small plastic cube. He commented that he did not know why he was using the weight of the objects rather than thinking of the density of the materials. I think that because the materials were there to be lifted, it was easier to use weight, and hence select the heaviness schema.

Givens can also affect selection if a given makes contact with a declarative proposition. For example, when Z.M. encountered questions with water, he would assert that water was the densest material at 4°C, and did not consider other approaches to the question. A similar case was observed with B.G. who asserted that diamond was the densest of all materials.

These examples show that the givens of a problem can influence a subject's approach, including using methods that they know are inappropriate or incorrect. This sometimes occurred even after subjects had recently noted the inappropriateness of a schema.

A second influence on the direction of reasoning is subject specification of givens. Most of the comparison questions presented materials such as aluminium, tin, copper, and candle wax without specifying a particular quantity or object. The subjects often specified the materials into particular forms such as a copper wire or a tin can. These specifications sometimes seemed to affect which component a subject selected by calling attention to properties of the specified object that the subject believed were indicative of density.

When B.G. was asked to compare the density of copper and tin, he started by specifying copper as a piece of wire and tin as a can. He first decided that tin was less dense because 'they want less dense cans' (copper > tin). This would be desirable, he reasoned, because less dense cans are less heavy. He went on to say that 'for copper they use things that are more solid' and tin is used for thin things such as cans. This specification led him to reverse his answer, claiming that tin must have a larger density than copper, because it 'can withhold things when it's thin' (tin > copper). This switch is based on his incorrect belief that density is directly proportional to hardness. This is why 'they use it for thin surfaces.' Finally, remarkably, he commented, 'I would think gee, why don't they use thin things with copper. I've never really seen anything with – thin things with – why don't they?'. Remember he had started his protocol by considering copper as a wire, which is a thin thing. This example shows clearly that B.G.'s specification of the class terms (copper and tin) affected the density belief he selected.

A comparable case of the effects of specification can be found with the same question for S.A. She was trying to imagine comparable tin and copper objects. She thought of tin cans, said that she could not think of copper cans and then tried to consider both a sheet of tin foil and a 'corresponding sheet of copper', but she was 'just having trouble imagining two things the same volume ...one made of copper, and one made of tin.' Because she could not imagine a tin and a copper object of comparable volume, she used her belief that harder things are denser, concluding that tin is less dense because 'tin ...is more malleable than copper.' This case shows how a specification, here an inability to form a representation, affected which belief was selected. Quite possibly, because S.A. represented tin as tin foil, she was more inclined to think of tin as more malleable, and this suggested the hardness schema.

These examples show that subject specifications of givens influence the density belief that is applied. This result extends the previous result about the effect of givens, and emphasizes the Hayes and Simon (1977) point about the importance of representation in reasoning.

The third factor that sometimes seemed to affect the direction of reasoning was an Einstellung-like phenomenon. Even though the questions were not constructed or arranged to induce Einstellung, some cases occurred in which subjects may have had their selection of components affected because of recently solved problems – perhaps even a single problem. For example, S.A. was comparing the densities of a *large* and *small* block, at 80°C and 20°C respectively. She started her protocol with an assumption that these blocks were the *same size*, which was consistent with the previous problem where she had set an assumption that two blocks were the same size. At one point she commented that 'Maybe we don't have to worry about volumes. Wait – maybe I've gotten off the – maybe that question prejudiced me when I looked at this one.... I'm making stupid mistakes. That last question prejudiced me.'

Another case can be found with B.G. who had solved six of the last twelve problems using some version of the idea of equal volumes and different masses. He had some difficulty when he encountered a problem in which the volumes were different and the masses were equal. He commented that, 'See, I'm getting used to, I've been working with, in terms of mass changing. OK, and so I'm thinking of the number on the top. Now I have to switch my thinking. I mean after a while, look at that stack [of question cards] there.' While this episode does not reveal any specific change in his thinking, it does show that solving several problems with one method may have affected the ease with which he could select another component to apply to this new case.

Evaluation of Solutions

The step-by-step reasoning model described above had an evaluation process in the construct-answer strategy that checked whether the result satisfied the goal. The model had no means to indicate whether a subject believed the answer they produced to a density problem. As I shall illustrate here, subjects engaged in activities that can be construed as deciding whether the produced answer was acceptable.

Logically, there are two ways to evaluate the correctness of an answer. Either the component that was used is deemed true or false in general, or the application of the component to a particular problem is appropriate or inappropriate.

Subjects sometimes evaluated whether an inference rule was correct. Other times they evaluated whether an inference rule should be applied to a particular case. As a consequence of these evaluations, subjects sometimes rejected the application of an inference; other times they qualified their belief in its validity. Evaluations are sometimes needed to select among alternative answers that the subject generated. This collection of evaluation processes stands beyond the inferential content of each component. The functional outcome in each case is to decide whether to accept an answer or not, and this affects the direction of reasoning.

I observed three tactics that subjects used to assess the *correctness of the component*. They are: (a) appeal to authority, (b) appeal to a component that one believes to be true, and (c) find a counter example. The first two tactics are distinguished by the source of the authority, external in the former case, personal in the latter. Applying these tactics, subjects produced three kinds of evaluations: certain; false; or true in general but uncertain.

One effect of a *certain* evaluation is to override the application of other components, thereby ending reasoning. For example, some subjects used some declarative propositions as certainties. The evaluation often came from an appeal to a higher authority: the subjects would report that their instructor had taught the proposition. They would use the proposition, sometimes overriding the application of schema-based inferences. An example is found in Z.M.'s protocol in which he compared the densities of lead, pinewood and water. He reported:

> S: All right, I know that the density of water is 1 and that's the most dense object, than the pinewood or the lead. Alright, and umm, between the lead and the pinewood, I would have to know the mass – and their volume because I haven't rememorized –
> E: Yeah so – but the water is denser than the lead and the wood?
> S: Pinewood.

In this remarkable protocol, Z.M. used his declarative proposition that water is the densest of all materials to decide that it is denser than lead or wood. Other protocols showed that he knew objects that sink in water are more dense than water. Nonetheless, the declarative proposition seemed to predominate here. A comparable case was observed for B.G., where he compared diamond, nickel, and silicon. He noted that diamond was the densest, mentioned that his instructor told him, and did not consider other components.

A second effect of the certain evaluation is to enable a decision between two density components that generate different answers to the same question. B.G. compared the density of a large block of iron at 80°C and a small block of iron at 20°C. He started by dismissing the fact that the blocks were two different volumes. He eventually answered that the smaller block was denser, arguing from a central schema and his belief about the effect of heat on the arrangement of the molecules. When the interviewer repeated B.G.'s conclusion, B.G. replied, 'It's usually opposite you know? When they tell you large and small it's – that's why I was like, wait a minute. Am I right? Yeah. I'll go with my logic rather than some tricks that are really trying to throw me off here. You know, like a double fool kind –.' In this episode, B.G. evaluated a component based on weight or volume alone against a central schema. He decided to follow the central schema, which he believed to be a true component.

Evaluation of certainty for other declarative propositions, that are not density components, can also interfere with density reasoning. This is a third effect. B.G. compared the density of 10g cubes of uranium and zinc, where the volume of the zinc is given as larger than the volume of uranium. He asserted that zinc must be denser than uranium because he thinks of uranium as a gas and zinc as a metal, and metals are denser than gases. The certainty here is his declarative proposition that uranium is a gas. This proposition, not universally true, inclined B.G. to select his solid-liquid-gas schema. However, he said that he was not even reading the question and went on to consider the givens. B.G. then used a central schema to decide that zinc is denser than the uranium, but was troubled by this conclusion. He reviewed his argument and reported, 'I'm getting confused because I'm thinking of zinc being much more dense than uranium because I can't think of uranium as being really solid.' In this case, a strong belief in a proposition that uranium is a gas yielded an answer that contradicted an answer produced by a central schema. B.G. accepted the answer produced by the central schema.

With an evaluation of *false*, subjects usually reject the component or its application, and often search for another component. I have seen subjects produce an evaluation of false by (a) finding a counter-example to the conclusion of the applied component, and (b) applying a definition based on a central schema, which is held to be certain, to show that a component is not adequate. Here are three examples in which subjects used counter-examples to reject potential density principles. For two problems, B.G. reported an intuition that denser materials are darker; once he supported this intuition with an argument, based on his particle schema, that perhaps closer molecules make an object darker. He criticized this intuition when asked to say more about it, saying that he never really used it, and that he wouldn't take it as a general rule. He noted that there were probably a lot of exceptions, and gave a counter-example of how one could colour a natural cork black, but that it still would not be very dense. M.R. used the counter-example tactic to refute a schema that density is directly related to hardness. He recalled that lead was not very hard, but that it was very dense. Similarly, Z.M. gave a counter-example of baking clay in the sun until it was superhard to refute the connection between density and hardness.

For the evaluation of *uncertain*, subjects reliably used particular density components, but were also aware of potential inadequacies in the beliefs embodied in these components. That is, subjects sometimes applied a component, even if they did not have a strong belief in its correctness. This phenomenon may be typical in that the subject must apply this component because of a demand for an answer and because nothing else is generated.

Subjects used an external authority and components they believed to be true when they gave uncertain evaluations, though sometimes they did not indicate an identifiable tactic. Here are two examples. B.G. decided that copper was more dense than aluminium, because copper is heavy and aluminium is light when he lifts them. He had specified aluminium as a can, and said that with copper he usually picks up 'something that's solid. So I think in terms of you know, it being more dense because it's heavier.' He evaluated his solution by saying: 'But I would have to say copper because I think of solid copper and that influences – you know that, gee, more mass, you know, more density but really I shouldn't go by that. But I am.' He was using his heaviness schema here, recognized that it was not adequate for a solution, but applied it anyway.

A second example occurred when S.A. compared the densities of balsa wood, peanut oil, and rubber. She used her solid-liquid-gas schema to decide that peanut oil, a liquid, was less dense than the two solids, but immediately said that her decision was 'strictly on that basis and I'm not sure that that's good thinking.' She mentioned that 'I think I learned it in chemistry. I guess that I'm not real clear on that, but that's how you'd think it would be and it seems like that's what we were taught.' This episode shows that her evaluation of this schema was based partly on an appeal to higher authority, and partly on an appeal to her personal knowledge. Her application of this schema seems to be a consequence of 'That's the only thing I can go on there.'

The other general strategy to evaluate answers focused less on the validity of the component and more on the validity of the *application of the component* in particular situations. Subjects would occasionally evaluate whether an applied component took all the relevant information into account. B.G. was asked to compare the density of sixty millilitres of water in a cylinder with the density of the remaining thirty millilitres after thirty millilitres had been poured out. His first, immediate answer was to assert that the density was the same, using the X is X schema. However, he then considered pressure differences. He focused on this aspect because he noticed that the height of the column of liquid is an important factor in determining the pressure at a given point in a liquid, something he had learned from university physics instruction. The X is X schema does not address the pressure differential caused by the height difference. I believe this inclined B.G. to search for another component that could take pressure difference into account. He eventually used the idea that the pressure difference produced a greater compression in the larger volume, hence it would have a greater density.

Discussion

At the opening of this paper, I noted both the importance of psychological models to instructional research, design and practice, and the current primacy of cognitive models. I then discussed two general processes, selection and evaluation, involved in physical-science reasoning. Selection and evaluation are fundamental in that they operate in each instance of problem solving. The selection process (qua theoretical concept) acknowledges that persons must access their knowledge, and that the most efficient solution does not always come even when it is available. The evaluation process acknowledges that we often treat our knowledge tentatively, and that this can affect its application.

Although the existence of the two above mentioned processes should be uncontroversial, they are not included in step-by-step cognitive models. Their inclusion critically shifts the kinds of psychological phenomena addressed. In particular, they draw attention to problems that people confront in applying their knowledge. The image of human problem solving that includes these processes contrasts qualitatively with the image embodied in a step-by-step model. The step-by-step model emphasizes structural or synchronic processes in a person's problem solving. Step-by-step models, to overstate the case a little, if treated as comprehensive, portray human problem solving as the provision of inputs followed by mental processing of these inputs by if-then rules until a goal is satisfied (or the person quits). They describe the inferential steps involved in applying information to produce an answer. There is no provision for the possibility that a person might have difficulty accessing a solution approach or trusting a produced situation. These possibilities are diachronic processes that affect when the operations described by the structural model occur. These diachronic processes reflect characteristics of the intellectual task that students face in solving and learning to solve problems in a topical domain.

In the remaining pages, I mention some considerations for further investigation of selection and evaluation, and consider three implications for instructional research. But first, I wish to delimit the scope of my claims in two ways. First, the analysis is limited to people who have had introductory instruction and a small amount of direct experience with the concept, probably in the order of weeks, though possibly distributed over a period of six to eight years. I am reasonably confident of the validity of this description for such persons, which includes virtually all compulsory school students and most university students. Second, I wish to limit my claims to situations in which a person has several solution methods available, and the problem is to select one of them. In short, the question is how individuals with adequate, but unpractised knowledge, attempt to apply their knowledge to a range of novel problems that sometimes challenge their ability to produce a solution. I believe this is a representative condition for most people engaged in learning new physical-science material.

Theoretical Development of Selection

For the delimited case under consideration, I reject a model that characterizes selection metaphorically as jigsaw puzzle solving, that is, as a matter of inspecting contemporaneously several jigsaw pieces to see which fits the empty space. In particular, I reject the comprehensive distance or reflection implied by this model for two reasons. First, the selection hypothesis and the informational access hypothesis mentioned above suggest that selection is a problem because we do not have access to the contents of our knowledge in a reflective way. Second, a first reading of a problem does not always reveal the structure of the problem. Consequently, subjects must select and attempt to apply a method to see if it is adequate for the problem. This was also observed with expert physicists solving a hard problem (Larkin 1983). The issue of selection is what factors influence this first choice. The concept of *priority*, mentioned earlier, is one approach to the selection issue, but it has several problems. First, its relation to the notion of access needs to be clarified. As the term is used, it conflates selection and evaluation as I have discussed here. It seems to refer to *conceptual* priority, rather than to be an indicator of how likely a person will be able to recall it. Second, any attempt at establishing such a priority must consider performance over a range of examples to defend against the possibility of transient effects like Einstellung. Third, as mentioned, the current formulation is a redescription of an empirical phenomenon. An interpretation grounded in a theoretical account of reasoning would be useful.

Theoretical Development of Evaluation

The evaluation process can be modelled using the same layers of control that were used to model the construct-answer strategy. That step-by-step model had four layers: intention, strategy, general tactics, and domain-specific tactics. Using the first three layers, the evaluation process can be characterized as: having an intention to evaluate a solution; having a strategy to establish the truth of the component or goodness of coverage of givens; and having general tactics, such as those discussed above, to realize these intentions and strategies.

It is encouraging that the same architecture can be used to model the step-by-step processes that operate with the subject-matter content and the evaluation process. This compatibility suggests that step-by-step models can be extended to incorporate evaluation.

Implications for Instructional Research

The results and analysis presented here are preliminary, but they provide some interesting considerations for instructional research.

First, if selection depends critically on the givens, then an important implication arises about the importance of using a problem set that covers a wide range of different given conditions. The suggestion is not new instructional wisdom, but the theoretical model clarifies some reasons for the validity of it. If successful conceptual performance is closely tied to specific givens within a similar question structure, then a mental representation of concepts that is abstracted beyond givens may require much experience or particular kinds of experience with a variety of structural features in the subject matter.

Second, attention to the process of evaluation may help in understanding the process of noticing conflicts and conceptual development. In the first place, many investigators have argued that conflict is an important process in the development of concepts (eg, Dewey 1933; Gunstone, Champagne and Klopfer 1981; Hewson and Hewson 1984; Inhelder, Sinclair and Bovet 1974; Murray, Ames and Botvin 1977; Piaget 1964; Sigel 1979). However, they have also noted the difficulty in inducing these conflicts for students (eg, Gunstone et al. 1981), and the processes of conceptual change remain opaque. My sketch of the evaluation process suggests that some problems in getting students to confront contradictions may be located here. Apparent contradictions can be resolved by an evaluation process that dismisses one of the solutions as inappropriate.

In the second place, components that subjects identify as possibly incorrect, even though they use them, may be a good starting point for instructional efforts to get subjects to modify or eliminate a component. DiSessa (1983) noticed this possibility in his formulation of learning as the development of different priorities. The notion emphasizes that not only must students acquire the inferential content of a component, but they must acquire, at least implicitly, an ability to assess when that component should be used.

Third, task performance is used as an indicator of knowledge or belief. Generally we take assertions generated in interviews and examination papers at face value as representing a person's beliefs. Most of the time, this is probably a reasonable assumption, but the selection and evaluation processes discussed here suggest some complications that may supplement our characterizations of the nature of a person's beliefs. In particular, I would want to assess a person's beliefs with a wide range of problems to minimize the possibility that a special feature in the givens has not predominated. Similarly, it seems important to recognize that students do not have equal degrees of belief in all the knowledge that they apply, but specific consequences for practice remain to be explored.

Summary

I have argued that a significant class of psychological processes that affect the direction of reasoning are not incorporated in contemporary cognitive models. The analysis showed that inclusion of these processes raises some questions relevant to instructional research, and the discussion indicated specific points for further theoretical development.

Acknowledgements

This chapter is derived from a doctoral dissertation submitted to the University of Pittsburgh. The examining committee was Professors James G. Greeno (Chairman), Audrey B. Champagne, Robert Glaser, Peter Machamer, and James F. Voss. The chapter itself was written while the author was at the Center for Research in Human Learning at the University of Minnesota.

The research was supported by the Office of Naval Research, Contract N00014-79-C-0215, Contract Authority Identification NR 667-430. Preparation of this chapter was supported by Grant T32 HD-07151 from NICHD to the Center for Research in Human Learning, and a special computing grant from Barbara Wolfe, Assistant Vice-President of Information Systems at the University of Minnesota.

I thank Patricia Zeller for transcribing the audio-recorded interviews, and Matthew Lewis for critical comments on the manuscript.

References

Anderson, J.R. (1983) *The Architecture of Cognition* Cambridge: Harvard University Press
Brown, J.S. and Burton, R.R. (1978) Diagnostic models for procedural bugs in basic mathematical skills *Cognitive Science* 2, 155-192
Bruner, J.S. (1985) Models of the learner *Educational Researcher* 14(6) 5-8
Chaiklin, S. (1984) *Reasoning with a Physical-Science Concept* Doctoral Dissertation, University of Pittsburgh
Chaiklin, S. (1985a) *Reasoning with a Physical-Science Concept* Paper presented at the meeting of the American Educational Research Association, Chicago
Chaiklin, S. (1985b) *Stability of Conceptions in Novice Physical-Science Reasoning* Paper presented at the meeting of the American Educational Research Association, Chicago
Champagne, A.B. and Rogalska-Saz, J. (1984) Computer-based numeration instruction. In V.P. Hansen and M.J. Zweng (Eds) *National Council of*

Teachers of Mathematics 1984 Yearbook 43-53. Reston, VA: The National Council of Teachers of Mathematics

Chi, M.T.H., Feltovich, P.J., and Glaser, R. (1981) Categorization and representation of physics problems by experts and novices *Cognitive Science* 5, 121-152

Dewey, J. (1933) *How we Think* (revised edition) Boston: Heath

diSessa, A.A. (1983) Phenomenology and the evolution of intuition. In D. Gentner and A. Stevens (Eds) *Mental Models* 15-33. Hillsdale, NJ: Erlbaum

Greeno, J.G. and Simon, H.A. (In press) Problem solving and reasoning. In R.C. Atkinson, R.J. Herrnstein, G. Lindzey and R.D. Luce (Eds) *Stevens' Handbook of Experimental Psychology* (revised edition) New York: Wiley

Gunstone, R.F., Champagne, A.B. and Klopfer, L.E. (1981) Instruction for understanding: A case study *The Australian Science Teachers Journal* 27(3) 27-32

Hayes, J.R. and Simon, H.A. (1977) Psychological differences among problem isomorphs. In N.J. Castellan, D.B. Pisoni and G.R. Potts (Eds) *Cognitive Theory* Vol.2, 21-41 Hillsdale, NJ: Erlbaum

Hewson, P.W. and Hewson, M.G. A'B. (1984) The role of conceptual conflict in conceptual change and the design of science instruction *Instructional Science* 13, 1-13

Inhelder, B., Sinclair, H. and Bovet, M. (1974) *Learning and the Development of Cognition* Cambridge: Harvard University Press

Kintsch, W. and Greeno, J.G. (1985) Understanding and solving word arithmetic problems *Psychological Review* 92, 109-129

Larkin, J.H. (1983) The role of problem representation in physics. In D. Gentner and A.L.Stevens (Eds) *Mental Models* 75-98 Hillsdale, NJ: Erlbaum

Larkin, J.H., McDermott, J., Simon, D.P. and Simon, H.A. (1980) Models of competence in solving physics problems *Cognitive Science* 4, 317-345

Larkin, K.M. (1978) *An Analysis of Adult Procedure Synthesis in Fraction Problems* (ICAI Working Paper 1) Cambridge, MA: Bolt Beranek and Newman

Murray, F.B., Ames, G.J. and Botvin, G.J. (1977) Acquisition of conservation through cognitive dissonance *Journal of Educational Psychology* 69, 519-527

Newell, A. and Simon, H.A. (1972) *Human Problem Solving* Englewood Cliffs, NJ: Prentice-Hall

Piaget, J. (1964) Development and learning *Journal of Research in Science Teaching* 2, 176-186

Resnick, L.B. (1976) Task analysis in instructional design: Some cases from mathematics. In D. Klahr (Ed.) *Cognition and Instruction* Hillsdale, NJ: Erlbaum

Resnick, L.B. and Neches, R. (1983) Factors affecting individual differences in learning ability. In R. J. Sternberg (Ed.) *Advances in the Psychology of Human Intelligence* 2, 275-323 Hillsdale, NJ: Erlbaum

Sleeman, D. (1984) An attempt to understand students' understanding of basic algebra *Cognitive Science* 8, 387-412

Stefik, M. (1981) Planning and meta-planning (MOLGEN, Part II) *Artificial Intelligence* 18, 141-170

Siegler, R.S. and Shrager, J. (1984) Strategy choices in addition and subtraction: How do children know what to do? In C. Sophian (Ed.) *Origin of Cognitive Skills* 229-293. Hillsdale, NJ: Erlbaum

Sigel, I.E. (1979) On becoming a thinker: A psychoeducational model *Educational Psychologist* 14, 70-78

Sternberg, R.J. (1985) All's well that ends well, but it's a sad tale that begins at the end: A reply to Glaser [Comment] *American Psychologist* 40, 571-572

8

Learning from Experience in Diagnostic Problem Solving

N.C. Boreham

Diagnostic ability is crucial in a wide variety of trades and professions. For instance, when a management consultant is asked why productivity in a factory has fallen, when a technician is given a piece of apparatus to repair, when a doctor is consulted by a patient, when an auditor notices discrepancies in a company's accounts, when an AA patrolman is called out to a stranded motorist – in all these situations, diagnosis is the basis for successful intervention. Despite the obvious differences between the content of the work, the structure of the diagnostic task in each field is the same: a system (whether it is the human body, an engine or an industrial company) presents signs and symptoms of malfunction, and the diagnostician has to find the cause by investigating the state of the system further.

It is a fundamental principle that diagnostic skill can only be acquired through extensive experience of the act of diagnosis itself. Whatever the importance of pre-requisite theory, practical experience is an essential component of any training programme in this cognitive skill. A central task for the educator is therefore to organize the students' early experiences of diagnosis in a way that maximizes learning. The aim of the present paper is to examine some of the implications of recent cognitive theory for this undertaking.

How we learn from experience is a question which has received a great deal of attention since the days of Dewey (1916) at least. Before we approach the central theme here, therefore, it might be helpful to review some of the important issues which have emerged from that debate.

First, the term 'learning from experience' really means learning from *reflection on* experience. Educators have found methods based on free group discussion and the Kolb Learning Styles Inventory useful for promoting such reflection (Abercrombie 1969; Kolb and Fry 1975).

Second, learning from experience is critically dependent on emotional involvement. The complex affective field within which reflection on experience ought to occur has been neatly described as 'comradeship in adversity', the essential element in the technique of action learning (Revans 1980).

Third, adults are, however, often resistant to the idea that they can learn from their own experiences (Usher 1985). This can be attributed to the nature of their formal schooling, which in most cases relied on reception learning to the exclusion of almost everything else, and played down the validity of intuitive ways of knowing. Educators wishing to promote learning from experience consequently have to revive in their students learning styles which may have been discouraged since primary school – learning from experience depends on learning *how to learn* from experience.

These are all necessary in any effective programme of learning diagnosis from experience. However, there is a further issue to consider – what aspects of the diagnostic task should be included in the range of experiences which the educator provides for the student? A basic assumption in training design is that not all components of a task are equally critical to successful performance of the task itself (Gilbert 1967). Admitting that diagnosis can only be learned from experience is consistent with recognizing that real life does not necessarily provide ideal conditions of practice. A representative sample of diagnostic problems taken from a professional's daily round will probably include environmental stressors that inhibit learning (Stammers and Patrick 1975), barriers to the effective reception of feedback (Einhorn 1980), and a large proportion of non-critical experiences which use up practice time without being particularly instructive (Gilbert 1967). To arrange a programme which will maximize the acquisition of diagnostic skill therefore requires judicious selection of an appropriate 'portfolio' of experiences.

Most diagnostic situations are complex, and afford the educator an opportunity to concentrate the learners' attention on certain aspects of the task rather than on others. Broadly speaking, the kind of practice available to trainee diagnosticians contains two elements – the rich set of background information about the case, and a rather limited set of hypotheses about the possible causes of the problem which can be tested against the available data. The pedagogical problem is how to make the best use of the trainee's time by achieving an appropriate balance between the two. Should he emphasize the former at the expense of the latter, or vice versa?

This dilemma was put to me forcibly by a junior hospital doctor, who was learning to be a diagnostician in the time honoured way as junior to a 'firm' of consultant physicians. The consultants worked in a highly efficient way, obtaining from each patient no more information than was needed to decide between the alternative diagnostic and treatment options which had to be considered. One way in which a junior can learn from participating in this process is by understudying the highly selective hypothesis testing of the consultants – imitation learning of this kind is strongly advocated in some textbooks (eg Cutler 1979). However, this particular junior doctor had a broader view. He spent a lot of time just sitting and talking to the patients about whatever aspects of their illness, medical history, lifestyle or life in general they wished to discuss. Whole afternoons spent this way, he believed, were not wasted but contributed more to the development of diagnostic insight than tracing the logical implications of patient data for individual hypotheses.

Knowledge-Based Models of Diagnosis

Increasing attention has been given in recent years to the role which knowledge plays in problem solving (Glaser 1984). Such work has clear implications for the present issue. Some modern cognitive theorists attribute expertise in reasoning to the possession of detailed knowledge of the problem domain, organized in the form of schemata or stereotypes. On this view, diagnoses are reached by recognizing the pattern of cues in the symptom display, and making implicit inferences to the cause of the problem. Models of diagnostic problem solving of this type have been developed by Feltovich (1981) and Johnson et al. (1981).

The mechanism by which recognition of a symptom pattern leads to a diagnosis was originally described in Minsky's (1975) theory of frames. A 'frame' is 'a data structure for representing stereotypical situations. Frames capture the essence of the situation but not the detail... *(and contain information) about how to act in this situation... the recognition of a frame automatically triggers the appropriate action*' (emphasis added). On this view, the basis of diagnostic expertise is a large memory store of symptom patterns, associated with each of which is a diagnosis. As Feltovich (1981) puts it, 'the expert recognizes the situation and calls forth actions that have proved efficacious in the same or analogous situations.' The model of diagnosis developed by Feltovich (1981) and Johnson et al. (1981) will be referred to here as the 'template model'.

An integral part of this model is that the hypothetico-deductive operations by which diagnosticians are presumed to evaluate hypotheses are not a critical element in their diagnostic expertise. Two specific pieces of evidence have been advanced in support of this. The first is that skilful and unskilful diagnosticians do not differ in their ability to perform the formal operations which the doctrine of mental logic presumes to be involved in hypothesis testing. For instance, it has been shown in expert-novice comparison studies that successful diag- nosticians generate better initial hypotheses (ie are quicker to recognize the cause of the problem) but show no particular superiority in hypothesis testing as such (Elstein et al. 1978). This has been widely replicated in other problem domains (Chi and Glaser 1985).

The second piece of evidence is research purporting to show that hypothesis testing is epiphenomenal, all that is needed to solve reasoning problems being 'contained' within the expert's memory store of situational templates (Frederiksen 1984). In this connection, reference is often made to Wason's findings concerning the selection task (Wason and Johnson Laird 1972). These showed that subjects could falsify a conditional hypothesis when it was presented in familiar concrete terms (ie embedded within a knowledge structure) but not when it was presented in the abstract. Many supporters of the knowledge-based theory have taken this to show that formal operations in themselves are not crucial to success or failure in hypothesis testing (eg Rumelhart 1978). As Feltovich (1981) puts it, 'extralogical knowledge factors dominate formal rules in reasoning. When, for a given setting, these other factors are consistent with formal logic, a person will appear formally rational... (but when the knowledge base is absent, as in the selection task) the relatively anaemic nature of content-free, "pure" reasoning is exposed'. Errors in diagnosis are attributed to incorrect knowledge about system malfunctions, rather than to inability to perform formal operations (Johnson et al. 1981).

Educational Implications

The template model of diagnosis presents a challenge to higher education. On the whole, university teachers tend to assume that problem-solving skills can be learnt by practising the relevant logical operations, and that familiarity with the problem domain is a mere ornamentation which the graduate can pick up for himself after he has been trained in the logic of the task itself. Accordingly, practice in diagnostic problem solving has often been designed to emphasize the testing of hypotheses against data, rather than the perception of patterns in symptom displays and the direct association of these with diagnostic solutions. Methods which have been devised to achieve such a logical emphasis include 20-Questions type tutorials and computer simulations which impose a hypothetico-deductive structure on the task. Obviously, if the template model is correct, then rehearsing the formal operations implicit in such hypothesis testing cannot be expected to bring about any improvement in diagnostic ability.

In an attempt to test the template model and its implications for higher education, two experiments will be described. One of these investigates whether practice at hypothesis testing improves diagnostic ability, while the other investigates directly whether experts rely on deductive logic to make their diagnostic judgements. The domain studied in both inquiries is the diagnosis of performance problems in industrial organizations.

Diagnosing Performance Problems

A performance problem is defined as the situation when a job in an organization is not being carried out to the required standard. This may be due to any of a large variety of factors, including the equipment, the work methods, the way in which personnel are selected, the training or the reward system. Management consultants are frequently required to solve such problems, which call for careful diagnostic thinking (Gilbert 1967; Mager and Pipe 1970).

The task was operationalized for this research in the form of tab item simulators. A tab item is a pencil-and-paper exercise comprising (1) a description of the system to be diagnosed, (2) a description of the symptom and (3) a list of questions supplying further information about the situation, the answer to each of which is covered by a sticky tab. Devices of this kind have been widely used for training physicians, maintenance engineers and other diagnosticians (McGuire et al. 1976). As a practice environment, the tab item provides opportunities for both learning about symptom configurations and practising hypothesis testing.

Practice in Hypothesis Testing

One way of evaluating the template model is to investigate whether practice in testing hypotheses against data results in a gain in diagnostic skill over and above anything which might be due to incidental learning about symptom configurations. A controlled experiment was therefore conducted in which the effects of the former on performance in a transfer task of diagnosis were isolated from the effects of the latter.

The subjects were forty-seven students of management science. They were randomly divided into two groups, one of which (experimental group) practised on a series of three tab item simulations of performance problems. These required the subjects to think up hypotheses for the problem given, and to test them by peeling off sticky tabs and interpreting the yes/no answers thus revealed. Since each case contained some fifteen separate hypotheses of which only one or two were true, this required a predominance of falsification as the subjects narrowed their search down to the causative factor. It should be noted that rejecting a hypothesis was not just a matter of uncovering a 'no' answer, for much of the disconfirming evidence was phrased positively. Thus to draw conclusions frequently involved the use of negation and double negation. Detailed descriptions of the test materials, subject responses and the scoring are given in Boreham (1983).

The control group practised on the same three cases, but were not asked to test any hypotheses. Instead, they were given a familiarization task which involved sorting the details given in the problem documentation into patterns centring around the different components of the system (training, selection, equipment, etc.) which might be faulty. This was not intended to be a complete pattern-recognition training programme in its own right. It was a control treatment, intended to provide an opportunity for acquiring knowledge about the configurations of data which might be associated with different causes of performance problems. As such, it controlled for the opportunity students in the experimental group might have had to acquire such knowledge incidentally.

Following the period of practice, both groups were given the same transfer task - a fourth tab item. This required freely constructed answers, which were content analysed by a team of three raters. The implication of the template model is that the experimental group would not show any superiority in diagnosis.

In fact, the experimental group performed significantly better than the control group on the transfer task. The principal difference between them was the frequency of misdiagnosis (ie attributing the problem to factors which had not been responsible for it and could have been eliminated by correct interpretation of the data available). In the experimental group, only 2 out of 21 students misdiagnosed, whereas in the control group as many as 10 out of 26 did so ($p=0.04$, two-tailed Fisher's exact test). A longitudinal analysis of the experimental group performance over the three practice exercises showed a gradual reduction in the frequency of misdiagnoses, which strengthens the conclusion that the hypothesis testing aspect of the tab item promoted acquisition of diagnostic skill over and above anything gained through familiarization with the case details.

The Cognitive Components of Expert Diagnostic Judgement

A further test of the template model is to ascertain directly whether experts rely entirely on pattern recognition when forming their diagnostic judgements, or whether they also make use of deductive logic. To investigate this, a process tracing study was conducted, with expert management consultants as subjects, and the transfer task of the previous experiment as the performance problem they were asked to diagnose. The subjects were tested individually and asked to think aloud while they solved the problem. Their efforts were tape recorded and transcribed, and the resulting protocols were analysed to identify the cognitive operations involved.

The experts' performance was best explained in terms of a bounded rationality model of reasoning similiar to the model proposed by Simon (1983). Full details of the protocol analysis, which is too lengthy to quote here in its entirety, will be found in Boreham (1983).

The subjects' expertise was quite obviously strongly dependent on their intuitive abilities to operate on mental models of what they implicitly recognized in the problem givens. Their initial problem spaces included constraints (not part of the problem givens, but recalled from the subjects' memory of similar situations) which drastically reduced the amount of the problem domain which needed to be searched for the causal factor. This was unmistakably the result of a pattern recognition process similar to those postulated in the knowledge-based theory outlined earlier.

However, the problem was not actually solved just by activating these templates. Despite the substantial prior experience of these consultants, and the fact that the problem was one which they had 'seen a lot of' in industry, the solution was not actually contained in the schemata which were activated. The intuitive processes were used only to generate a problem space which isolated the crucial aspects of the problem and guided subsequent search.

In order to model the consultants' problem-solving behaviour accurately, it was necessary to represent the process of diagnosis as an alternation between knowledge-driven operations on a mental model of the situation, and sensory-driven operations on the problem givens. Insights gained in the former type of episode narrowed down to the cause of the problem remarkably quickly, but the management consultants still felt the need for local search to verify that what they suspected was actually the case, and to delineate the nature of the problem exactly.

It was at the stage of local search that they utilized inferential procedures which conformed more closely to the process of hypothetico-deductive reasoning than to the process of pattern recognition. The subjects' reasoning from the yes/no answers to the truth value of particular hypotheses followed the classical laws governing inferences from categorical propositions (propositions which refer to classes). During the initial work-up, the subjects categorized each individual hypothesis into a class, eg all the hypotheses referring to aptitudes were placed by one subject into a group which he called 'Selection'. Having established this categorical framework, they used it to decide the truth of certain groups of hypotheses en masse without having to test each one individually. This was done by asking a general question which referred to such a category, and using the answer to infer the truth values of the hypotheses which had been designated members of that class. The subject's inferences followed the general law of Modus Tollens $((p \supset q).\sim q)$ $\supset \sim p$, where p is a specific hypothesis, and q is a statement meaning 'something in this class of organizational functions contributed to the performance problem'. Having allocated (for instance) a hypothesis about a specific aptitude to the class of selection factors, this established the truth of the entailment $p \supset q$. By then establishing the truth of $\sim q$ (ie that it is not a selection problem), it was possible to eliminate the hypothesis about a specific aptitude by logical deduction – for if $p \supset q$, and we know that $\sim q$, then the classical laws of logic tell us that $\sim p$ is certainly the case.

That the subjects were correctly applying this logical law is clear from the fact that they avoided making the invalid inference of affirming the consequent $((p \supset q).q) \supset p$. It is a common fallacy in this kind of categorical reasoning task, having established that q is true, to infer from this that p must also be true. But the subjects carefully avoided this error: if the answer to a general question *confirmed* the categorical proposition q, they 'unpacked' that category by recalling all the hypotheses they placed in it during the initial work up, and then tested each one individually.

Conclusion

In recent years, the concept of high-level knowledge structures has been reintroduced to cognitive psychology in an attempt to explain human problem solving. In the field of diagnosis, it has been hypothesized that expertise depends on a memory store of 'templates' which yields problem solutions when activated by recognition of the relevant symptom patterns. This model is sometimes offered as a sufficient explanation for all observable diagnostic judgement, both the expertise and the error. If the template model is accepted in its full rigour, the formal operations of hypothetico-deductive logic are downgraded to the status of mere epiphenomena.

The findings described above question whether such a monolithic knowledge structure really does provide a complete explanation for the phenomena of diagnostic reasoning. The rock on which the template model founders is that not even an expert's memory store can contain sufficient detail to predict everything which will happen in the future. Or, to put it in a different way, if sufficient detail is supposed to be stored in memory to solve every problem by pattern recognition alone, then this simply translates the difficulty of explaining problem solving into new terminology without actually eliminating it.

In the light of recent research (Chi and Glaser 1985) it is clear that human judgement is more dependent on knowledge than was previously believed. The experts in the present study relied heavily on pattern recognition and mental models of the state of the malfunctioning system. But they used this knowledge as an executive programme to guide local search, not to produce a diagnosis. The diagnosis itself was the outcome of the local search, the data thus generated being interpreted by inferential processes which are more accurately modelled by logical deduction than by pattern recognition. The implication of this study, then, is that formal operations are an irreducible component of expertise in diagnostic judgement, at least in the problem domain investigated. This conclusion is corroborated by the finding that practice in the formal operations involved in hypothesis testing substantially reduced frequency of misdiagnosis in the sample of students.

Where does this leave the educator? Anybody wishing to provide a suitable practice environment for learning diagnostic skills will certainly have to ensure that all the conditions mentioned earlier are met – the learners should be stimulated to reflect on their actions, the practice environment should involve them emotionally as well as intellectually, and their ability for self-directed, self-initiated learning should be developed to the full. The focus of the present paper has been on a fourth consideration – which aspects of the diagnostic task should be included in the portfolio of practice material? While admitting that exposure to symptom configurations might prove to be an important part of diagnostic training, the present results show that practice in testing hypotheses against data is likely to be beneficial too.

References

Abercrombie, M.L.J. (1969) *The Anatomy of Judgment* Harmondsworth: Penguin

Boreham, N.C. (1983) *The Effectiveness of High and Low Fidelity Training Techniques* Unpublished PhD Thesis, University of Manchester

Chi, M.T.H. and Glaser, R. (1985) Problem solving ability. In R. J. Sternberg (Ed.) *Human Abilities* New York: W.H. Freeman

Cutler, P. (1979) *Problem Solving in Clinical Medicine* Baltimore: Williams and Wilkins

Dewey, J. (1916) *Democracy and Education* New York: Macmillan

Einhorn, H.J. (1980) Learning from experience and suboptimal rules in decision making. In T.S. Wallsten (Ed.) *Cognitive Processes in Choice and Decision Behaviour* Hilldale, NJ: Erlbaum

Elstein, A.S., Shulman, L.S. and Sprafka, S.A. (1978) *Medical Problem Solving* Cambridge, MA: Harvard University Press

Feltovich, P.J. (1981) *Knowledge Based Components of Expertise in Medical Diagnosis* University of Pittsburgh, Learning Research and Development Centre: Technical Report PDS2

Frederiksen, N. (1984) Implications of cognitive theory for instruction in problem solving *Review of Educational Research* 54, 363-407

Gilbert, T.F. (1967) Praxeonomy: A systematic approach to identifying training needs *Management of Personnel Quarterly* 6, 20-33

Glaser, R. (1984) Education and thinking: the role of knowledge *American Psychologist* 39, 93-104

Johnson, P.E., Duran, A.S., Hassebrock, F., Moller, J., Prietula, M., Feltovich, P.J. and Swanson, D.B. (1981) Expertise and error in diagnostic reasoning *Cognitive Science* 5, 235-283

Kolb, D.A. and Fry, R. (1975) Toward an applied theory of experiential learning. In C.L. Cooper *Theories of Group Processes* New York: Wiley

McGuire, C.H., Solomon, L.M. and Bashool, P.G. (1976) *Construction and Use of Written Simulations* New York: Harcourt Brace Jovanovich

Mager, R.F. and Pipe, P. (1970) *Analyzing Performance Problems* Belmont, California: Fearon

Minsky, M. (1975) A framework for representing knowledge. In P. Winston (Ed.) *The Psychology of Computer Vision* New York: McGraw-Hill

Revans, R. (1980) *Action Learning* London: Blond and Briggs

Rumelhart, D.E. (1978) *Schemata: The Building Blocks of Cognition* La Jolla, California: Centre for Human Information Processing

Simon, H.A. (1983) Search and reasoning in problem solving *Artificial Intelligence* 21, 7-29

Stammers, R. and Patrick, J. (1975) *The Pyschology of Training* London: Methuen
Usher, R.S. (1985) Beyond the anecdotal: Adult learning and the use of experience *Studies in the Education of Adults* 17, 59-74
Wason, P. and Johnson-Laird, P. (1972) *The Psychology of Reasoning* London: Batsford

Part 3

Learning as Construing

9

The Educational Construction of Learning

Roger Säljö

A Swedish officer celebrating his 100th birthday was interviewed on the local television some time ago. On being asked the perfectly ordinary and inevitable question of how he felt about being so old, he gave a very distinct, and in my view unforgettable, answer: 'I feel fine, thank you', he said 'considering the alternative.' Empirical research in the modern sense on thinking and learning is by now celebrating its first centennial. Since the appearance of the epoch-making *Über das Gedächtnis* by Hermann Ebbinghaus in 1885, researchers in the behavioural sciences have been studying in well-designed and impeccable experiments the intricate issues of how people learn, remember, solve problems, and manage other related cognitive phenomena.

Looking today across the various branches of research that deal with such essential human phenomena as thinking and learning, the uninitiated but inquisitive novice is bound to experience considerable confusion. A process of continuous proliferation of subcommunities of researchers with their own paradigms of thought and accompanying vocabularies characterizes the development over the past decades. Theoretical perspectives once sunning themselves at the centre of public attention, widely recognized as the long-awaited breakthrough in the struggle for improving and understanding human learning and thinking, can find that their glitter is fading when tested against the multifaceted and complex reality of real-life cognitive activity, and, if unlucky, they become marginalized as the cherished intellectual pastime of small groups of researchers still managing to pay adherence to their original intellectual premisses.

Whether this first era of cognitive research has been successful or not is difficult to say, since we have nothing to compare it with. At one level research activities are flourishing, as judged by the increase in the number of journals and books published. In this respect prospects look good, and, like the Swedish officer cited above, we need not for the moment worry about the alternative. Yet many people, especially perhaps those with a practical interest, would argue that there seem to be difficulties in reaching clear cut and definitive answers to the issues addressed in all these studies. In the area with which I am most familiar, education, burning issues such as 'How should we teach?', 'What problem-solving strategies are the most efficient?' or 'How should text books be designed to optimize learning?' still await unambiguous answers. The harsh, but knowledgeable, critic of cognitive research might make a comparison with other human sciences, for example medicine, that seem to have managed to deal with questions of health and illness more successfully than we have been able to deal with the easily recognized problems of learning and thinking in modern society.

Even people with a theoretical interest in these areas of research could point to certain unsatisfactory experiences in the past. The school of thought that has had the clearest impact in education, the Skinnerian version of behavourism, was built on the assumption that mental phenomena, if they existed, were outside the realm of interest of the behavioural scientist. Even today there are signs that are worrying. Disputes between representatives of various schools of thought or proponents of supposedly competing models of learning and thinking miss the beauty and intrigue of genuine theoretical confrontation, since empirical studies of 'memory systems' and 'information processing capacities' merely mirror the assumptions of the models and theories from which they emerged. The fundamental ambiguity of cognitive phenomena allows, for example, for the 'interference theorist' to conceive human forgetting as the consequence of various kinds of interference, while the student of mechanisms of learning and forgetting in the sixties and seventies would seek refuge in the intricacies of the various memory systems postulated as explanatory constructs.

My own first experiences of studying human learning were of participating in a project devoted to the study of how people, mostly university students, go about their everyday business of learning. For me, as a student of cognition, the outcomes of this work were critical with respect to the theoretical frameworks then in vogue. What I had learned, bookishly, to regard as crucial theoretical differences in the design of the human intellectual make-up, did not seem to form any identifiable part of the problems that we were observing among students. For example, one of the main findings of this semi-anthropological attack on normal learning was that the most decisive factor determining study success was if students actually read their text books or not. Those who did were generally quite successful, while those who for some more or less acceptable reason chose not to, usually – although not always – ran into troubles in their examinations (cf Svensson 1976). What could be understood as in some way purely intellectual differences in an abstract sense did not seem to be particularly powerful factors in explaining achievements, and, in fact, the unsophistication of the matters that really seemed to make a difference for study success was in many ways shocking, given the perspective of cognitive research.

However, what I have said so far should not be seen as an attack on the merits and contributions of cognitive research, but rather as an argument for reconsidering some of those 'practical problems and natural settings' to which psychology's answer so far has been a 'thundering silence' as Neisser (1982, p.5) put it in his well known opening address at the congress on 'Practical Aspects of Memory' some years ago. By returning to the complex phenomena of learning and thinking in the dynamics of everyday life, consciously putting prevalent theories and models in parenthesis, we may begin to readdress basic issues, and on the way engage in stimulating discussions on reasonable models of human thinking.

Since empirical research in these areas by now has a long tradition, it might seem somewhat strange to attempt to create enthusiasm for readdressing the issue of what constitutes the object of inquiry in studies of learning and thinking. However, in my view, such a step back from the flood of research findings appearing, is both necessary and warranted, should we wish to establish contact with everyday life. When Ebbinghaus laid the foundation for empirical research in these areas, he did so by pursuing a perspective upon learning, remembering and forgetting that enabled him and all his successors to study such processes in their 'pure' form and without the confounding influences and ambiguities characteristic of such phenomena in their everyday appearance. In inventing the nonsense syllable, Ebbinghaus was, as Hilgard (1964) phrased it, 'all ahead of his times' (p.vii) paving the way for research which maintained a strict division between form and content in the study of human thinking.

From an historical perspective, it is interesting to understand why Ebbinghaus' work did have such a resounding impact. The answer is that there already existed a fairly clear understanding of what constituted the decisive criteria of being scientific. Thus, as Giorgi (1983, 1985) points out, 'a history of research practice, including guidelines and criteria, preceded psychology's adoption of the experiment as the ideal form' (1983, p.147). Method thus preceded content, and the problem Ebbinghaus solved was making diffuse and ambiguous phenomena accessible to empirical study in line with the conceptions of research characteristic of the Zeitgeist. Thus, 'the primary motivation for inventing the nonsense syllable was to provide as homogeneous a material as possible,' and consequently Ebbinghaus, since he 'could not control language or the past history of the subject, introduced material as devoid of meaning as possible' (Giorgi 1985, p.33).

In this process, the research subjects became ahistorical and asocial beings, whose ways of interpreting the world were consciously put aside. In the laboratory setting, they were condemned to temporary ignorance, stripped of the intellectual tools and conceptual frameworks through which one normally makes sense of the world. Stripped of the *culturally derived* cognitive equipment, the activities left to study in the scientific laboratory, we should argue, carry very little of the flavour of what educators have to deal with as practical issues.

Empirical studies and theorizing in the fields of learning and thinking have, of course, developed tremendously over the years. Yet, in curious ways, they seem to preserve many of the hidden assumptions of the nature of their object of inquiry. Behind the wide range of terminologies used to describe human thinking, there still remains an isolated mind contemplating the world and an ahistorical individual whose 'information processing system', 'memory storage' or 'cognitive apparatus' is studied per se. The epistemological underpinning of such a distinction between form and content, between thinking and its object, was firmly established in our world view by the philosophical works of Descartes, who by his famous statement 'I think, therefore I am', separated the mind and the body. In what has become known as Cartesian dualism, the 'mind and the body are two independent entities, the mind exercising intellectual activities, the body being governed by mechanical laws' (Markova 1982, p.20). Following this, the individualistic mind and its assumed properties became the natural objects of study for cognitive researchers, and in this sense Cartesian man is 'a *thinker* rather than a *doer*', who contemplates the world and 'acquires knowledge through the passivity of perception and understanding rather than by any form of activity' (ibid. p.62).

The unwillingness of students of cognition today to devote attention to natural learning, memory and intelligence thus reflects the assumption that to concentrate upon the general issues of the 'mental mechanisms' assumed 'to underlie these behaviors' (Sternberg 1983, p.204) is an inherently more theoretical undertaking.

However, the postulation of 'mental mechanisms', though firmly accepted in many branches of the behavioural sciences, rests on fragile and largely pretheoretical assumptions. Regularities observed in empirical research on how people solve problems, learn, and use their intellectual resources, are not necessarily indicators of 'underlying mental mechanisms'. Instead, I would argue, they indicate that human beings when orienting themselves in the world, and when drawing on their previous experiences, tend to interpret similar situations along similar lines.

To restrict the discussion solely to learning, it is obvious that the meaning of this concept is highly ambiguous and not susceptible to any analytically satisfactory definition. That this concept has remained defiantly opaque across a variety of situations – as is generally acknowledged by distinguished theorists (cf for example Bower and Hilgard 1981; Hill 1963) – is thus no temporary state of affairs; it is a genuine characteristic. The meaning of the concept of learning thus is to be sought in the socially and culturally established conventions with respect to what counts as learning in specific educational environments (cf for example Becker, Geer and Hughes 1968; Säljö 1982, 1984). Acts of learning in a culture which is illiterate by necessity have to be oriented towards reproducing significant, cultural documents such as religious texts, laws, etc. In a literate culture, where for obvious reasons the demands for reproducing can be relaxed, reflection and analytical thought became a more prominent mode of learning. However, cultural barriers need not be as large as that. Even in rather homogeneous educational contexts, students can be seen to entertain differing conceptions of what it means to learn.

Our dawning insights into this area of subjective conceptions of phenomena such as knowledge and learning, we owe to the pioneering observations of William G. Perry. His work, based on genuine participant observation of students trying to orient themselves in the world of the university, shows that behind the learning difficulties encountered at university there may not necessarily be insufficiencies in 'processing capacities' or 'motivation', but rather conceptions of knowledge that are at variance with those held by the faculty. Since the students he observed when they entered university generally equated knowledge with what is commonly referred to as 'facts', ie statements about the world that are accepted as unequivocally 'true' and 'correct', they failed to see the point of much of the teaching they were exposed to. Tacitly interpreting their task at university as one of essentially memorizing the 'Answers' to a finite set of 'Questions', they misconstrued many of the teachers' intentions. Presentations of alternative perspectives or conflicting explanations so characteristic of the scientific mode of construing knowledge, were regarded as unnecessary detours, as refusals on the parts of teachers to 'tell it like it is'. What Perry describes in his celebrated book *Forms of Intellectual and Ethical Development in the College Years: A scheme* (1970) is a gradual, and sometimes rather painful, shift in students' conceptions of knowledge from an absolutistic and reified conception of knowledge as consisting of discrete entities, of 'Rights' and 'Wrongs', to a *relativistic* one, where knowledge is seen as dynamic and as relative to certain perspectives and premises. Conflicting 'truths' become a possibility and, as a function of this, the learning task students set for themselves changes.

The development Perry pins down in such detail represents a powerful change in a person's outlook on the world, as powerful as many of the developments described by psychologists studying cognitive growth among children. In my own research, as in that of others (cf Marton and Säljö 1976a, b; Marton, Hounsell and Entwistle 1984), it has become evident that there is a *functional* relationship between the mode in which people subjectively construe learning and the way they go about dealing with learning tasks (Marton and Säljö 1984; van Rossum and Schenk 1984; Watkins 1983). An absolutistic conception of learning (and knowledge) has thus been found to be associated with an approach to learning, in our terminology defined as a surface approach, which, in turn, has been shown to lead to difficulties in understanding what one learns and also to poor long-term retention. In particular, a surface approach with its strong emphasis on rote learning seems to cause problems in academic areas where there are extensive amounts of texts that have to be digested by the student (cf Svensson 1976). Construing knowledge, ie the end-product of learning, as a matter of storing 'facts', or more generally, 'information', many of the students we observed saw no obvious criteria for selecting what to attend to amongst the hundreds, perhaps thousands, of pages that have to be covered for an examination in, say, political science or history. In this sense, and in the perspective of the learner, conceptions of learning and knowledge at the micro-level, ie at the level of the cognitive activity, serve as premises for the approach a person uses. In this perspective, our cognitive processes, ie our 'sense-making activities' (Merleau-Ponty 1962), reflect what we assume is being required. In a slightly different language, the way we learn can be understood to be guided by the 'socially and institutionally established premises for communication' (Rommetveit 1974) that we assume to be valid in the context in which we act.

To emphasize the social nature and origin of human approaches to learning, we might draw an even wider circle and inquire as to the basis of this conception of learning. Here it is obvious that the static and absolutistic conception of learning and knowledge can be understood as 'a fundamental part of Western thought' (Douglas 1971, p.39). In other words, it would appear that everyday thinking is characterized by a way of conceptualizing learning which people tacitly come to conceive as 'given', and which may not be identical to the way endorsed by a subcultural group, such as a research community. Again referring to the research of my colleagues and myself, it can be seen that the difficulties Swedish students have with handling large masses of text in the kinds of academic fields mentioned above, have to do with the fact that they have no experiences of this particular *version of learning*. At preceding levels of the school system, they live in a completely ordered educational environment, where what is to be learned is neatly packed and arranged. Modern text books with frequent underlinings and heavy use of bold-type have left very little to learning except memorizing and reproducing discrete units of 'information'.

One consequence of the view advocated here is that learning does not exist as a general phenomenon. To learn is to act within man-made institutions and to adapt to the particular definitions of learning that are valid in the educational environment in which one finds oneself. As an example, the learning problems that physics students experienced in some of our studies were very different from those briefly described above as having to do with the problem of how to extract something sensible out of hundreds of pages of text. Here the genuine problems of learning – although not necessarily of passing tests – have more to do with accepting the way of organizing reality that physicists have found convenient, and which at times is at variance with what we assume to be valid in our everyday life. Some of my colleagues, to take an example, have done extensive work on students' understanding of the concept of force (eg Johansson, Marton and Svensson 1981). These studies illustrate the considerable difficulties even advanced students have in leaving their everyday – and within that context perfectly adequate – interpretation of force, and accepting the physicists' version of this concept. Again, however, this difficulty does not seem to be related to limitations in processing capacities or intelligence among students. What seems to be the problem is that our everyday thinking about phenomena that relate to force is Aristotelian in nature. In our everyday life we thus 'know' a lot of things about how physical objects like balls, cars or aeroplanes behave in various circumstances. We tend to explain the motion of such objects by forces that we assume to be somehow stored up in these objects and that cause them to move and eventually stop. However, the physicist as physicist when facing an identical situation does not feel that he has to explain why the object in question is in motion. Instead a long development and considerable intellectual investments have led to the conclusion that it is more feasible for theoretical purposes and for the knowledge interest of physics, to consider motion as a natural condition, and thus to reserve the concept of force for the explanation of *changes* in motion. To realize this at an abstract level is maybe not so difficult, but to realize what it means in various instances turns out to be quite a struggle for many students, since the Aristotelian world view seems to hold a firm grip over our thinking.

I have taken these few examples to illustrate my main point: learning problems of the kind encountered in real-life are generally not capacity problems or problems of intellectual deficits; they are communication problems and have to do with the diversification of knowledge and the rapidly increasing ways of understanding and explaining the world. For me as a researcher, this point of departure has important consequences. The object of inquiry in studies of learning and thinking changes from 'mental mechanisms' and 'information processing devices' and is replaced by an equally fascinating study of 'conceptions of reality' (Marton 1981), or, as Goodman (1978) phrased it, of different 'ways of worldmaking'. In other words, and still following the footsteps of Goodman, there is a need for a complementary line of research, where the approach would be guided by 'simply this: never mind mind, essence is not essential, and matter doesn't matter. We do better to focus on versions rather than worlds' (ibid. p.96).

What are potential contributions for praxis of focusing on 'versions rather than worlds'? In my view, and since educational processes are not 'rational' in the sense that methods of teaching and learning are adapted to research findings, a valuable contribution is the provision of a language with suggestive metaphors in terms of which cognitive processes as aspects of complex phenomena such as educational transactions can be fruitfully discussed. Research thus has an important function in increasing the possibilities of inter-subjectivity on such matters. It is precisely in this respect that the findings in traditional research such as learning and retention curves, problems of transfer, etc. have been so disappointing. They form no basis for saying anything intelligent about human learning in everyday circumstances precisely because they do not capture any significant aspects of such processes. It is also obvious that I am a bit suspicious about the usefulness of some variants of the computer-metaphors of today. Accounts of cognitive processes should not alienate us from the world of the learners by providing abstract meta-languages where their perspective is lost. We might then, if unlucky, find ourselves in a situation analogous to the legendary person in charge of the time-tables for the buses in an English town. His response to the complaints of angry citizens that the buses often did not stop at the bus-stops, was to say; 'if they did, it would disrupt the timetables.' Refusing to attend to the 'life-world' of the would-be passengers or, in our case, the teachers and learners, we may risk ending up putting cognitive research in a position similar to the one which modern technology-based industry is in: it has a lot of solutions to tricky technical problems, and it is currently engaged in persuading people that they have problems that match these solutions.

Rather, in my view, genuine insight into human learning is dependent on the provision of a language that is not only analytically clear, but also *sensitive* to the decisive characteristics of learning and thinking as these phenomena evolve in educational contexts. Should this be a feasible mode of reasoning, the cognitive processes we will be talking about in future will be those of students trying to come to grips with the versions of the world that research has produced and that are inherent in our culture although not visible to everyone. Our basis for intervention will lie in our knowledge about what constitutes learning problems in our particular field, and the knowledge we draw on will come from many sources; including the history of ideas and studies of differences between what is valid knowledge in a lay perspective and what it is in a scientific subculture. In other words, it will be about how people succeed in expanding their intellectual repertoires to encompass new, and previously unseen, 'ways of worldmaking'. However, they do this as *cultural beings* with experiences of reality and equipped with a language in terms of which these experiences are intelligible. This is not an easy road to tread, I admit, but according to my almost certainly unreliable Swedish sources, a former Australian prime minister is supposed to have said 'Life was not meant to be easy.'

References

Becker, H., Geer, B. and Hughes, E. (1968) *Making the Grade* New York: Wiley

Bower, G. and Hilgard, E. (1981) *Theories of Learning* (5th edition) Englewood Cliffs, NJ: Prentice-Hall

Douglas, J. (Ed.) (1971) *Understanding Everyday Life* London: Routledge

Ebbinghaus, H. (1885) *Über das Gedächtnis* Leipzig: Duncker and Humboldt

Giorgi, A. (1983) Concerning the possibility of phenomenological psychological research *Journal of Phenomenological Psychology* 14(2) 129-169

Giorgi, A. (Ed.) (1985) *Phenomenology and Psychological Research* Pittsburgh: Duquesne University Press

Goodman, N. (1978) *Ways of Worldmaking* Hassocks, Sussex: The Harvester Press

Hilgard, E. (1964) Introduction to H. Ebbinghaus *Memory* New York: Dover

Hill, W. (1963) *Learning: A Survey of Psychological Interpretations* San Francisco: Chandler

Johansson, B., Marton, F. and Svensson, L. (1985) An approach to describing learning as change between qualitatively different conceptions. In A.L. Pines and L.H.T. West (Eds) *Cognitive Structure and Conceptual Change* New York: Academic Press

Markova, I. (1982) *Paradigms, Thought, and Language* Chichester: Wiley

Marton, F. (1981) Phenomenography – Describing conceptions of the world around us *Instructional Science* 10, 177-200

Marton, F. and Säljö, R. (1976a) On qualitative differences in learning: I – Outcome and process *British Journal of Educational Psychology* 46, 4-11

Marton, F, and Säljö, R. (1976b) On qualitative differences in learning: II – Outcome as a function of the learner's conception of the task *British Journal of Educational Psychology* 46, 115-127

Marton, F., Hounsell, D. and Entwistle, N. (Eds) (1984) *The Experience of Learning* Edinburgh: Scottish Academic Press

Marton, F. and Säljö, R. (1984) Approaches to learning. In Marton et al. (1984)

Merleau-Ponty, M. (1962) *Phenomenology of Perception* New York: Humanities Press

Neisser, U. (1982) Memory: What are the important questions? In U. Neisser (Ed.) *Memory Observed* San Francisco: Freeman

Perry, W.G. (1970) *Forms of Intellectual and Ethical Development in the College Years: A Scheme* New York: Holt

Rommetveit, R. (1974) *On Message Structure* London: Wiley

Säljö, R. (1982) *Learning and understanding* Göteborg: Acta Universitatis Gothoburgensis

Säljö. R. (1984) Learning from reading. In Marton et al. (1984)

Svensson, L. (1976) *Study Skill and Learning* Göteborg: Acta Universitatis Gothoburgensis

Sternberg, R.J. (1983) Componential theory and componential analysis: Is there a Neisser alternative? *Cognition* 15, 199-206

van Rossum, E. and Schenk, S. (1984) The relationship between learning conception, study strategy and learning outcome *British Journal of Educational Psychology* 54, 73-83

Watkins, D. (1983) Depth of processing and the quality of learning outcomes *Instructional Science* 12, 49-58

10

Essay Writing and the Quality of Feedback

Dai Hounsell

The idea of feedback has a long and distinguished patrimony. It was Edward L. Thorndike, at the end of the nineteenth century, whose Law of Effect first established a relationship between learning and a knowledge of the consequences of one's actions. Subsequently, the notion occupied a central position within the behaviourist pedagogy of B.F. Skinner in the form of 'contingencies of reinforcement'. For Skinner, knowledge of results and immediate reinforcement of the correct answer were fundamental to learning (Skinner 1953, 1954). But the term 'feedback' stems from control engineering and seems to have been given wider currency by Norbert Wiener in his work on cybernetics (1961). Wiener was able to define feedback precisely and succinctly as follows:

> When we desire a motion to follow a given pattern the difference between this pattern and the actually performed motion is used as a new input to cause the part regulated to move in such a way as to bring its motion closer to that given by the pattern. (Wiener 1961, p.6)

In contemporary pedagogy – indeed, in everyday discussions of the teaching-learning process as well as in academic texts – the importance of feedback seems to be widely accepted. But the construct has broken free of its earlier conceptual anchorage. The condition of immediacy is no longer considered mandatory, the advocacy of feedback is not confined to any particular body of psychological thought – one is as likely to find it espoused by Carl Rogers (1969) as by neo-Skinnerians (see for example Keller and Sherman 1974) – and the term itself, in present-day usage, has a much looser meaning than that given to it by Norbert Wiener. To the higher education lecturer, 'providing feedback' essentially means giving students information on how well, or how poorly, they are doing in their academic work. And as the adoption of coursework assessment has steadily gained ground since the 1960s, so providing written and sometimes oral comments on students' assignments has become a familiar and often time-consuming part of everyday teaching. Yet despite the increasing incidence of feedback of this kind, the phenomenon itself has gone largely unexamined. Only

Mackenzie (1974) in a small, informal survey of Open University tutors, has explored comments on assignments, finding evidence of very considerable quantitative and qualitative variations. The aim of the present paper is to consider the quality of feedback in the light of the findings of a study of undergraduate essay-writing in the social sciences.

The investigation (Hounsell 1984a, 1984b) adopted the experiential perspective of an evolving tradition of research into student learning (see for example Hounsell and Entwistle 1979; Marton, Hounsell and Entwistle 1984). In effect, it was therefore concerned to understand and describe qualitative differences in students' experiences of the activity of essay-writing, following an exploratory, phenomenographic methodology.

The Empirical Study

Two groups of second-year university students took part in the empirical investigation: seventeen whose main subject was history and sixteen whose main subject was psychology. The principal source of data was a series of semi-structured interviews, but in addition information was collected on students' coursework essay marks and final degree results, the students completed the Lancaster Approaches to Studying inventory, and the essays discussed in the interviews were selectively analysed. The students were interviewed on two occasions, with an interval of approximately one academic term in between. Each interview was linked to a specific coursework essay prepared for a particular course unit within the relevant major scheme of study. Questions raised in the interview dealt not simply with the content of that essay and how the students had gone about preparing and writing it but also with other recent essays, whether submitted for the focal course unit or for others being studied. Students were also asked about such matters as tutors' expectations, marks and comments on returned essays, their perceptions of the contribution of essay-writing to their learning, and their experiences of undergraduate studying in general. The interviews were subsequently transcribed and underwent intensive qualitative analysis.

The main findings stem from analysis of the interview accounts. Within each of the two subject groups, a fundamental difference was identified between the students' *conceptions* of what an essay was and what essay-writing involved. The full set of categories of description derived (Hounsell 1984b) cannot be presented here for reasons of space, but Table 1 provides a summary of the main differences in conception. Some history students conceived of essay-writing as a question of *argument*, coherently presented and well-substantiated; others saw it as concerned with the *arrangement* of facts and ideas. And amongst the psychology students, essay writing was seen by some as a matter of *cogency*, where substantive discussion was rooted in a solid and coherent core of empirical findings, and by others as *relevance*, in the sense of an ordered presentation of material pertaining to a topic or problem.

As Table 1 also shows, the sub-components of four conceptions could be distinguished in terms of the stance adopted towards three core elements of

A History

	Level I Conception 'ARRANGEMENT'	Level III Conception 'ARGUMENT'
GLOBAL DEFINITION	Define an essay as an ordered presentation embracing facts and ideas	Define an essay as the ordered presentation of an argument well supported by evidence
SUB-COMPONENTS		
a Interpretation	An acknowledgement that it is useful or important to express any ideas or opinions you may have	A concern to take up a distinctive position or point of view on a problem or issue
b Organization	A concern with organization as such, but without reference to the aptness of organizing principles	a concern with an essay as an integral whole
c Data	Concern with data, but quantitatively, with no explicit criteria of selection	A concern with data as evidence, substantiating or refuting a particular position or viewpoint

B Psychology

	Level I Conception 'RELEVANCE'	Level II Conception 'COGENCY'
GLOBAL DEFINITION	Define an essay as an ordered discussion of relevant material on a topic or problem	Define an essay as a well-integrated and firmly grounded discussion of a topic or problem
SUB-COMPONENTS		
a Interpretation	An acknowledgement that essays entail the expression of any ideas, thoughts and opinions you may have	A concern to present a consolidated view of a topic or problem within which your own ideas and thoughts have been integrated
a Organization	A concern with organization in the sense of linking parts to one another rather than structuring a whole	A concern with an essay as an integrated whole
c Data	A concern with coverage of relevant material, where relevance is viewed as if it were an inherent characteristic of the psychological literature	A concern to build an essay upon a firm empirical foundation

Table 1
Conceptions of essay writing: global definitions and components.

essay-writing: interpretation (the meaning(s) given to the essay material); organization (the structuring of the essay material into a particular sequence or order); and data (the raw material which forms the basic subject-matter of the essay). This tripartite dissection also helps in considering the two pairs of conceptions as comprising two cross-disciplinary groups.

In the first group are the two *interpretative* conceptions of argument (history) and cogency (psychology). What these two conceptions share is a concern with the making of meaning: an essay is seen as a mode of discourse through which one makes sense of a topic or problem in a way which is individually distinctive. The pivotal element is therefore that of interpretation, whether this takes the form of a consolidated view (in psychology) or of a distinctive point of view or position (in history). The elements of organization and data are thus viewed as subordinate to and harnessed to interpretation: they serve to convey a chosen interpretative stance in a form which is coherent and well-substantiated. This is directly reflected in the students' accounts of their essay-writing procedures (Hounsell 1984a) where the coherence aspired to in the finished product grows out of the interplay between thoughts and ideas on the one hand and a corpus of potential evidence or empirically verified data on the other. The student is thus the arbiter of the content and form of the essay, making personal choices about the selection and organization of material, whether in the light of an explicit interpretive stance which had crystallized at an early stage or of a steadily growing sense of the dominant theme. Introductions and conclusions are not simply conventions but devices through which a unity of form and content can be facilitated.

The second group of conceptions comprises the two *non-interpretative* ones of arrangement (history) and relevance (psychology). In each, an orientation towards the establishment of meaning is absent, and each is correspondingly less explicit than its interpretative counterpart. Although there is an acknowledgement that essays are a medium through which one's own ideas, thoughts and opinions can be conveyed, these tend to have an almost incidental status or are seen as 'value added' rather than as the essay's main justification. They do not (as the interpretative conceptions do) occupy a central position, or invest the activity with its essential character or its chief justification. Moreover, since interpretation is not uppermost, the conceptions lack what, in the interpretative conceptions, is the driving force and the conceptual base underpinning a hierarchical structure. Instead of being welded together in a unified structure, the three core elements of interpretation, organization and data, though individually valued, tend to be seen as hermetically isolated constituents whose relationship to one another remains unexplicated. Thus organization is viewed as the joining of parts to one another rather than the structuring of a whole, while data-gathering is seen as amassing a quantity of material or striving for completeness of coverage – an essay is written *from* rather than *with* the sources one has tracked down, and conclusions tend to be treated as afterthoughts or conventions followed in form rather than in substance. In consequence, students' descriptions of their essay-writing procedures appear flat and mechanical, a series of steps which seem uninformed or undirected by considerations of meaning. And the students' accounts of the content of their essays typically do not include a substantive reference to a conclusion.

No less importantly, such differences in conception seem to have a more general association with students' grasp of a discipline. Students ascribed to an interpretative conception tended to see the craft of essay-writing as mirroring the practice of the discipline (in history) or (in psychology) as an activity both fostering and demonstrating one's mastery of the accumulated knowledge of the discipline. The non-interpretative conceptions, by contrast, do not have these associations. There are instead abundant indications of vagueness and uncertainty about the nature of essays and essay-writing and a perceived gap between aspiration and what is achieved in a finished essay.

Accounting for Differences in Conception

It is not difficult to find parallels between these differences in conceptions of essay-writing and other findings from research into student learning. The concern with the abstraction of meaning characteristic of the interpretative conceptions has evident affinities with a deep approach to learning (see for example Marton and Säljö 1984), contextual relativistic reasoning (Perry 1970) and a thematic conception of learning (Säljö 1982). Similarly, the non-interpretative conceptions of essay-writing share the quantitative and reproductive associations of a surface approach, a taken-for-granted conception of learning, and some aspects of the pre-relativistic positions within Perry's scheme of intellectual development. But how can such differences be accounted for – and in particular, how is it that the non-interpretative conceptions of essay-writing both subsist and apparently persist?

One possible source is the course context within which the activity of essay-writing takes place. At the most obvious level, the interview analysis pinpoints contextual features which could be considered dysfunctional. In both subject groups, the traffic of comment on essays was almost overwhelmingly from tutor to student and in written form. It was only very seldom that one-to-one oral discussion of essays took place, and there was virtually no substantive discussion of essay-writing amongst peers: whatever discussion did occur was confined to close personal friends and touched upon deadlines, choice of essay topics or useful sources, rather than weightier issues such as options in the treatment of an essay theme or essay-writing strategies. Nonetheless, and despite some variation in the amount of written feedback given, both groups of students were issued with written guidelines on departmental expectations of essays and received page-specific and general comments on individual pieces of work. Broadly speaking, then, it does not seem plausible to attribute differences in conception to a manifest lack of guidance on what essays entailed. I would suggest that the problem lies deeper and more subtly in what Rommetveit (1974, 1979) has called 'the architecture of inter-subjectivity'.

The Architecture of Inter-subjectivity

Rommetveit is a psycholinguist who has been critical of the Chomskyan transformational perspective on language for its neglect of the social context within which language is produced and interpreted. As Säljö (1982) has observed, for Rommetveit:

> the meaning of (an) utterance does not reside in the utterance per se but has to be seen relative to the situation of which it is a part and to the presuppositions about the nature of this situation which the agents hold. (Säljö 1982, p.173)

The term 'presuppositions' is particularly crucial here. Rommetveit argues that communication is based upon 'mutual faith in a shared social world' (Rommetveit 1979, p.96) and its cornerstone is a 'commonality of interpretation'. If, therefore participants in a communicative act are to converse effectively, there must be shared or complementary premises or assumptions (which themselves tend to be tacit and taken-for-granted):

> It presupposes complementarity and reciprocal role-taking. The speaker must monitor what he says on the premises of the listener, and the listener must listen on the premises of the speaker. Both of them, moreover, must continually relate what is said at any particular stage of their dialogue to whatever at that stage has been jointly presupposed. (Rommetveit 1979, p.102)

Applying this perspective to the present findings, it would suggest that where students' conceptions of essay-writing are qualitatively different from those of their tutors, communication cannot readily take place because the premises underlying the two disparate conceptions are not shared or mutually understood. Students misconstrue a tutor's comments or guidance or fail to grasp the import of these because they do not have a grasp of the assumptions about the nature of academic discourse underlying what is being conveyed to them. Similarly, tutors fail to acknowledge 'the subtle interplay between what is said and what is taken for granted' (Rommetveit 1979, p.96) and so do not seek to close the gap between their own and the students' understanding of expectations.

Bearing in mind that the inter-subjective character of feedback was not an explicit focus within the original research design, indications of this gulf in communication can nonetheless be found within the interview accounts. Perhaps the most telling of these show up in students' reactions to specific comments. One psychology student, for example, finds herself thrown by comments which in effect challenge her understanding of expectations, but she also apparently interprets argument in a literal and everyday sense rather than an academic one:

Ellie: I felt, in actual fact, I'd covered the area very comprehensively, by trying to bring in as many angles as I could. I tried to cover all the different areas. But one of the tutor's criticisms was why did I just keep going from one to the other. But I thought that's what I was supposed to do.

Interviewer: So did you feel you had a clearer sense of what the tutor was looking for when you got the essay back ?

Ellie: Well, from the comments on the essay, I gathered the tutor wanted me to argue, about something, but I mean, by presenting the material as the research had demonstrated, it was a mild form of argument. I wasn't going to get aggressive, in an essay.

Feedback also evidently fails to 'connect' (to borrow E.M. Forster's term) in the case of another psychology student, whose literalist stance does not appear to acknowledge that disciplines have characteristic modes of discourse in which the pertinence of 'how' and 'why' questions is presupposed:

Gail: I felt pretty satisfied with it. I thought I'd get a brilliant mark for it. I was really put off when I saw (the tutor's comments on my essay). I just thought it was 'What limits a person's ability to do two things at once?' Not why, or how it was done. What I did I thought was very relevant, I just answered the question, which the tutor didn't think was right, 'cos the tutor wanted 'how' and 'why' factors, and I didn't quite answer that.

Two examples from history, similarly, suggest that guidance about generalization and a concern with detail is not firmly apprehended because, for the students concerned, there is not an appropriate conception within which it can be readily construed:

Interviewer: What did you think the tutor was looking for in this essay?
Pattie: Ah... well, this is what's confusing me. I know the tutor likes concise work, but doesn't like generalizations, and doesn't like too much detail, although I think on the whole he'd like more detail than generalizations. And because it was such a general question, I thought, 'oh help!', I don't know what he's looking for.

Interviewer: What do you think the tutor was looking for in this essay?
Sue: He's obviously looking for a much more sort of, detailed approach, I would say. Although on my last essay he did say that I spent too much time explaining things, and I ought to be arguing and interpreting more, and so I was trying to argue and interpret all the way through this, as well as obviously having to bring in details. And I just wondered if by doing that I haven't tended to generalize a bit. Because when I start to argue and interpret I generalize a little bit....I think he's looking for argument and interpretation, I just think he's expecting a lot of, uh, more detail perhaps as well.

Analysis of the interview accounts also indicates that the definitional and process aspects of essay-writing are in some way bound up with one another, such that acquiring a new conception may entail not just apprehending what seems to be required but being able to realize this in the finished essay. Thus students may indicate their awareness (at least, embryonically) that something different is expected, but feel powerless to achieve it:

Wendy: (Psychology)	I think really that what the tutor wanted was for us to say what has been said, and then what you think – Is there a reason for it? But I don't really think I did that. (Laughs) I think it was just what other people said.
Brenda: (History)	I don't really have a structure to (my essays). They say you're supposed to, and some of the tutors like you to have, you know, themes, where you deal with various themes as you go along, but mine don't, they just... as it occurs to me. On the whole I just write it down as it comes to me.

Indeed, nowhere is this important (and seemingly baffling) awareness of expectations more apparent than in what is perhaps the crucible of an academic essay, the conclusion.

Rick: (History)	I might draw a conclusion, if I have time, and draw all the threads together. If not, I might just finish, you know, just finish, like that.
Brenda: (History)	Sometimes I can finish with a quote, sometimes I can sum up with my own feelings, or sometimes it just kind of gets to where there's nothing more to write, but you can't think of anything to sum up with.
Rosemary: (Psychology)	My conclusions are always terrible. The tutor said if I rewrote the conclusion – 'cos it was one of those I didn't conclude, he would re-mark it.
Ellie: (Psychology)	I'd done this amazing structure (laughs) and then I hadn't put any ... evaluative conclusion.

But we should also note the dysfunctional side-effects of feedback which does not seem to engage with the student's understanding of the activity. A specific consequence is to see tutors' comments as marginal:

Donna: (History)	I never really find them very helpful. (Laughs) Just irrelevant, really.

or as having nothing to offer beyond the confines of a particular essay assignment:

Interviewer: Holly: (Psychology)	Generally speaking, do you find tutors' comments helpful? Not unless you get that title again, no.

| Peter: (Psychology) | Sometimes I do read the comments but I find that, I'll never write the same essay again anyway....I tend to ignore them in some ways, unless there's something very startling. |

But there is an even more worrying consequence of repeatedly low marks and of feedback which is critical in tone and opaque in its signification. This is to treat essay-writing extrinsically, as a chore which deserves only minimal effort or an activity whose value lies elsewhere. For example:

| Rick: (History) | If I knew I could do a good essay, I'd do more research. Sometimes I just give up. |

| Ellie: (Psychology) | Most students really dread (essays). Perhaps they could be of use, but I am going to just treat them... with the view in mind that I'm going to try and use them for revision. And that's it. |

| Frank: (History) | It's just work, in a way. Just all these essays, and reading's the worst part, it's just labouring really.... I think it tends to kill the interest, in fact. |

| Peter: (Psychology) | I find that my main objective, when turning out an essay, is just to get two and a half thousand words and finish. |

Such comments suggest firstly, that motivation may be less a personal attribute than a function of the relations between an individual and a situation, and secondly, that some students may be locked into a 'cycle of deprivation' as far as constructive feedback is concerned. Since feedback fails to connect, it comes to be viewed as insignificant or invalid, and so is not given considered attention. At the same time the activity within which it is offered is seen increasingly as unrewarding, and so it is approached perfunctorily, thus further lessening the likelihood that a more appropriate conception might be apprehended.

Conclusions

Though ostensibly concerned with essay-writing as a learning activity, the findings I have discussed are concerned at base with the nature of academic discourse. The interpretative conceptions, which match or approximate to premisses for academic discourse in the two disciplines concerned, point to the primacy of meaning-making and to the crucial supporting roles played by organization and data in conveying meaning in a form which is both adequately substantiated and coherent. But some students, as we saw, seem to hold conceptions of a fundamentally different anatomy. These latter conceptions are not embedded in premisses about disciplined meaning-making but take instead the form of loose constellations of relatively undifferentiated criteria about interpretation, organization and data. Such divergent conceptions may present a formidable obstacle to feedback: conventional attempts to guide students, whether through general guidelines or comments on specific essays, may founder because the exigences of communication – a complementarity of premisses between tutor and student – are unfulfilled. The nub of the problem is that substantive comments about what constitutes academic discourse cannot have a Wiener-like clarity and precision. Such characteristic comments by tutors as 'you don't make your points clearly enough', 'this essay lacks structure' or 'too much irrelevant detail', do not have a meaning which is self-evident. They are best seen as connotative not denotative, and thus not as particularized observations but as invocations of norms. Such comments allude to a mode of discourse which is largely tacit and so invisible to students who have not already grasped its contours.

From the perspective of teaching, therefore, attempts to improve the quality of students' essays (and perhaps also, their broader mastery of their chosen discipline) must spring from and turn upon dialogue about the nature of academic discourse. And since grasping what constitutes academic discourse represents the kind of personal intellectual revolution charted in Perry's developmental scheme (Perry 1970), we cannot make this revolution happen but only try to create conditions under which it might be facilitated. Foremost among these would be a recognition by lecturers of the inter-subjective as well as constructive character of learning as an activity. Feedback which amounts to information-giving rather than an attempt to articulate and explore premisses – on the student's as well as the tutor's terms – is unlikely to connect.

More specifically, it may be helpful to offer feedback in which observations which are content-related and those which address norms for discourse are more sharply differentiated. The use of discipline-specific 'assignment attachments' (McDonald and Sansom 1979), in which achievement is related to an explicit set of expectations, is one possible avenue forward. Yet it is difficult to see how any re-focusing of effort will be successful without a concomitant attempt to regear the context of essay-writing. In this investigation, as we have noted, essay-writing appeared to be an almost overwhelmingly private and solitary activity: there was no substantive peer discussion and communication from tutors to students appeared to be largely formal, post hoc, product-oriented and limited in scope. Essay-writing thus appeared to be a central assessment activity but a peripheral pedagogical one – and this despite an evident association between accomplishment in essay-writing and students' broader mastery of a discipline. A more open, collaborative and process-orientated approach, designed to bring essay-writing into the mainstream of day-to-day teaching, would seem highly desirable.

Finally, from the standpoint of research into student learning, these findings further outline the constructive and contextualized character of undergraduate study so manifest in other investigations. They also challenge the comfortable assumptions that the provision and reception of feedback form an unbroken cycle of communication. Clearly, a searching examination of the quality of feedback is urgently required.

Acknowledgements

The larger study on which this paper draws benefited very considerably from the helpful advice of Noel Entwistle and Ference Marton, and of Roger Säljö, who first drew my attention to the work of Ragnar Rommetveit. This paper was written while the author was Senior Research Officer at the Institute for Research and Development in Post-Compulsory Education at the University of Lancaster.

References

Hounsell, D. (1984a) Essay planning and essay writing *Higher Education Research and Development* (Australia) 3 (1) 13-31

Hounsell, D. (1984b) *Students' Conceptions of Essay Writing* Unpublished PhD, University of Lancaster

Hounsell, D. and Entwistle, N. (1979) *Student Learning* Special issue of the international journal *Higher Education* 8 (4)

Keller, F.S. and Sherman, J.G. (1974) *The Keller Plan Handbook* Menlo Park, California: W.A. Benjamin

McDonald, R. and Sansom, D. (1979) Use of assignment attachments in assessment *Assessment in Higher Education* 5 (1) 45-55

Mackenzie, K. (1974) Some thoughts on tutoring by written correspondence in the Open University *Teaching at a Distance* 1, 45-51

Marton, F. and Säljö, R. (1984) Approaches to learning. In Marton et al. (1984)

Marton, F., Hounsell, D. and Entwistle, N. (1984) *The Experience of Learning* Edinburgh: Scottish Academic Press

Perry, W.G., Jr. (1970) *Forms of Intellectual and Ethical Development in the College Years: A scheme* New York: Holt Rinehart

Rogers, C. (1969) *Freedom to Learn* Columbus, Ohio: Merrill

Rommetveit, R. (1974) *On Message Structure* Chichester: Wiley

Rommetveit, R. (1979) On the architecture of intersubjectivity. In R.Rommetveit and R.M. Blakar (Eds) *Studies of Language, Thought and Communication* 93-107. London: Academic Press

Säljö, R. (1982) *Learning and Understanding* Göteborg: Acta Universitatis Gothoburgensis

Skinner, B.F. (1953) *Science and Human Behaviour* New York: Macmillan

Skinner, B.F. (1954) The science of learning and the art of teaching *Harvard Educational Review* 24, 88-97

Wiener, N. (1961) *Cybernetics, or Control and Communication in the Animal and the Machine* (2nd edition) New York: Wiley

11

Teaching Dialectical Thinking through Model Construction

Yrjö Engeström

Models as Instruments of Dialectical Thinking

According to Harré (1970) and Wartofsky (1979), the central intellectual tools of science are models. I suggest that the historical development of scientific thinking may be understood as a gradual evolution of five basic types of models, briefly characterized as follows:

1 *Spontaneous* gestural and iconic models are typical of the 'primitive' cultures where the world is perceived as an organic unity and functional relationships prevail. A single case functions as a causal model of a whole domain or network of events and phenomena.
2 As societal practice grows in complexity, the relative specificity and undifferentiated nature of gestural and iconic models becomes an obstacle. It is resolved through the invention of writing, specifically of the phonetic alphabet, making possible the linear storage of information and the effective classification and hierarchization of the world. Thus, normalistic and *classification* models become the dominant form: everything is given a name and a place.
3 The written word paves the way for the reflective recording of regularities and laws in nature. The emergence of modern natural science means also the emergence of the *procedural* models, fixating the stepwise logic of movement and action. The systematic construction of machines is the triumph of algorithmic thinking.
4 Algorithmic thinking, however, is unable to grasp the probabilistic and reciprocal nature of real systems, most forcefully brought into the open by the revolution in physics. The ideas of feedback and self-regulation open the era of *systems* models.
5 The age of computers brings us to see the world as a universal network of interdependencies, forcing man to ask for the initial basic relations and contradictions behind bewildering systemic complexities. Hegel's classical idea of genetic *germ-cell* models, explaining the source of the self-movement and diversification of systems, gains actuality and impetus.

In this paper, I shall concentrate on the implications of the last type, germ-cell models. The form of scientific thinking that corresponds to this type is *dialectical thinking*. The psychological quality of dialectical thinking, as the emerging form of modern scientific thought, has only recently become an object of serious research in the West (see Basseches 1985; Markova 1982; Mitroff and Mason 1981; Riegel 1975). The existing studies tend to neglect the essential tool aspect of dialectical thinking – namely the construction and application of germ-cell models as the psychological kernel of this mode of scientific thinking.

A germ-cell must be (a) historically the earliest and genetically the first simple form of the system, (b) logically elementary and commonplace, present in each concrete manifestation of the system, (c) internally contradictory, revealing the basic tension between the essential elements of the system, giving rise to the development and multiplication of the system. The germ-cell is a unity of opposite moments which both depend upon and rival each other. It is by working out the tensions and interactions between the elements of the system that it becomes possible to explain and foresee the development of the system, that is, to reconstruct it in its concrete diversity and richness.

Dialectical thinking as a disciplined form of theoretical thought proceeds through certain necessary steps or intellectual actions. In the context of investigative, research-like learning activity, Davydov (1982) identifies the following actions: (1) transformation of the problem situation in order to find out the initial basic relation of the system; (2) modelling of the relation in enactive, graphic and symbolic forms; (3) transformation of the model in order to investigate its properties and behaviour in 'pure form'; (4) derivation and construction of series of concrete and practical tasks and problems that can be solved on the basis of the basic relation found and modelled; (5) control of quality of the actions mentioned above; and (6) evaluation of the acquisition of the general solution method embedded in the germ-cell model. I have suggested that a seventh essential action be added, namely (7) critique and further development of the model found and applied (Engeström and Hedegaard 1985).

One more essential ingredient of dialectical thinking must be mentioned, namely its *dialogic* nature. Dialectical thinking must be seen as internalized dialogue, as continuous transition between competing and complementary views of the object of study.

> (...) inner speech (and its elementary form of mono-dialogue) may be represented as the dialogue of those cultural-historical models of thinking (activity) that are internalized in the different voices of my own 'I', the argument among these functioning as a kind of positing, the creation of new cultural phenomena (knowledge, ideas, works of art). (Bibler 1984, p.53)

But it is not only a question of internal dialogue. As Lektorsky points out, knowledge that is inseparable from the individual subject appears as something static and complete, while science as productive activity requires that knowledge is in principle incomplete, pointing toward unsolved problems and inviting further explorations. 'That, in its turn, is only possible under division of research work and organisation of a special system of scientific communication (...). In other words, the modes of treatment of objectified knowledge are collective in their nature' (Lektorsky 1984, p.234; see also Finocchiaro 1980).

The Context and Design of the Case Study

A group of thirteen third-year students in the 'adult education' discipline at the University of Helsinki received a 16-hour course in instructional theory. The main part of the course consisted of an analysis of research-oriented learning activity, as well as of a discussion of the properties of the five types of models presented in the preceding section of this paper. The course took place in the spring semester of 1985.

At the end of the course, the students were divided into four groups. Each got the assignment of working out their own models representing the central idea of their discipline. The groups were instructed to work out their models according to their own conceptions about the future of the discipline, not just as descriptions of the presently existing curriculum. The lecturer was present but did not interfere with the work.

These four models (see Figures 1-4) functioned as the initial problem material to be transformed by the students (compare Davydov's first learning action in the previous section). The further course of the experiment was the following. The first phase consisted of a joint discussion and critique of each model. It will be called *external dialogue*. The four groups debated each other's models, while the lecturer summarized the arguments but refrained from a personal evaluation. The discussion of each model followed a three-step structure: (1) the group's *argument*, (2) *critique* from the others, (3) the group's *defence*. Thus the dialogue was external in two senses. It took place between various real subjects; and it was mainly concerned with the conflicts and comparisons *between* the models, not so much with the essential contradictions *within* the common object of the models.

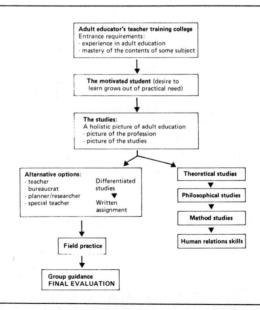

Figure 1
The model of Group 1.

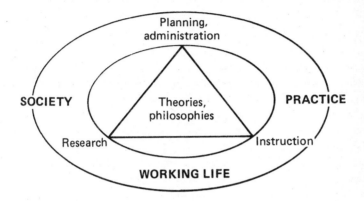

Figure 2
The model of Group 2.

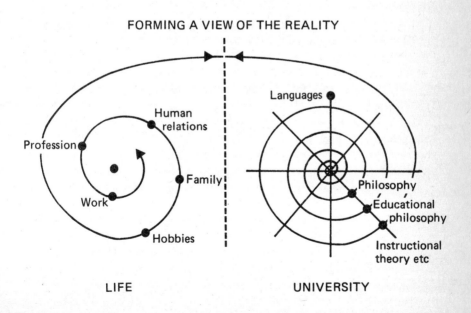

Figure 3
The model of Group 3.

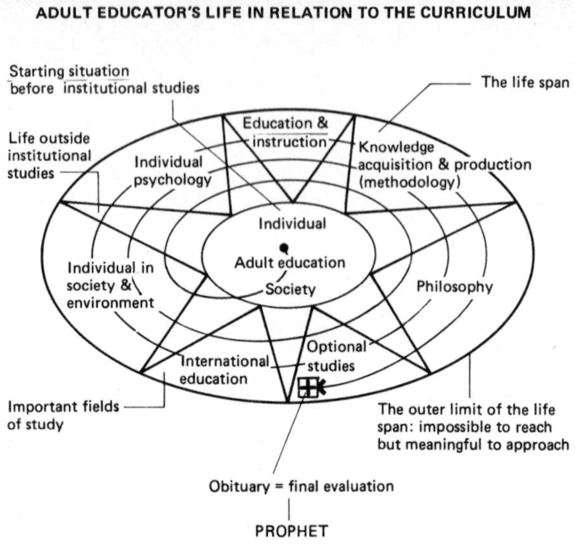

ADULT EDUCATOR'S LIFE IN RELATION TO THE CURRICULUM

Figure 4
The model of Group 4.

The second phase took place three weeks after the completion of the course, in connection with the regular written examination set by the course. Instead of traditional essay questions, the students received tasks demanding *internal dialogue*. The instruction read as follows:

1 Enclosed you'll receive the models worked out in groups during the course. Give your own personal evaluation of these four models (and of the discussion concerning them).

2 Present your own conception of the most essential inner contradiction of the studies and/or discipline of adult education.

3 On the basis of that contradiction, formulate your own new germ-cell type model for the studies/discipline of adult education.

Notice that you must leave at least 30 minutes for completing a fourth test. You'll get that fourth test after you have finished with the three above.

The total amount of time available for the examination was three hours. All the students used at least two hours, and five students worked up to the time limit.

This second phase was aimed at moving to internal dialogue in both senses characterized above. The tasks demanded not only external comparison but, above all, identification of the internal contradiction of the object system. Furthermore, they demanded modelling of the germ-cell type (Davydov's second learning action). I was especially interested in whether individual students could in this phase consciously depart from the model of their group and proceed to a more developed or sophisticated version.

The third phase demanded the *conscious application* of the model the student had just formulated. This was a step forward ascending to the concrete, towards reconstructing reality as conceptually grasped concreteness. The students received a fourth examination task with the following instruction:

> From the new model you have just designed, derive an analysis and a solution to the following problem:
>   A personnel trainer (or planner of training) who has studied adult education plans and realizes presently training which is split into separate short courses, over the contents of which he has no mastery. His work easily becomes superficial, formal arranging and administering of courses which does not require the application of theoretical knowledge of adult education, nor does it stimulate to develop that theoretical knowledge further. What is to be done?

The task describes a realistic problem situation, commonly experienced among Finnish adult educators in various types of organizations. The task was deliberately formulated so as to question the validity of conceptions treating adult education restrictively as the inside problem of the university.

Results of the External Dialogue Phase

The essential contents of the three-step discussion of each model will be presented below in a condensed form.

The Model of Group 1

The argument The students graduating as adult educators will find themselves helpless in their working life if and when they do not have a substantial mastery of any content-discipline which they could teach. The present curriculum of adult education guarantees no such content mastery. The new curriculum must be built on two premisses: practical experience and content-mastery of some subject to be taught. This will give the students a real professional identification and competence.

The critique The two premisses will make the studies in adult education something like a vocational school. Certainly many students who do not have prior practical experience are less prejudiced and more innovative than some experienced ones. Even though the content-mastery of a subject is often an advantage, there is no reason to demand it from everybody and especially not prior to studies in adult education. The model is a typical procedural or algorithmic description of the course of study. It describes adult education one-dimensionally and narrowly, like a pipeline. It gives no clues concerning the essential ideas within adult education.

The defence It was not the intention of the group to go deep into the content of the studies. The group only wanted to attack and solve the primary practical dilemma at that time undermining the identity of students.

The Model of Group 2

The argument Adult education must prepare the students to master the practice of adult education comprehensively. The three main aspects or fields of this practice are administration/planning, instruction, and research. The studies must aim at a balance between these three. Based on a solid theoretical and philosophical grounding, the studies must penetrate into the social practice and reality of work in all the three fields.

The critique The model is deceptively simple and harmonious. It is too closed and balanced. Where are the inner contradictions? Admittedly it looks like a germ-cell. But isn't it all too formal? It is nearly like the current official ideology of the curriculum. As all movement and tension is lacking, the model is most likely to function in the manner of a classification model. What are the substantial ideas or concepts of the discipline – they cannot be found in the model.

The defence Perhaps it could be made more dynamic and realistic by pointing out that there are contradictions and tensions between all the three corners. Otherwise, it is definitely understandable and clear.

The Model of Group 3

The argument This is a model of conscious study. The students' lives and the development if their consciousness is continual movement back and forth between two major poles, namely life outside the university and study inside the university. The essential contradiction is just between these two poles. The task of the university – and especially of the students themselves – is to work out consciously the relationship between these poles. This is the real germ-cell of university study, though perhaps in a metaphorical form.

The critique This model may be exciting, but it has nothing to do with the specific object of adult education. Furthermore, isn't there life inside the university, too? Actually, even the most formally organized studies are saturated with private communication and life-experience. Thus the model is both too far away from adult education and too mechanically dualistic.

The defence Essentially this same model can be applied to any field of study, including adult education. The content and form of the adult education curriculum must be put into interaction with the life-world of the students. The mechanistic dualism is not true: the two-way arrows indicate that ingredients of life enter the university and vice versa.

The Model of Group 4

The argument The curriculum of adult education must expand the horizon and abilities of the students to the maximum. The studies must draw the students from their initial state of ignorance into ever broadening cycles of knowledge.

The whole life-span of an adult educator is continuous studying. In an ideal case, such a life-span will redefine the curriculum for later generations.

The critique The life-span is pictured within a closed circle. It gives the impression of predetermined fixed limits, with no possibility of surprises or breakthroughs. The dynamism of the model is illusionary – it is actually just a classification model of the different 'branches' of study. The model is also highly moralistic and individualistic. According to it, everybody should become a 'great man'. There are no contradictions and no substantial ideas peculiar to adult education in the model. It is almost comical that the area reserved for life outside institutional studies gets progressively smaller as the life-span proceeds towards its noble end.

The defence The star form indicates expansion. The spiral indicates continuous learning. These are not static features. The static aspects are due to difficulties in graphic expression.

The above outcomes of the external dialogue phase may be summarized as follows:

1 As expected, each group insisted on defending its product. In a way, this phase ended in a stalemate. However, such a stalemate may be not just a dead end. It may also function as a cognitive conflict giving rise to attempts at new models.

2 The students very consciously pointed out: (a) the lack of substantial ideas peculiar to the discipline adult education in the models (ie the relative formality of the models); (b) the lack of inner contradictions and dynamism in the models of Group 2 and Group 4 (the model of Group 1 was also criticized for this but it was also praised for pointing out very clearly the lack of content-mastery as the essential contradiction in adult education).

Results of the Internal Dialogue and Modelling Phase

To overcome the stalemate of the previous phase, the students would have to be able to delineate the *internal* contradictions of adult education in more or less common terms, enabling a substantial debate and a testing of alternatives. Therefore, the first interesting question in this phase concerns the quality of response to the second task set by the examination. In the analysis, five distinct conceptions of the inner contradiction emerged (see Table 1):

1 *Mastery of teachable contents vs. general methods and theories*
   The lack of the knowledge=facts that the student could *teach* to adults in the future. In the same way, for the development and planning of education one needs the substantial mastery of some branch of knowledge, which is not given by the adult education studies today. (Group 1 student)

   For some reason, I feel that the main contradiction is whether the students of adult education should already have a teachable substance mastery and practical experience or can the students come straight from school. (Group 4 student)

2 *Demands of production vs. humanistic aims*
The most important inner contradiction of our discipline is caused by attempts to direct the studies towards the interests of production on the one hand and by the humanistic strivings, on the other hand. (...) One superficial expression of this is the debate between qualitative and quantitative research methods. Within our discipline, we are trained as instructional technicians and simultaneously we are taught philosophy. (Group 2 student)

The question is, can education/adult education at all support the realization of humanistic values in the world when the prevailing social system, production and other background factors determine the direction anyhow. (...) Thus, it is not so much a question of an inner contradiction as of a collision between the external determining factors directing the reality of adult education and the inner values. (Group 3 student)

3 *Positivist objectivity vs. taking sides and responsibility*
In education, a strong positivist approach still dominates. It prevents science from influencing practice and taking responsibility for world problems. (Group 3 student)

4 *Theory vs. practice in general terms*
The biggest problem is that the connection between theory and practice is unsatisfactory. The connection with practice, with adult education in the field, is established by too superficial and easy means. (Group 4 student)

5 *The weak theoretical foundation of the discipline*
As a strong scientific foundation and clear achievements are lacking, there appear to be doubts about the meaningfulness of the whole discipline. (Group 2 student)

Type of conception	Group 1	Group 2	Group 3	Group 4	Total
1 Mastery of teachable contents vs. general theories & methods	3	–	–	2	5
2 Demands of production vs. humanistic aims	–	1	1	1	3
3 Positivist objectivity vs. taking sides & responsibility	–	1	1	–	2
4 Theory vs. practice in general	–	–	1	1	2
5 Lack of strong theoretical foundation	–	1	–	–	1
TOTAL	3	3	3	4	13

Table 1
Conceptions of the inner contradiction of adult education according to the original group of the student.

The students' third task was to model the essential inner relations of adult education. In the analysis, three quite clear categories of models emerged: (1) models of the desired course or organization of the studies, or *administrative* models; (2) models of individual student's/adult educator's tasks, options, or fields of competence, or *individualistic* models; (3) models of the relationships between adult education and society, or *societal* models. The administrative models look at adult education as a matter of university teaching and studying only. The individualistic models look at adult education as the field of knowledge and activity of the individual. The societal models look at adult education as a tension-laden relationship between a discipline and/or an educational practice and the larger society or economy. The distribution of the models into these categories is presented in Table 2.

Type of model	Group 1	Group 2	Group 3	Group 4	Total
1 Administrative models	2	–	–	2	4
2 Individualistic models	1	1	1	2	5
3 Societal models	–	2	2	–	4
TOTAL	3	3	3	4	13

Table 2
Models of the inner relations of adult education to the original group of the student.

The contents and quality of the models remain formal in this phase too. No substantial ideas or concepts peculiar to adult education are used as a basis for the models. This is a rather depressing result. The students don't seem to have acquired or constructed any strong organizing scientific concepts that would function as content-bound guidelines or an orientation basis of their emerging scientific thinking. In several models, the term 'theories' (in plural) is used as a substitute for the scientific kernel of the discipline. Even familiar educational concepts, such as 'learning' or 'development', are totally absent. This finding seems to indicate conceptual confusion and inflation in the curriculum of adult education. Even the societal models can only be seen as quite abstract and 'thin' attempts at determining the general direction of the identity search of the discipline and its students.

Results of the Application Phase

The solutions suggested by the students in the fourth task of the examination were analysed and six types were found (see Table 3):

1 The *traditional* solution: it suffices to have a general picture of the course content plus co-operation with specialist lecturers.
2 The *content-mastery* solution: one must somehow educate oneself to obtain the mastery of the subject-matter taught in the courses.
3 The *elevation* solution: the work of the adult educator must be elevated to a level where it no longer deals with specific contents but rather with broader, holistic planning and coordination.
4 The *societal development* solution: the socio-economic development, especially the growing complexity of work and organizations, forces organizations to understand the fruitlessness of separate short courses.

5 The *job change* solution: one can only look for a job where there still are more degrees of freedom and possibilities to influence the way training is realized.
6 The *developmental teamwork* solution: since the individual mastery of the content is impossible, one must build up teams which integrate training into broader development projects of the work processes and organizational structures, eventually drawing even the personnel to be trained into the planning process. This demands new types of knowledge and skills (especially concerning the analysis of work processes) from the adult educator.

The solutions of the students fell into these categories in the manner shown in Table 3.

Type of solution	Group 1	Group 2	Group 3	Group 4	Total
1 Traditional solution	–	–	1	2	3
2 Content-mastery solution	2	1	–	–	3
3 Elevation solution	–	1	–	1	2
4 Societal development solution	–	1	–	–	1
5 Job change solution	–	–	1	–	1
6 Developmental teamwork solution	1	–	1	1	3
TOTAL	3	3	3	4	13

Table 3
Solutions to the application problem according to the original group of the student.

The most sophisticated and original solution was that of Type 6. Here is an example of the reasoning representing it:

Points of departure for the analysis:
   – The educational planner does not have to be a specialist in every branch.
   – Most important is a view of the whole system.
   – Education and training cannot be separated from the total functioning of the organization.
Analysis and solution:
   – The personnel trainer starts discussing the function of training in the organization with the management.
   – The disjointed short-course training is given up.
   – On the basis of the ideology or goal-setting of the organization, a development plan is worked out. It is discussed with and among the whole personnel. A common goal-setting emerges.
   – The knowledge and consciousness of all members of the organization concerning the 'whole' of it are systematically raised.
   – Training is planned along with the development project.
   – At this stage, the personnel trainer has a fairly deep insight into the

substantial problems and prospects of the different branches of the
organization (this insight is continuously completed).
- The trainer may also keep up his/her competence by acquiring
specialization in some substance area.
- The central idea of the analysis is to change the piecemeal work
(organizing courses) into developmental activity. (Group 4 student)

It is somewhat surprising that this most advanced solution (Type 6) was
produced by two students who had constructed individualistic models and
by only one student who had constructed a societal model. In other words,
the same advanced solution type was reached on the basis of two different
types of models. If we trace these three students back to their contradiction
answers, we find that the first one of them (from Group 1) saw the
contradiction between content mastery and general theories and methods –
and she quite logically produced an individualistic model. This student,
then, came to a societally advanced solution from a rather pragmatic-
individualist background conception. The second student (from Group 3)
saw the contradiction between positivist objectivity and taking responsibility
for world problems. She produced the societal model, thus being a 'pure
societal type'. The third (from Group 4) saw the contradiction between
demands of production and humanistic aims. He produced a detailed
individualistic model stressing the effect of internalized humanistic values on
the process of study. Thus he represents a mixture of societal and
individualistic orientation.

One reason for the relatively 'weak' performance of the producers of
societal models in the application task seems to be their pessimistic view of a
mainly repressive or one-way effect of the society and economy on adult
education. This view easily leads to solutions like 'job change' or 'societal
development' imposed from without.

Conclusions

The study reported in the preceding sections does not aim at proving or
disproving the validity of the theoretical constructs of dialectics. Rather, it
aims at disclosing some of the possibilities and problems involved in teaching
dialectical thinking through model construction and model application.

One central problem in the procedure employed in the study was brought
up by a student in her answer to the second examination task:

> I do not know the historical background of the studies of adult education,
> thus I do not know what problems were originally supposed to be solved by
> the introduction of these studies. (Group 1 student)

Dialectical thinking is concrete-historical thinking. In the construction of
germ-cell models, a historical study of the genesis of the object is necessary. In
this experiment, the students were not required to perform such a historical
analysis. The only historical material they had available was their own
experiential life history as students of adult education. This kind of
unobjectified, tacit material is difficult to elaborate. It will take special

instructional efforts and certainly more time than was available for this experiment to ensure that systematic and consciously mastered historical analysis enters into the process of model construction.

In spite of the preliminary nature of this research, I am quite convinced of the need for instructional experiments where students are led into analysing and reconstructing the central genetic models behind the conceptual diversity of their disciplines and fields of study. In fact, this might be a very useful exercise for most university teachers and researchers. Adult education as a discipline is unlikely to fare successfully in this kind of experiment. It lacks well established conceptual and methodological structure. The results of this study point to the urgency of the need for conceptual clearance in the field, at least from the viewpoint of student learning. It will be interesting to compare the present results with the outcomes of similar experiments in other fields of university teaching.

References

Basseches, M. (1985) *Dialectical Thinking and Adult Development* Norwood: Ablex

Bibler, V.S. (1984) Thinking as creation (Introduction to the logic of mental dialogue) *Soviet Psychology* 22, 33-54

Davydov, V.V. (1982) The psychological structure and contents of the learning activity. In R. Glaser and J. Lompscher (Eds) *Cognitive and Motivational Aspects of Instruction* 37-44. Berlin: Deutscher Verlag der Wissenschaften

Engeström, Y. and Hedegaard M. (1985) Teaching theoretical thinking in primary school: The use of models in history/biology. In E. Bol, J.P.P. Haenen and M.A. Wolters (Eds) *Education for Cognitive Development* 170-193. Den Haag: SVO/SOO

Finocchiaro, M.A. (1980) *Galileo and the Art of Reasoning: Rhetorical foundations of logic and scientific method* Dordrecht: Reidel

Harré, R. (1970) *The Principles of Scientific Thinking* London Macmillan

Lektorsky, V.A. (1984) *Subject, Object, Cognition* Moscow: Progress

Markova, I. (1982) *Paradigms, Thought and Language* Chichester: Wiley

Mitroff, I.I. and Mason, R.O. (1981) *Creating a Dialectical Social Science* Dordrecht: Reidel

Riegel, K. (Ed.) (1975) *The Development of Dialectical Operations* Basel: Karger

Wartofsky, M. (1979) *Models: Representation and scientific understanding* Dordrecht: Reidel

Part 4

Improving Student Learning

12

Using Cognitive Psychology to Help Students Learn how to Learn

Michael J.A. Howe

In recent years psychology has thrown up a substantial number of ideas that seem to have implications for the practical issue of helping people to learn. But where some of the ideas will land is hard to see: certain current claims appear to be mutually contradictory. I shall look at a number which appear interesting and promising. I shall start by looking at some recent ideas about the organization of human abilities, and consider some implications for education. Secondly, I shall raise the problem of deciding on the most appropriate level of analysis to attempt when trying to identify basic components for necessary mental skills. One way to deal with this issue will be described. My third topic concerns the need to deal with people as individual learners, if they are to receive genuine assistance. Fourthly, I shall mention some studies which illustrate the importance of motivational influences on individual achievements. The fifth and final point I shall make is that if new learning skills are to be fully utilized, opportunities must be provided for them to become familiar and habitual.

The Organization of Abilities

Turning first to the organization of human abilities, many of us assume, implicitly or explicitly, that underlying people's different abilities is a commodity (which we might decide to call intelligence, or 'g') that, broadly speaking, determines the level of our achievements. The reasonable assumption is that people differ in how intelligent or how 'bright' they are: a person who is good at some intellectual skills will usually be good at other intellectual skills, success at various different abilities being limited to some extent by the amount of general intelligence the individual possesses. The fact that moderate correlations are observed between people's learned achievements in different intellectual spheres appears to be consistent with this view of human abilities.

But there are people in whom the level of performance at one or more kinds of intellectual task appears to be unrelated to their other abilities. Consider, for instance, those mentally retarded individuals labelled as 'idiots savants'. The term refers to people who despite being mentally retarded according to most criteria nevertheless perform exceptionally well at certain particular intellectual skills. Their feats can take any of a variety of forms. Sometimes a person will memorize whole pages from a telephone directory, or a railway timetable. Some idiots savants can perform highly complicated arithmetical calculations at lightning speed, by mental arithmetic. Very occasionally, exceptional artistic abilities are encountered. A number of idiots savants have been highly gifted musicians. I recently participated in an investigation of one whose main skill (as happens in a substantial proportion of these people) took the form of calendar calculating (Smith and Howe 1985). If you told him the date of your birth, he would inform you, immediately, the day on which it fell, and he could do this for any date in the present century.

The important point to which the various feats of idiots savants draw attention is that it is possible for individual intellectual skills in humans to be separate from other skills, and independent of them to a surprising extent. No matter that in most people the correlations between one's performance in different areas may strongly suggest that the different skills must function in conjunction with one another, the feats of idiots savants show that it is quite possible for certain mental abilities to exist independently.

Evidence like this encourages us to take a hard look at our everyday assumptions about the organization of the different human abilities of capable individuals. One psychologist who has done so is Howard Gardner, and his investigations have led him to draw attention to the relative autonomy of different abilities. In his recent book *Frames of Mind* (1984), Gardner argues that it is reasonable to speak of different human abilities as constituting separate intelligences which are relatively independent of one another. For obvious reasons such a view has strong implications for education at school and beyond.

This all looks rather like a revival of nineteenth-century faculty psychology. In certain respects it is (and Jerry Fodor's recent book *The Modularity of Mind* is actually subtitled 'An essay on faculty psychology'). Gardner supports his case by noting that a number of different areas of competence can be seen to meet each of a variety of further criteria in addition to the fact that they can be encountered in relative isolation, as in the idiot savant cases. For example, there are numerous findings from studies of brain damage showing that certain abilities may be selectively destroyed or selectively spared. Gardner mentions six other criteria by which the merits of a particular kind of ability can be judged for its suitability to be considered as a separate intelligence, but in practice it would be hard to specify in a hard and fast manner the particular conditions for meeting some of these criteria.

Gardner has drawn up a preliminary list of competences which he thinks qualify as separate intelligences. These are: linguistic intelligence, musical intelligence, logico-mathematical intelligence, spatial intelligence, bodily-kinaesthetic intelligence, and a group of abilities which he terms 'the personal intelligences'. He does not consider his list to be exhaustive or final.

Even though we may fail to be convinced by Gardner's claims, he succeeds in making us examine our own assumptions about the manner in which our different abilities are related to one another. One possible objection to Gardner's position is that whereas, as in idiots savants, certain intellectual skills *can* operate in relative isolation, their doing so is itself a symptom that things are wrong. On the whole, it might be argued, people function best when their different abilities operate with a degree of coordination. In idiots savants, although the individual skills may be highly impressive, they are virtually never applied to any situations that are particularly useful, let alone innovative. It may be that most abilities are more independent than we normally assume, but that the effective utilization of human capacities depends upon those abilities being coordinated with one another.

Norman Geschwind once suggested that 'the brain really is a kind of federation and, furthermore, a loose federation; it is not perfectly connected. The extent of the disunity varies from person to person' (Miller 1983, p.127). What might be the advantages of having such a federation? This question is rather convincingly answered by Paul Rozin (1976). He points out that special abilities, which are often highly impressive and very complicated, are to be found in many organisms, including ones that we do not think of as being at all intelligent. For example, impressive special abilities (Rozin calls them 'adaptive specializations') can be observed in the behaviour of insects such as the honey bees originally described by von Frisch. The brain of the bee must contain astronomical data, and some kind of clock, and a mechanism for relating information from the different sources. As a result, the distance of the food source from the hive and the angle of direction with respect to the sun is calculated, and through dance-like movements it is subsequently communicated to the other bees in the hive.

However, as Rozin argues, adaptive specializations in the form of mechanisms of this kind (which appear to be largely pre-wired), however numerous and however complicated, would not be equal to the task of controlling human abilities. For us to be competent and to adapt to the varying circumstances that people face it is necessary for the different functions of the brain to be more highly coordinated. Our mental capacities need to be multi-purpose in nature, in ways that are not possible in the case of the bee, which cannot utilize its impressive navigational and directional signalling capacities for different, newer, tasks. It has all that computing power, but it cannot decide to use it for other purposes. What makes humans so able, Rozin claims, is the fact that to a considerable extent we are able to draw rather widely upon our mental capacities and make use of a particular skill in a range of different circumstances. This multi-purpose aspect of the different parts of the human brain is possible, Rozin argues, because the different systems are relatively *accessible* to other demands and other systems. In intelligent humans, instead of brain mechanisms being restricted to a particular job they can be applied to a number of different purposes. The brain's components function together as a kind of construction kit: each can be used in various ways, to meet the demands of varying tasks.

For Rozin the key to the flexibility and adaptability which are the hallmarks of an intelligent organism lies squarely in the accessibility of the brain's specialized mechanisms. He feels that certain kinds of pathology, in which functioning intelligence is decreased, are explicable in terms of the absence, or loss, of such accessibility. For example, he says that one sometimes encounters children who are generally lacking in intelligence and problem-solving ability, but who are linguistically very fluent. He believes that this is due to the language system becoming disconnected from the other systems involved in cognition. Brain damage can lead to the loss of access to certain systems, even when the actual processing systems remain intact. For instance, a sudden loss of ability to read is occasionally encountered, associated with blindness in the right visual field but normal sight in the left visual field. The result is produced by a lesion which has the effect of cutting the connections between intact parts of the cortex. Thus the cause of reading loss is not a lack of the processing capacity, but a loss of access to it.

Rozin feels that the notion of accessibility is relevant also to the practical endeavour of learning to read. He argues that a cause of difficulty in learning to read lies in the fact that language is an adaptive specialization which, whilst impressive in all kinds of ways, is nevertheless relatively inaccessible. Thus, for example, it is not available to conscious awareness: we are not at all aware of how language works and we cannot use the mechanisms underlying language to help with non-language tasks. Of course, for most purposes we do not need to have a detailed understanding of our language systems in order to deal with food and drink. But, Rozin claims, reading is one important ability for which inaccessibility to our language mechanisms does create problems. The difficulty, he says, lies in getting access to the phonological system. Rozin calls it a matter of pulling the phonological system out of the cognitive unconscious. In connecting seen words to their sounds we have to form associations between the visual system and the relatively inaccessible phonological system.

This claim, that the difficulty of gaining access to the phonological system is a reason why some children have great difficulty in learning to read, is not one which is easy to prove or disprove, but Rozin cites some evidence which appears to support it. For example, in an experiment by Marion Blank (1968) children had to judge whether two consecutive spoken words were the same or different, for instance *web* and *wed*. (The words always differed in one phoneme.) The children were later required to say aloud the same words after each was spoken by the experimenter. Blank found that, quite frequently, words were repeated correctly by the children even if their judgements had been incorrect when they had been asked to say whether or not the word items were identical. Thus the children's performance at *using* certain words gave evidence of successful discriminations that were not apparent when they were asked questions *about* them. Also, it emerged that children who could discriminate between different words might nevertheless have a lot of trouble understanding that two different word items, such as *dog* and *dig*, started with the same sound. Again, it seems that children who can perform a word discrimination task may have more difficulty with a task that involves knowing things about the words.

Rozin also draws attention to the fact that the earliest writing systems were logographic rather than phonological, based on pictures representing meanings, not symbols for word sounds. Furthermore, Rozin found that children who were having very great difficulty with learning to read English experienced no unusual difficulties in a learning task in which they had to associate thirty Chinese characters with their spoken English equivalents. It seems that learning tasks involving language sounds can present practical difficulties that are absent from other learning tasks of equivalent complexity.

Rozin has put forward a number of ideas about how to help children learn to read, in the face of the difficulties which, he claims, are presented by the need to get access to the phonological code. Very briefly, he suggests helping children to gain the idea of reading and decoding in circumstances that use non-phonological methods, for example ones based on pictures and then syllables. Later, the alphabet-based aspects of reading which give so much difficulty are gradually introduced.

Components of Ability

I have discussed the organization of abilities at some length because the ways in which the different computing systems of the brain are coordinated are highly important in determining what people actually achieve. Let me now turn to another issue, the components of mental abilities. One unresolved problem is how to decide what size of units to look for and what level of analysis to attempt when we try to identify basic components that we can refer to in specifying the mental skills people need. Should we look at the processes underlying apparently simple tasks such as letter identification or simple and choice reactions? Or ought we to define basic components of thinking and learning on the basis of task descriptions? Or should we give emphasis to the kind of analysis of mental operations favoured by Piaget? Is it generally helpful to try to identify extremely small and simple components which might form building blocks for more complicated processes, or is it more fruitful to attend directly to the larger units that are so formed? It is by no means inevitable that looking for the simplest, smallest, or most basic units involved in human cognition is the most effective research strategy if we are interested in producing findings that have practical applicability.

Another question to be answered, in deciding upon the kinds of components to look for, is whether it is most useful to concentrate on processes that seem to have a relatively straightforward role in learning as such, or whether to give emphasis to factors such as attentional processes, which whilst not being so directly involved as components of cognitive skills may nevertheless be crucial for the acquisition of human abilities. Reuven Feuerstein, a psychologist from Israel who has long been interested in compensatory education, has put forward useful ideas about some of the pre-requisite component skills necessary for the kinds of intellectual achievements that are highly desirable for life in the present century. Having observed that some compensatory approaches have been successful and others not, he argues that in order to ensure success it is essential first to identify fairly precisely the ways in which mental functioning is inadequate in those individuals who are educationally backward or retarded, as reflected in low scores at achievement or intelligence tests. Feuerstein believes that a compensatory programme needs to be based on a model of learning and thinking that incorporates careful specification of the particular skills that need to be taught. He also insists that if any remedial programme is to be successful the teachers concerned need to be given considerable training, and that the programme needs to be both intensive and prolonged. And he rejects the idea that any brief programme can function effectively in the way that a shot in the arm may serve as a kind of immunization.

For Feuerstein (1980) a key concept is the *modifiability* of the individual. By modifiability he refers to the extent to which the person is capable of learning from his environment. Feuerstein points out that the fact that a person's environment may be highly stimulating is not sufficient to guarantee that the person actually learns from it. For that to happen it is also necessary for the learner to undertake certain mental operations, which are themselves learned. Many disadvantaged children fail to learn, he claims, because they lack essential pre-requisites, in the form of necessary skills for learning.

What are some of these pre-requisites? They include various character-istics, some of which can be regarded as skills as such, others as being habitual ways of responding to situations. Examples are attending to and concentrating closely on what is seen or heard, reflecting, and delaying any immediate response until necessary thought has occurred. As Robert Sternberg points out (Chapter 5), making a snappy response is not always the intelligent thing to do. Other essential learning skills include: utilizing information in memory in order to make comparisons; remembering the past and imagining the future; understanding and looking for relationships between perceived objects; organizing items and seeing patterns, regularities and other relationships based on qualities such as size, shape, colour, texture and direction.

According to Feuerstein, most children learn to do these kinds of things largely but not exclusively from their parents and families. Some children do not learn them, because, says Feuerstein, they lack what he terms *mediated learning experiences*. He explains this concept by saying that for most children, in their earliest years, other people, typically the parents, perform the function of mediating between the environment and the child, through talk, play, reading out loud, playing games, giving directions, serving as models, asking and answering questions, having various kinds of temporally organized interactions and dialogues with the child, directing the child's attention to rules, regularities and various attributes of objects in the environment. These kinds of activities, if they occur, serve to direct the child's attention to those aspects of the environment which are significant, and encourage the child to perform necessary mental operations on the child's perceptions, making comparisons possible and enabling relationships to be discerned. The child, as a result of the mental activities thus encouraged, acquires skills and habits of attending and thinking, and is able to perform operations of thought on items that are in memory, rather than simply being able to react, without reflecting, to concrete events. (Having summarized Feuerstein's views I should point out, however, that some researchers have questioned the value of trying to teach cognitive skills on their own. Bob Glaser (1984), for example, cites evidence (eg Siegler and Klahr 1982) indicating that thinking abilities are most effectively developed in the context of specific bodies of knowledge and related skills. Similarly Paul Ramsden has been critical of the notion of what he calls 'detachable skills'.)

Feuerstein argues that however stimulating the environment, the child will suffer if there is no one to act as a guide and interpreter, directing the child's attention to what is significant: without this mediation the environ-ment simply presents a noisy mass. In its absence the child will be disadvantaged. The compensatory training programmes Feuerstein has devised are based on the assumption that such a child will remain at a disadvantage, and lack 'modifiability', until appropriate mental skills and habits of thinking are acquired.

People as Individuals

The next, and third, point to be discussed concerns the importance of thinking about people as individuals. Any practical steps that are taken in order to increase learning need to reflect an understanding of the needs of individuals, not just those of a non-existent 'average' learner. A preoccupation with norms and averages can sometimes lead to our depending on forms of data, such as average developmental growth curves or learning curves, which show how scores at various cognitive skills increase smoothly and systematically as the *average* child gets older, but which have little relationship to what actually happens in any particular *individual*. Changes in children are in fact typically irregular, characterized by sudden improvements followed by a steady state until the next sudden change, which might be one week later or several years afterwards, smooth progressions being unusual (Belmont 1978).

There are further reasons for being concerned with individuals as such, if we want to help people learn more efficiently. In a recent article I suggested that,

> When we try to answer practical questions about what to do in particular individual circumstances, it is invariably necessary to start with a phrase such as *it depends upon*...
>
> Hence if we were to ask, say, how breaking a limb would influence intellectual capacity in a seven-year-old, it would be fruitless to seek a universally correct answer. In one recorded instance, that of the young H.G. Wells, the effect was to encourage an already bookish child, confined to bed by his injury, to devote even more time and attention to the written word, indirectly contributing to his becoming unusually knowledgeable in early life and an outstanding savant in adulthood. Ought we to inflict a similar injury on every seven-year-old we can find? Clearly not. (Howe 1982, p.1072)

As a rule, knowing that a particular event, or a particular combination of events, have had a certain effect on one person may tell us little or nothing about the likely outcome of similar events on someone else. As Howard Gruber has expressed it, every individual seems 'to incorporate the flow of experience into the existing structure of his own knowledge in accordance with his own purposes' (Gruber 1981, p.255). In consequence, the general knowledge that psychologists possess about the environmental causes of various skills and achievements will not always be sufficient for making accurate predictions concerning the effects of educational interventions on individual people.

Motivation

The emphasis on individuality leads to the fourth aspect of human learning, motivation. The importance of motivation is hard to over-estimate. (This is true not only for learning and cognition: much the same conclusion emerges from studies of the effectiveness of methods for combating social problems such as alcoholism, obesity, and drug taking.) What really matters in all of these is the individual's commitment to making the changes that are sought after.

The term motivation covers a range of phenomena, and even when we give them labels that are apparently more precise ('needs', 'drives', 'wants', 'incentives', 'interests', and so on) I suspect we are still mixing up a variety of causes for people's actions. Such causes can influence behaviour in very different ways, depending upon the particular individual and the precise circumstances concerned. The fact that motivational influences are so diverse contributes to the difficulty of measuring them, and this in turn may be one reason why motivation receives less attention in research into learning and instruction than its importance would justify. I have a strong feeling that motivational factors are crucial whenever a person achieves anything of significance as a result of learning and thought, and I cannot think of exceptions to this statement (Howe 1980, 1982, 1984). That is not to claim that a high level of motivation can ever be a *sufficient* condition for human achievements, but it is undoubtedly a necessary one. And, conversely, negative motivational influences, such as fear of failure, feelings of helplessness, lack of confidence, and having the experience that one's fate is largely controlled by external factors rather than by oneself, almost certainly have effects that restrict a person's learned achievements.

These impressions about the importance of motivation are not based on any readily quantifiable observations. However, the findings of some recent studies of the training and development of outstanding individuals provide convincing evidence. A number of investigations are described in a recent book edited by Benjamin Bloom (1985). In each study around twenty of the most outstanding young American people in an area of expertise were interviewed at some length, as were their parents, in order to gain fairly detailed accounts of the circumstances in which the skills and abilities were acquired. There are investigations of concert pianists, Olympic swimmers, research mathematicians, sculptors, and neurologists. In looking at those accounts it is hardly surprising to find that motives are always important. But what *is* surprising is the sheer extent to which, in at least some stages of a person's development, motivational influences appear to have been more important than other crucial factors, such as technical expertise on the part of instructors.

For instance, in two very different areas of expertise, playing the piano and playing tennis, remarkably similar kinds of incentives seem to have played a vital part in the progress of most of the individuals who were studied. Of these people, the tennis players were right at the top of their profession and the concert pianists had all been finalists in at least one of the international competitions in which the most outstanding young players can be identified.

The particularly remarkable point of similarity in the early lives of virtually all the young pianists and the young tennis players – who formed two strikingly different groups in most respects – lay in the nature of the personal and social relationships with their first teacher. Writing of the different coaches who first taught each of the tennis players, usually in middle childhood, Judith Monsaas, the psychologist who carried out the investigation (Monsaas 1985) noted that these first tennis coaches were mostly not outstanding players. However, they had one thing in common: the attribute of being very good with young children. The players thought of them as extremely nice people.

When we turn to the very different skill of playing the piano, we find that the first teachers of the concert pianists are described in remarkably similar terms. As with the earliest tennis coaches, by no means all the children's first piano teachers were particularly good performers: the author of this investigation, Lauren Sosniak (1985), reports that over sixty per cent of them were considered to be no better than average among local teachers. But once again, what did matter were the personal relationships which they established with the young learners: the teachers are described as being warm and kindly people, who were good at giving children support and encouragement.

Maintaining the existence of benign motivational influences in people's changing lives is not easy. This is an especially difficult source of problems for classroom teachers. They may have little power to control many of the motivational factors that are potentially most powerful for helping particular children to attend more closely to classroom affairs, to study harder and to achieve more. And for many children there is a limit to what can be done to motivate them more effectively without making substantial changes in the kind of society we live in. Nevertheless, whenever we think about how children and adults can be helped to learn, it is useful to keep in mind the fact that the extent to which any individual will take advantage of available educational opportunities will depend very much upon the degree to which the individual is motivated to succeed.

Forming Learning Habits

The fifth and final point to be emphasized is the necessity for the skills that are involved in effective learning not only to be learned but to be used and repeated until they become habitual. This is essential if a person, especially an immature one or one whose educational background is not characterized by success, is to continue to use newly acquired skills in the future, or to apply them to new tasks that are not identical to those in which the skill in question was originally gained. The reason is simple: when things get difficult we tend to fall back on actions which are tried and tested, familar and comfortable, and which we may perform with a degree of automacity. We avoid activities that are relatively unfamiliar, not so well-tried, and which demand all our concentration. For reasons of this kind it is not uncommon to find learners, particularly if they are children, reacting to a new and difficult task by regressing to earlier and less sophisticated methods, such as trying to memorize information by rote, rather than making use of more recently acquired strategies. In his excellent book about classroom learning, *How Children Fail*, John Holt (1964) gives numerous examples illustrating the tendency of anxious children to revert to the tried and familiar, abandoning considerably more effective methods if the latter have not been assimilated to the extent that the child feels secure with them. In unfamiliar and stressful conditions even an adult is likely to abandon a new approach if the very activity of using that method itself demands more than a certain amount of attention. In such circumstances, abandoning the new approach may be an intelligent strategy. And, as Paul Ramsden has remarked, it is sometimes 'intelligent' for a smart student in higher education to adopt a surface rather than a deep approach to learning (cf Chapter 15). Newly-learned strategies are soon dropped, even when the user has been able to observe their effectiveness, if there has been no opportunity for the kind of practice that leads to such strategies becoming habitual (Belmont and Butterfield 1977). Typically, it is much easier to teach a useful new learning or memory strategy than it is to ensure that people are able to go on using it.

For practical purposes, the remedy lies in ensuring that new strategies, methods and techniques for study and learning are not simply learned, but are used again and again, and thoroughly practised, in a range of different circumstances, until they become a well-established part of the individual's habitual repertoire, and performed as readily and easily as previously were the more primitive alternative approaches. But giving sufficient practice does take time. Moreover, simply saying that there is a need to practise is not enough: ill-designed tasks can be very tedious and boring, serving only to alienate the young learner. It is easy to ensure that opportunities are numerous enough for a new skill to become established, and varied enough to keep the learner's interest.

Having emphasized the need for sufficient practice to be provided to enable acquired cognitive strategies and skills to become familiar, let me proceed to a brief conclusion. I have stated, first, that we need to have a good understanding of the manner in which intellectual abilities are organized, related to one another and coordinated. Second, in order to teach learning and thinking skills we need to have some practical specification of the components of mental abilities, choosing the level and the size of those components with down-to-earth considerations in mind. Third, we have to bear in mind the limitations of normative knowledge for helping individual human beings. Fourth, we must avoid underestimating the importance of motivational influences in everyday cognition. And fifth, newly acquired cognitive strategies and new learning skills must become habitual if they are to be fully utilized: care is needed to ensure that there are sufficient opportunities for repeated use.

To incorporate these essential features (and that list is by no means exhaustive) into programmes for helping individuals to learn requires both a good understanding of the psychology of human cognition and considerable practical know-how about the ways in which people actually deal with learning experiences in school and in daily life. Clearly, a good combination of psychological knowledge and practical expertise is necessary. In finishing, let me illustrate this by mentioning one way in which Reuven Feuerstein solves a problem encountered in attempting to motivate educationally retarded adolescents. He points out that in any learning task based on the kinds of materials encountered in school learning, educationally backward adolescents will be at a disadvantage and realize they are backward. So Feuerstein uses learning materials that are unlike ones normally encountered in school. There is no big disadvantage in doing this, since he feels that it is the cognitive skills, not the particular information in them, that is important. At the same time, Feuerstein avoids having tasks that are too easy: the students have to work hard at them. But, with these unfamiliar materials, learning is almost equally difficult for the teacher. This is important. It means that the students can see themselves as being on something like an equal footing with the teacher.

The moral to be drawn is one that is widely applicable: if you wish to help students to learn you must know something about the underlying cognitive processes, and you also need to have some psychological insight into the individuals you want to help.

References

Belmont, J.M. (1978) Individual differences in memory: the cases of normal and retarded development. In M.M. Gruneberg and P. Morris (Eds) *Aspects of Memory* London: Methuen

Belmont, J.M., and Butterfield, E.C. (1977) The instructional approach to developmental cognitive research. In R.V. Kail and J.W. Hagen (Eds) *Perspectives on the Development of Memory and Cognition* Hillsdale, New Jersey: Erlbaum

Blank, M. (1968) Cognitive processes in auditory discrimination in normal and retarded readers *Child Development* 39, 1091-1101

Bloom, B.S. (Ed.) (1985) *Developing Talent in Young People* New York: Ballantine

Feuerstein, R. (1980) *Instrumental Enrichment: An intervention program for cognitive modifiability* Baltimore: University Park Press

Fodor, J.A. (1983) *The Modularity of Mind: An essay on faculty psychology* Cambridge, Massachusetts: MIT Press

Gardner, H. (1984) *Frames of Mind* London: Heinemann

Glaser, R. (1984) Education and thinking: the role of knowledge *American Psychologist* 39, 93-104

Gruber, H.E. (1981) *Darwin on Man: A psychological study of scientific creativity* (2nd edition) Chicago: University of Chicago Press

Holt, J. (1964) *How Children Fail* New York: Pitman

Howe, M.J.A. (1980) *The Psychology of Human Learning* New York: Harper and Row

Howe, M.J.A. (1982) Biographical evidence and the development of outstanding individuals *American Psychologist* 37, 1071-1081

Howe, M.J.A. (1984) *A Teacher's Guide to the Psychology of Learning* Oxford: Blackwell

Miller, J. (Ed.) (1983) *States of Mind* London: British Broadcasting Corporation

Monsaas, J.A. (1985) Learning to be a world-class tennis player. In B.S. Bloom (Ed.) *Developing Talent in Young Children* New York: Ballantine

Rozin, P. (1976) The evolution of intelligence and access to the cognitive unconscious *Progress in Psychobiology and Physiological Psychology* 6, 245-280

Siegler, R.S. and Klahr, D. (1982) When do children learn? The relationship between existing knowledge and the acquisition of new knowledge. In R.

Glaser (Ed.) *Advances in Instructional Psychology* (Vol. 2) Hillsdale, New Jersey: Erlbaum

Smith, J., and Howe, M.J.A. (1985) An investigation of calendar-calculating skills in an 'idiot savant' *International Journal of Rehabilition Research* 8, 77-79

Sosniak, L.A. (1985) Learning to be a concert pianist. In Bloom (1985)

13

Effects of Verbal Participation in Small Group Discussion

Jos H.C. Moust, Henk G. Schmidt, Maurice L. de Volder, Jan J. Beliën and Willem S. de Grave

Research into small group learning has flourished during the past few years, and has been conducted from an interactional and a cognitive point of view.

Recent research from the interactional perspective has generally shown that the achievements of students working in cooperative settings are superior to those of students in competitive and individualistic settings. In particular, those models of small group learning in which decentralization of authority and clear cooperation reward structures were implemented have proved to lead to superior performance (see, for example, the extensive reviews by Sharan (1980) and Slavin (1980)).

Research that systematically investigates the effects of group interaction variables on achievement has been executed by Webb (1980a, 1980b, 1982a, 1982b) and by Peterson and Janicki (1979). These researchers demonstrated that some interaction variables are more beneficial to the learning of individual members of a group than others. Those that turn out to be the most beneficial are 'giving help' and 'receiving help'. Both show a positive relation with achievement. Students who give help, that is explain difficult subject-matter to their peers, learn more than students who do not. The effect on achievement of receiving help depends on (a) whether the help is given in response to a student's need, and (b) whether the help includes explanations as well as the correct answer. Receiving no help when asking for it appears to be markedly detrimental to achievement.

Research by Webb (1980a, 1980b) has further shown that the amount of off-task behaviour in a group is negatively but non-significantly related to achievement while the amount of passive behaviour, defined as a lack of any discernable involvement in the group task, also shows a negative relationship with achievement. Thus, merely observing other students' working activities and listening to others' explanations appears not to be sufficient for learning the material.

In their conclusions Webb (1980 a, b) and Peterson and Janicki (1979) stress two points: (a) students have to be actively involved in the learning process, and (b) the mere act of giving or receiving help is not a sufficient condition for learning. It is the way in which this is done by the students that is important. Giving or receiving help consisting of explanations has a greater effect on learning than does help consisting only of a correct answer.

Although these results are interesting, they do not explain what kinds of cognitive processes mediate between the interactional behaviour and the superior learning results. In other words, *how* do students learn while giving or receiving explanations. To get a deeper insight into these processes we have to turn to the cognitive perspective on group learning.

Bargh and Schul (1980) have shown that students who have to learn subject-matter with the aim of teaching it to another student score higher on an achievement test than students who learn the material only for themselves. Their findings indicate that people studying for a teaching role perform better both on peripheral detail items and on items measuring the central message of the material. Bargh and Schul suggest that students preparing to teach someone else construct a more highly organized cognitive structure than students trying to learn the material only for themselves. They further suggest that the former students may reorganize the material not only when preparing for its presentation, but also while teaching.

The mechanism that could be responsible for this cognitive restructuring is elaboration on existing knowledge. Elaborations are subject-produced inferences that describe previously unseen or un-understood relationships between concepts or real-world phenomena. According to Anderson and Reder (1979) information is better understood, processed and retrieved when students are given an opportunity to elaborate on that information. Elaborations provide redundancy in the memory structure. Redundancy can be looked upon as a safeguard against forgetting and an aid to retrieval.

If one accepts this explanation for the findings of Bargh and Schul (1980) one might hypothesize that the same mechanism underlies the superior learning of students who are actively engaged in small group discussion. A study by O'Donnel, Damsereau, Rocklin, Hythecker, Lambiotte, Larson and Young (1985) provides support for this hypothesis. They investigated the impact of the frequency of elaboration on the text processing performance of dyads using technical text. Students in the frequent elaboration group were requested to elaborate four times while studying the passage; students in the infrequent elaboration groups elaborated once. The amount of elaboration engendered by small group discussion had a clear effect on the learning of the students.

Of particular significance to the present study is research done by Schmidt (1982). Schmidt investigated the role of elaboration of prior knowledge during discussion by presenting a problem description to a small group of students. The problem described a set of phenomena which can be observed in reality. Students were asked to explain these phenomena in terms of underlying processes, principles or mechanisms. Subsequently, they processed a problem-relevant text, which aimed at clarifying any ambiguities that turned up during the initial analysis of the problem. Schmidt found that groups of students working to this problem-analysis approach showed superior recognition and transfer of information as compared with control groups which had not been presented with the same sort of problem. These effects were attributed to the activational and restructuring properties of the problem-analysis procedure. Schmidt concluded that elaboration of prior knowledge through small group discussion in general has a positive effect on subsequent text processing. Recent research by De Grave, Schmidt, Beliën, Moust, De Volder and Kerkhofs (1984) confirmed these results.

The investigations summarized here can be used to explain why students who actively participate in small group discussion show superior learning. Their participation can be interpreted as elaboration on prior knowledge which contributes to the construction of a richer cognitive structure of the topic. But what happens to those who participate less actively in the discussion? Large differences in the amount of active involvement among students in tutorial sessions are no exception, as anyone who attends such groups may confirm. Do students who elaborate less learn less? This question was investigated in the present study, using the activation-of-prior-knowledge approach developed by Schmidt (1982). A problem was presented to several groups of students, which they were asked to discuss. The discussion was recorded on tape. Subsequently, the students read a problem-relevant text. Learning was assessed by achievement on a recall and a completion test. The relationship between achievement and participation in the discussion was assessed.

Method

Subjects

The subjects were twenty female and two male first-year students from two schools for health sciences. All subjects had enjoyed the same type of secondary education, their final examination including biology. The average age was 18.9 years, with a standard deviation of eleven months.

Procedure

The students were randomly assigned to discussion groups: four groups of about six students. In each of the groups a male experimenter was present. He briefly explained the problem-analysis approach by means of a written example describing a plant releasing oxygen in daylight but not in the dark. In a hand-out of one and a half pages, the phenomenon was analysed from a few viewpoints, and a number of more or less elaborate explanations were offered. The experimenter actively involved subjects in order to check their understanding of the way they were to proceed with the next problem. He emphasized that they were to brainstorm on possible explanations for the problem and to analyse the explanations coming up while discussing them with each other. This briefing took five to ten minutes.

The experimenter then announced that the next problem-analysis should not take longer than fifteen minutes, and the problem was given in writing. It read: 'A red blood cell is placed in pure water. Under the microscope we can see it swell very quickly and burst finally. Another blood cell is placed in salt water and begins to shrink'.

When students had finished reading the problem, the discussion started. The experimenter acted as a discussion leader, asking questions, paraphrasing answers and summarizing. It was essential that, while leading the discussion, he did not provide new information. The discussion was recorded on tape.

After discussion time was over all students were given a text of six pages on the topic of osmosis and diffusion. The text contained no formulas, tables, figures or other didactic features on the subject. Students were instructed to study the text for fifteen minutes.

After this, they were told how the experiment would carry on. Since no time limits were set for the next phases, students were allowed to raise a hand after completion of a phase and to proceed to the next phase. When this was clear to students, they received a booklet (the free-recall test) consisting of three blank pages and a front page with the following instruction: 'Write down everything you remember about osmosis and diffusion. Write in sentences, do not use single words or drawings'. When students indicated they did not remember anything more than they had written down, they were given a second booklet. This contained a cued recall or completion test consisting of forty-four items related to the text, such as: 'Diffusion proceeds quicker when molecules are ...' (answer: smaller); and 'When two concentrations possess the same maximum osmotic pressure, they are called ...' (answer: isotonic).

Alpha reliability of the completion test was calculated at 0.73. Inter-rater reliability for the scoring of free recall, calculated for a number of randomly selected, free recall protocols, was 90 per cent and higher, counting only the number of correctly recalled propositions.

A verbatim transcription was made of every tape-recording of the problem-analysis, which was then analysed. The following independent variables were constructed:

1   The *number of propositions* every group member produced during the problem-analysis. (According to Mayer (1985) propositions are subject-predicate units which express one single idea.)

2   The *number of clauses* every group member produced. Every *new* contribution of a group member in relation to the subject-matter under discussion was counted as a clause. This is a useful alternative measure of participation because one person may contribute to the discussion only once by means of a long monologue, consisting of many propositions, while another may produce a large number of short interventions, also meaning many propositions. Without measuring the number of clauses produced these two categories of students could not be distinguished.

3   The *relative number of propositions*. Since the amount of discussion time in every group was variable, a measure was needed to compare the relative contribution of each group member. The relative number of propositions was computed by dividing the number of propositions produced by individuals by the total amount of propositions produced by their group.

These three independent measures are expected to be interrelated. Dependent variables were a) the number of correct propositions every group member produced in free recall, and b) the amount of correct answers in the completion test.

Results

Table 1 shows the means and standard deviations of the variables of interest. Looking at those of the discussion variables, one can conclude that the participants' contributions vary widely. Variance in achievement is less.

		Mean	**SD**	**NP**	**NC**	**PP**
DISCUSSION	– Number of propositions (NP)	16.05	10.16	–	–	–
VARIABLES	– Number of clauses (NC)	6.67	3.87	0.84	–	–
	– Percentage of propositions (PP)	19.06	11.91	0.99	0.76	–
ACHIEVEMENT	– Completion test	37.23	4.37	−0.30	−0.30	−0.29
VARIABLES	– Number of propositions in free recall	34.07	10.72	0.02	−0.14	–

Table 1

Discussion and achievement variables: means, standard deviations and correlations.

The table also shows the correlations between and among the discussion and achievement variables. First, there are high intercorrelations between elaboration measures, indicating that they are actually all measuring the same construct. Second, it can be concluded that no correlations exist between the elaboration and achievement variables. In fact, slightly negative – although not statistically significant – correlations exist between the amount of elaboration and achievement scores on the recall and completion test.

Discussion

Conceptualizations of learning in terms of an elaboration hypothesis (Anderson and Reder 1979; Reder 1980) predict that the more subjects elaborate while processing information, the richer the resultant cognitive structure will be, or, in other words, the better the learning. Applied to small group learning this theory suggests that the amount of elaborative activity during discussion has a positive influence on achievement.

In the present study this hypothesis was tested. Subjects analysed a problem in a small group. The discussion was recorded on tape and a verbatim transcription produced. Subsequently, subjects read a problem-relevant text and took a free recall and cued recall test. The study failed to demonstrate any relationship between the discussion variables, that were utilized as an operationalization of amount of elaboration, and achievement. These data seem to imply that the amount of elaboration during small group discussion has no effect on learning whatsoever.

Superficially, the result is at variance with previous research in this area. Schmidt (1982) and De Grave et al. (1984), for instance, have found that elaboration of prior knowledge by discussing a problem generally facilitates the processing of new information. O'Donnell and her associates (1985) have shown that the achievements of frequently elaborating dyads were superior to those of their less frequently elaborating counterparts. These studies indicate that the amount of elaboration is indeed a major variable in learning by small group discussion.

The reader should be aware, however, of the differences in design between the investigations concerned. The studies reviewed here were experimental in nature and employed between-groups comparisons in order to investigate the influence of elaboration by discussion. In one case (that of Schmidt and his collaborators) means of elaborating groups were compared with those of non-elaborating control conditions, while O'Donnell et al. (1985) controlled the amount of verbal elaboration by their subjects by means of experimental manipulation. The present study utilized a *between-subjects* approach to the problem. In principle, it is possible that a relationship which exists at the group level might be absent at the individual level.

There is a more plausible alternative explanation, however, for this apparent discrepancy. It is possible that subjects not – or less – participating in the discussion elaborate as much as those who do participate, without *verbalizing their elaborations to the same extent as the latter*. This covert-elaboration hypothesis could explain why no relation could be demonstrated between amount of elaboration, as measured by the number of utterances by group members, and achievement.

An implication of this point of view is that the amount of verbal participation in a discussion may not be such a valid indicator of the amount of elaboration carried out as is often suggested in the literature.

Indirect support for a covert-elaboration hypothesis comes from data provided by Webb (1980a, 1982a), Peterson and Janicki (1979), and recent research by Peterson and Swing (1985). These investigators have shown that not only do interactive behaviours like giving explanations or providing information (the behaviours they usually summarize as 'giving help') have a facilitative effect on achievement, but so also is the mere act of listening to others ('receiving help') beneficial to the learners as compared with off-task behaviours. So not only the talkers benefit from their efforts, but also the listeners, because both groups are cognitively active.

This conclusion that the more silent students may learn as much from small group discussion as the more talkative ones may come as a relief to those who worry about the involvement of the silent in small group activity.

The investigation described here suggests certain avenues for further research. One is to verify the extent to which non-participants in small group discussion are really elaborating covertly. This can be done in several ways, one of which is to utilize a stimulated-recall procedure. By this procedure subjects are shown a videotape of a discussion in which they participated and are asked to stop the tape whenever they recall a thought they had during the discussion. The method has been used with some success in research into clinical reasoning processes (Elstein, Shulman and Sprafka 1978). Another investigation that could be made is into the extent to which the specific nature of the elaborations influences learning. There are some indications that explanatory elaborations are particularly successful in the promotion of learning (Britton and Black 1985), which suggests that learning groups should be presented with tasks that stimulate the production of explanations. More detailed analyses are necessary, however.

Dedication

This paper is dedicated to the memory of Jan J.J. Beliën, who died during the preparatory stage.

Acknowledgements

The contributions of Bert Kerkhofs and Karin van Ee-Ten Horn to the analysis of the data, and of Karin van Ee-Ten Horn to the translation of this paper are acknowledged.

References

Anderson, J.R. and L.M. Reder (1979) An elaborative processing explanation of depth of processing. In L.S. Cernak and F.I.M. Craik (Eds) *Levels of Processing in Human Memory* Hillsdale, NJ: Erlbaum

Bargh, J.A. and J. Schul (1980) On the cognitive benefits of teaching *Journal of Educational Psychology* 72 (5) 593-604

Britton, B.K. and Black, J.B. (1985) *Understanding Expository Text* Hillsdale, NJ: Erlbaum

Elstein, A.S., L.S. Shulman and S.A. Sprafka (1978) *Medical Problem-Solving, an Analysis of Clinical Reasoning* Cambridge: Harvard University Press

Grave, W.S. de, H.G. Schmidt, J.J.J. Beliën, J.H.C. Moust, M.L. de Volder, B. Kerkhofs (1984) *Effecten van Verschillende Typen van Activatie op Recall, Gemeten met een Aanvultoets* (Differential effects of three types of activation of prior knowledge on recall, measured by a completion test) Paper presented at the Annual Dutch Educational Research Association Meeting, Tilburg

Mayer, R.E. (1985) Structural analysis of science prose: can we increase problem-solving performance? In B.K. Britton and J.B. Black (Eds) *Understanding Expository Text* Hillsdale, NJ: Erlbaum

O'Donnell, A.M., Dansereau, D.F., Rocklin, T.R., Hythecker, V.I., Lambiotte, J.G., Larson, C.D. and Young, M.D. (1985) Effects of elaboration frequency on cooperative learning *Journal of Educational Psychology* 77, 572-580

Reder, L.M. (1980) The role of elaboration in the comprehension and retention of prose: a critical review *Review of Educational Research* 50, 5-53

Peterson, P.L. and T.C. Janicki (1979) Individual characteristics and children's learning in large-group and small-group approaches *Journal of Educational Psychology* 71, 677-687

Peterson, P.L. and S.R. Swing (1985) Students' cognitions as mediators of the effectiveness of small-group learning *Journal of Educational Psychology* 77, 219-312

Schmidt, H.G. (1982) *Activatie van Voorkennis, Intrinsieke Motivatie en de Verwerking van Tekst* (Activation of prior knowledge, intrinsic motivation and text processing) Apeldoorn: Van Walraven

Sharan, S. (1980) Cooperative learning in small groups: recent methods and effects on achievement, attitudes and ethnic relations *Review of Educational Research* 50 (2) 241-271

Slavin, R.E. (1980) Cooperative learning *Review of Educational Research* 50 (2) 315-342

Webb, N.M. (1980a) Group process: the key to learning in groups *New Directions for Methodology of Social and Behavioral Science* (6) 77-87

Webb, N.M. (1980b) A process-outcome analysis of learning in group and individual settings *Educational Psychologist* (15) 69-83

Webb, N.M. (1982a) Group composition, group interaction and achievement in cooperative small groups *Journal of Educational Psychology* 74, 475-484

Webb, N.M. (1982b) Student interaction and learning in small groups *Review of Educational Research* 52 (3) 421-445

14

Learning Skills, or Skill in Learning ?

Elaine Martin and Paul Ramsden

During the last few years, increasing interest has been shown in methods of improving student learning within the natural context of teaching and assessment. Such interventions, which may take the form of individual counselling or various types of group activities, are typically additional to normal teaching activities and vary in the extent to which they embody subject content or concentrate on detachable skills. They may be organized by study skills counsellors, external experts on studying and learning, by the staff themselves, or perhaps by a combination of subject experts and study skills advisers (Hills 1979; Frederick et al. 1981; Tabberer 1982). The theoretical basis and practical organization of these interventions also vary a great deal. Some programmes are grounded in ideas from cognitive psychology (Weinstein and Mayer, in press); others draw on psychoanalytic models (Raaheim and Wankowski 1981). Some emphasize a 'discovery' approach in which students learn from each other, and have foundations in personal construct theory, with a leavening of concepts from recent research in student learning (Gibbs 1982; see also Entwistle and Ramsden 1983, pp.206-208). Still others are based chiefly on experience and on commonsense notions of good study habits – time organization, essay-planning skills, note-taking techniques, the 'right' way to read a book – and so on.

For the purpose of this paper we wish to identify two contrasting types of interventions, both of which involve students in group activities rather than in individual counselling or the application of advice from study skills books. We do not pretend that these two types of programme represent all kinds of learning skills activities in higher education. However, they do represent two very different approaches to improving student learning and both are quite widely used in the UK and elsewhere. The main question we address is: What are the effects on undergraduate student learning of different kinds of learning skills interventions? Having examined the influence of the programmes on two groups of first-year students, we then consider the implications of our findings for future intervention strategies.

Theoretical Background

The purpose of learning skills interventions is to improve the process and outcome of student learning. In simple terms, the organizers of such programmes hope that their participants will increase their motivation for academic learning, acquire specific techniques that may be implicated in successful studying (such as methods of note-taking), and perform more satisfactorily in assessments.

Such relatively crude measures of the effects of interventions can now be supplemented by more sophisticated criteria derived from recent research into student learning. Differences in the ways in which students approach learning tasks are now well established. Students differ in the way they relate to a learning task – whether they intend to understand it and extract personal meaning from it or attempt merely to reproduce its content (or apply a memorized algorithmic procedure to its solutions). In addition to this referential distinction, generally characterized as a distinction between a deep and a surface approach to a task, students differ in the organizational principles they apply to their learning. A holistic approach involves the use of integrating principles to relate new content to old and to build internal connections in new material; an atomistic approach engages the student with the subject matter by focusing on its details in isolation and in sequence (Svensson 1984). These approaches (deep/holistic versus surface/atomistic) are logically and empirically linked to qualitatively different learning outcomes, as well as to broader indicators such as course grades.

Approaches to learning are highly context-dependent. They vary within the same student between different tasks and are functionally related to students' perceptions of teaching and assessment (see Ramsden 1984; Laurillard 1984). However, students bring to learning tasks their past experiences of similiar situations; they have preconceived ideas of what makes for learning (Marton and Säljö 1984). Säljö (1979) identified five qualitatively different conceptions of learning in interviews with adults. Learning was seen as:

1 A quantitative increase in knowledge
2 Memorizing
3 The acquisition of facts, methods, etc., which can be retained and used when necessary
4 The abstraction of meaning
5 An interpretative process aimed at understanding reality.

Observed variations in approaches to learning are linked with variations in conceptions of learning at this more general level. Van Rossum and Schenk (1984) demonstrated that deep approaches were associated with conceptions 4 and 5 and surface approaches with conceptions 1 to 3.

It is of interest to note that Säljö's categories reflect similar categories used to describe developmental processes in student learning, such as those in Perry's scheme (Perry 1970). The main distinction in Säljö's scheme between an absolutistic concern with facts as something separate from everyday reality and a pluralistic view of knowledge embodying the notion of alternative ways of understanding reality is close to Perry's contrast between dualistic thinking and relativistic reasoning. Indeed, Gibbs, Morgan and Taylor (1984) have shown that students may shift during a programme of study from a less sophisticated to a more sophisticated conception of learning.

Most lecturers in higher education would probably agree that one of the aims of their teaching is to encourage students to develop more sophisticated conceptions of learning. The difficult educational issue is how such development might be encouraged. So far little evidence has emerged from student learning research which bears on this question. A supportive teaching and assessment context appears to be a necessary condition, at least for some students (Ramsden 1984). Unfortunately, direct attempts to induce deep approaches may have the opposite effect from that which was intended (Marton and Säljö 1976; Ramsden, Beswick and Bowden (Chapter 15)). Entwistle and Ramsden (1983), among others, have suggested that the teaching of study strategies, in a form which draws attention to the existence of contrasting styles and approaches to learning which are idiosyncratic but effective, might prove to be advantageous. The increased use of study skills programmes concentrating solely on techniques, however, may help students to perform more effectively in certain assessments, but may be detrimental to the development of more complex conceptions.

The Present Study

Learning skills interventions which focus on discrete skills, detached from the content and context of learning, might reinforce students' tendencies to see learning as memorization and the acquisition of facts. On the other hand, an emphasis on increasing students' awareness of their own learning processes and developing an armoury of suitable approaches to be used in appropriate conditions might expedite change from the lower to the higher levels of Säljö's scheme. Differences in interventions are not easy to research because interventions which are part and parcel of a teaching programme are contaminated by the pervasive effect of the normal context of assessment and teaching. However, interventions not so contaminated are not only difficult to arrange with any degree of realism, but will have limited relevance to improving learning in other normal teaching contexts.

The present study examined two programmes designed to improve student learning in two departments of history at British universities. Each department arranged a voluntary learning skills programme for its first-year students. Of the total number of students in the first year (N = 120 and 150) thirty were enrolled on a first-come-first-served basis. Both departments were anxious to assess the success of the interventions and made it clear that students who enrolled would be expected to complete the course, although not every student attended every session. From time to time staff from both departments found it necessary to remind students of their promise of commitment to the course. Because of this diligence on the part of the staff it was possible to obtain data from all sixty students. As we shall show below, the two programmes differed in important ways. However, both were organized and taught entirely by subject specialists (ie there were no study counsellors or learning skills advisers involved).

Lecturers in the programmes were interviewed about their reasons for running them and their expectations for the students who participated. Students were interviewed on four occasions: before the programme began, in order to identify their pre-course conceptions of learning and to examine expectations for the programme; during the first term, to assess their initial responses to the experience; during the second term; and finally, at the end of the programme, in order to discover to what extent they had made use of the skills presented or developed in their normal studying. The final interviews also provided evidence of students' conceptions of learning after one year of undergraduate history. Conceptions of learning were examined by asking 'What do you actually mean by learning?' (cf Säljö 1979).

In addition to the interview and observation data, information on students' pre-course and year one academic attainment was collected. The index of pre-course attainment was their 'A' level grade score. Two measures of year one progress were available: students' mean assignment grade and their examination mark. Both departments gave equal weight to essays and examinations in determining students' overall first-year grade. Data on first-year progress were collected for the whole first-year group including students who participated in the interventions.

The main dependent variables were changes in conceptions of learning during the first year and students' end of year grades. It was hypothesized that participants in either intervention would perform better (after controlling for differences in entry attainment) than non-participants. However, students in the 'learning to learn' programme would be more likely than those in the 'study skills' programme to develop from seeing learning as an 'increase in knowledge or memorization' to conceiving of it as 'the abstraction of meaning or understanding reality' (Säljö 1979).

The Two Programmes

Both programmes were organized by subject staff with a commitment to helping their first-year students to learn more effectively. The study skills programme (so called by its teachers) was based largely on the experience of a senior lecturer in the department who had attended a three-day course on the teaching of study skills in 1980. The structure and materials for the programme derived from exercises devised by Buzan (1974), modified by the organizer in the light of his experience in running a similar course during the previous two years.

The previous year the programme had been a compulsory one for first-year students, but doubts about its effectiveness in improving students' performance, together with staffing difficulties, had caused it to be cut back in the year of this study to thirty students only. However, it did now extend over two terms instead of one.

The programme was arranged in such a way that each skill area (note-taking, reading, writing, examinations, organization of time, etc.) was introduced with a lecture. Students were provided with handouts summarizing the main points to be observed in developing the skill. Thus, for example, the session on writing began with a lecture on purpose, planning, content, writing English, and presentation, supported by a handout covering each of these topics. Students then made a plan for a short essay entitled 'Writing an Essay', and went on to read and compare two articles on the use of metal detectors on historical sites. For homework, they made a list of clichés, spelling mistakes, and grammatical errors they often made.

The learning to learn programme (again so called by its teachers) was quite different. It was modelled on the structured group-discussion methods for improving student learning devised by Gibbs (1981), an approach which can be seen as a reaction to unease about the usefulness of earlier 'how to study' advice that involved prescriptive statements on study technique. While the sessions had similar titles to those in the study skills programme, the resemblance ended there. It is of particular importance, in view of the findings obtained, to note that explicit attempts were made in the programme to take account of students' existing approaches to learning and to use materials directly related to the content of students' studies in their first-year courses. In the session on writing, for example, students began by reading two essays, written by first-year students, on Henry VIII's qualities of kingship – a similar, although not identical, assignment to one they had themselves to prepare. Students compared their analysis of the similarities and differences between these essays with each other, first in pairs and then in fours, before moving into a plenary session in which the qualities of the essays as history essays were identified by the groups and shared with the views of the teachers who were present at the session. The focus was thus on the nature of historical argument and on the relationship between students' approaches and the lecturers' expectations.

The organizers of the learning to learn programme made a conscious effort to select material of direct relevance to the curriculum and to link it to the process of studying history. The study skills course, in contrast, focused on skills *separately* from the content of the curriculum, an approach that brought a certain amount of student criticism:

> I find it a bit boring sometimes.... I think if the stuff we were using was more in our field, was just more interesting to us, then I might be able to stomach it more easily.

> I wish we could deal more directly with our present problems... Last week, I had to break off from a real problem with planning my next assignment and working on it... and come to a session on writing which I thought might help me, but really didn't, well it might do in a general way, but I had, still have, a specific problem of knowing how much I can generalize from these inventories... I get, we get, no specific help like that.

In contrast a student from the learning to learn programme remarked:

> We did a sort of general course in the sixth form at the beginning of the sixth form on study skills ... but this is much better I think it's better because it's really getting down to what you do in your subject.... The course we had was for everybody... and there were people doing arts and people doing sciences and it had to be pretty general. Here we're talking about the problems we have in history .... We're all history students faced with the same assignments and the same problems.

The Two Departments

The interventions were not experimentally controlled, but formed part of the naturally-occurring variation in the context of learning in the two departments. Field notes on the observations of the researcher, who was in regular contact with the teaching and learning process in both departments throughout one academic year, were systematically collected. In addition, interviews with staff and students included questions about the teaching process and the students' perceptions of assessment and teaching.

It was clear that the two departments provided different learning contexts. In summary, the study skills department, although demonstrating concern with and commitment to its first-year students, offered a more formal teaching pattern, less choice over assessed work, and a heavier workload than the learning to learn department. Although staff stated that they were always accessible to students, the students felt that they in practice erected constraints and were often dismissive of students' ideas. Students in this department had five assessed assignments to submit during the year, and there were additional compulsory pieces of written work to be done. Tutorials often followed the pattern of a mini-lecture rather than a discussion.

The atmosphere in the learning to learn department was rather more relaxed, with more regular contact between students and staff outside formal class time. Students were less afraid to voice problems and test out ideas. Assignment topics were generally negotiable. There were no compulsory assignments beyond the five essays that formed the continuously-assessed component of the first-year course.

Results

Students' Comments

The student interviews highlighted a clear pattern of response to each of the courses. There were some students whose comments were at variance with the general trend of responses, but in this paper it is the general trend that is discussed.

The majority of students on the study skills programme were initially keen and committed and generally said complimentary things about the course. For instance,

> Yes I think it's working well for me ... there's quite a lot to learn really, but I think I'm getting the hang of it all .... I've found the speed reading very useful... I used to take ages to get through things, now I find I get through them in a lot less time.... No I'm really pleased with the way things are going so far.

This sort of enthusiasm was maintained by the majority of students for all of the first term. During the second term, however, it diminished:

> I think it's useful to be shown these various techniques and what have you.... To be honest I'm not all that taken with all of them ... I think you've got to pick and choose a bit....

While I feel its probably beneficial to come here, I do find it a bit of a chore... I've got a lot of work at the moment and I could use these two hours ... it's a bit of a drag at the moment.

Interviews in the third term, carried out after the course had finished, showed that only five of the students who had attended the course admitted to regularly using the techniques they had been taught:

> I can do all the things we've learnt, well I can if I try... I must admit I often don't bother... I mean I think the thing is that they're there if you need them but you don't have to use them.

> I know what I ought to do, like when I'm writing an essay, using the library and looking through books and taking notes and doing the plan... I mean I can do all that stuff if I have to, the thing is that when I don't have to I find that I don't do it ... I know it's silly because it would help me, but somehow it just doesn't seem to make sense in terms of the immediate problem of getting this assignment in for the next morning.

The opposite pattern of responses was found in the learning course. At first the course was not popular. By the end of the first term twenty of the thirty students said they felt they were not getting out of it what they had hoped for and that they would not recommend it to other students:

> It's not what I expected ... I thought we'd be told how to take notes, for instance ... I'm not sure what we're supposed to be doing, but I don't think it's really helping me ... I know its hard to say at this stage, but, ... I'm a bit disappointed.

> Frankly I don't think they've got any idea what they're about.... They don't tell us anything, they leave it all to us to tell each other ... well they're supposed to be the experts, what's the point of having experts if they won't tell you what to do... won't try to help you.

By the middle of the second term students began to admit that the course sometimes helped them in thinking about their assignments:

> It's certainly not the course I thought it was going to be ... I'm not sure I've learnt anything about the things I expected to learn about ... I mean I still take the most awful notes, I'm still a disorganized mess, but I think I'm beginning to get something out of it... It's hard to say what ... Perhaps a proper understanding of me as a student.

> We like coming because it's a pleasant group. We get to know each other really well and the staff. When you come in here you really reveal yourself ... I don't know if talking about learning as we do makes me a better learner ... Sometimes I think it helps ... I don't know if I'm a better more efficient learner for it really.

But by the third term twenty of the thirty students said that they were regularly using the advice and insights gained through being on the course.

I really think this course has helped me tremendously....When I think back to the things I said about it at first ... I think I've changed my whole understanding of what I'm here for since then... I honestly think this course has had a lot to do with that.

I've enjoyed it. I've got insights rather than skills .... I suppose if it's skills I want I can always go and get one of those books on how to study from the library. Insights are not so easy to come by, unless you're guided in the way that we have been in this course.

These general responses must be seen in the context of comments students made about their expectations of the courses. Students from both programmes typically said they expected to be taught specific skills. Some of them had already had experience of skills courses from their sixth forms. Others had seen books giving conventional skills course advice. In common with students in other studies (eg Frederick et al. 1981) these expected and wanted advice that would help them take more effective notes, read quicker, and write better essays. It seems likely that when students from the skills programme found themselves confronted with an experience that offered this type of help, they felt satisfied. After a while they were dubious whether the acquisition of these skills did help them to learn more effectively.

Students from the learning to learn programme, on the other hand, initially felt cheated because the course they were presented with bore no resemblance to their preconceptions of a course aimed at helping them to improve their learning. Only later did it become clear to them what the programme could offer. There is a 'mythology of study skills' shared by first-year students which conditions their expectations (see Ramsden 1985).

Changes in Conceptions

What changes in students' conceptions of learning took place during the period of this study and to what extent are these changes associated with the two programmes? It may be useful to characterize the conceptions in more detail by referring to the descriptions and illustrative quotations provided by Säljö (1979).

Conception 1: Learning as the increase of knowledge. The main feature of this first category is its vagueness, in the sense that what is given in the answers is merely a set of synonyms for the word learning, eg 'It's to increase your knowledge'.

Conception 2: Learning as memorizing. The meaning of learning is to transfer units of information or pieces of knowledge, or facts from a teacher or book, into the head.

To learn ... sort of to listen and to get inside ... acquired knowledge kind of... quite simply to learn it ... to get things in one's head so they stay there.

Conception 3: Learning as the acquisition of facts or procedures which can be retained and/or utilized in practice. Some facts and principles are considered to be practically useful and as a consequence they are given special attention and remembered for a long time.

Yes to learn so that you know it and so that you can make use of it. It shouldn't be just learning something which disappears immediately after you've learnt it, but you should be able to make use of it even after a while.

Conception 4: Learning as the abstraction of meaning. With this conception the nature of what is learned is changed. Learning is no longer an activity of reproduction but a process of abstracting meaning.

For me... learning does not mean that you should learn all those petty details but instead it means learning about a course of events and how things have developed and reasoning within my subject but it does not mean sitting down and memorizing trifles such as dates and such things....

Conception 5: Learning as an interpretative process aimed at the understanding of reality. This conception is similar to conception 4, but there is an additional suggestion that learning should help you interpret the reality in which you live.

In the present study transcripts of students' responses to the question 'What do you actually mean by learning' were analysed by three independent judges. A 68 per cent level of agreement between pairs of judges was obtained for the pre-course conception categorization and a 72 per cent level for the post-course categorization.

Examination of Table 1 will show that no student held a level one conception either before or at the end of the first year. It is also clear that the conceptions were similarly distributed within the study skills and the learning to learn groups prior to the programmes. However, there is a definite movement towards higher level conceptions among the learning to learn students.

Unfortunately, it was not possible to examine the conceptions of learning of the students who did not participate in the programmes. As we have already indicated, the two departments appeared to have different expectations of their first-year students and offered different kinds of support. We should therefore be cautious about attributing the changes in conceptions to the interventions alone; the interventions can perhaps be seen as an additional factor, enhancing a departmental environment already somewhat more conducive to the development of more sophisticated conceptions of learning in the first year.

As well as the obvious result that the learning to learn students more frequently advanced their conception of learning, the data show that students from both programmes found it difficult to move beyond a level three conception. On the learning course only three students did so, compared with eight moving from level four to level five. On the skills course no student moved through the level three conception.

Säljö himself has suggested that conceptions one, two and three are the most common amongst students adopting a surface approach. Conceptions four and five on the other hand are usually those of students adopting deep approaches. This is again supported by van Rossum's study (van Rossum and Schenk 1984).

It seems as though what is being highlighted in the results of this study is the pedagogical problem of how to move students from a surface to a deep approach. Clearly the study skills course team have little or no success, while the success of the learning to learn course team, although better, is only small.

Conception	Learning to Learn		Study Skills	
	pre	post	pre	post
1	0	0	0	0
2	3	0	3	1
3	10	10	11	16
4	15	10	14	9
5	2	10	2	4
TOTALS	30	30	30	30

Table 1

Changes in conceptions of learning.

First-Year Performance

There were no significant differences in the mean A level grade scores of participants and non-participants, or in the mean scores of students in the two departments.

Two outcome measures were available in each department: students' mean assignment grades and students' end-of-year examination marks. The results are comparable within the departments but not between them. There was no significant difference between the performance of participants and non-participants in the study skills programme on either the essay or the examination measure. In the other department, the learning to learn participants obtained similar examination marks to the non-participants. However, they performed significantly better than the non-participants in their history assignments. The participants' mean essay grade was 19.0; the non-participants' mean essay grade was 17.6 ($t = 2.2$, $p < 0.05$).

Conceptions of Learning and First-Year Grades

Examination of the relationship between students' conceptions of learning and their first-year performance reveals a positive association between grade and conception. For example, in the learning to learn programme the five students with the highest combined examination and assignment grades concluded the course with level five conceptions; while the five students with the lowest grades concluded with level three conceptions. In the study skills programme the only four students to conclude the course with level five conceptions attained the four highest combined scores; while the four students with the lowest grades concluded with level two or level three conceptions.

The association between grades and conceptions for all sixty students is summarized in Table 2.

Combined Essay/Examination Grade	Conceptions of learning		Totals
	Conceptions 1–3	Conceptions 4–5	
< 16	10	0	10
16–20	17	16	33
> 20	0	17	17
	27	33	60

Table 2
Conceptions of learning and first-year grades.

Discussion and Conclusion

It is a truism that first-year students in higher education often experience difficulty in studying and learning. But to recognize that students might need help in coping with academic demands is not the same thing as knowing how to help them (Hounsell 1984). All too often, learning skills programmes and advice give solutions to problems that have not been clearly defined, much less understood. Learning difficulties are frequently a function of inadequacies in teaching as much as inexperience in students (Gibbs 1981). The recognition that study techniques training may be misleading or harmful to students, and that the advice given is idealized, often irrelevant, and not based on our knowledge of how effective student learning actually takes place, has led to an advocacy of 'integrated' learning skills programmes (ie study skills courses in which teaching staff are involved), and to learning to learn guides and courses which emphasize awareness of purpose and of the ends, rather than a selection among the means, of studying (see Marshall and Rowland 1981).

In this small investigation of history departments, we have compared the effects of two examples of the newer approaches to improving students' learning. Our results do not permit us to feel sanguine about the prospects of these interventions for improving student learning in general. It seems clear that the integrated study skills course was not particularly successful in its aims. Not only was it eventually regarded in negative terms by its participants (despite their initial enthusiasm), but there was no apparent influence on student's grades. In comparison with the learning to learn students, moreover, the study skills students were less likely to develop more complex conceptions of learning during their first year of studying university-level history.

At first sight, the learning to learn programme was more successful. Some students who undertook it did seem to develop 'skill in learning' (Svensson 1984), in so far as their changed conceptions of learning can be regarded as reflecting deep and holistic approaches to their subject. These changes were manifested in assignment performances that were better than those of non-participants in the programme. The strong association between the categories of conceptions at the end of year one and average grades, in both the study skills and the learning skills groups, lends support to the validity of the categorization of conceptions of learning as an indicator of learning outcome. But why did the learning to learn interventions have a positive effect on students? There seem to be two reasons. First, the content of the programme was tightly linked to teaching and curriculum. For example, the assignment-writing exercises discussed history essays written by earlier cohorts of students; these were on topics very similar to the topics of essays students were writing at the time. It seems likely that interaction between students and lecturers during these sessions helped to make explicit teachers' expectations for their students' essays, and at the same time increased teachers' awareness of the approaches to writing used by their students. As Hounsell (1984) and Biggs (in press) have recently shown, the quality of an essay in history is partly a function of the students' conceptions of what an essay is and what essay writing involves. A major difficulty for beginning students is that they may not be familiar with the process of realizing the genre of an essay in a particular subject. Guidance in essay writing which fails to confront students' current grasp of what is meant by 'an essay' is of limited usefulness. The study skills sessions on assignments concentrated briefly on the word-sentence level of composition, an approach which is unlikely to help students develop deep approaches to writing (see Biggs, in press).

The second, related reason for the greater success of the learning to learn programme was probably its embeddedness within the supportive departmental context. It would have been possible to run similar types of sessions in a less satisfactory environment, but whether they would have helped students is more doubtful. It was partly the openness and relative freedom from stress characterizing the department's assessment and teaching which allowed the learning to learn interventions to work. The learning to learn programme was effectively an additional form of teaching in the department.

In practical terms, our findings indicate a need for caution in recommending a more general use of learning skills programmes in higher education. The focus on specific courses in learning skills may be misplaced. Our results do, however, offer tentative support for further experimental interventions which adopt a holistic approach to improving learning and teaching. Such an approach (see Ramsden 1985) entails recognition that activities designed to improve student learning are a proper part of the whole process of teaching.

References

Biggs, J.B. (In press) Approaches to learning and to essay writing. In R.R. Schmeck (Ed.) *Learning Styles and Learning Strategies* New York: Plenum Press

Buzan, T. (1974) *Use Your Head* London: BBC

Entwistle, N.J. and Ramsden, P. (1983) *Understanding Student Learning* London: Croom Helm

Frederick, J., Hancock, L., James, B., Bowden, J. and Macmillan, C. (1981)

Learning Skills: A Review of Needs and Services to University Students Melbourne: Centre for the Study of Higher Education, University of Melbourne

Gibbs, G. (1981) *Teaching Students to Learn* Milton Keynes: Open University Press

Gibbs, G., Morgan, A. and Taylor, E. (1984) The world of the learner. In F. Marton et al. (Eds) *The Experience of Learning* Edinburgh: Scottish Academic Press

Hills, P.J. (1979) *Study Courses and Counselling: Problems and Possibilities* Guildford: SRHE

Hounsell, D. (1979) Learning to learn: Research and development in student learning *Higher Education* 8, 453 - 469

Hounsell, D.J. (1984) Learning and essay-writing. In Marton et al. (1984)

Marshall, L. and Rowland, F. (1981) *A Guide to Learning Independently* Melbourne: Longman Cheshire

Marton, F., and Säljö, R. (1976) On qualitative differences in learning, II – Outcome as a function of the learner's conception of the task *British Journal of Educational Psychology* 46, 115 -127

Raaheim, K. and Wankowski, J. (1981) *Helping Students to Learn at University* Bergen: Sigma Forlag

Ramsden, P. (1984) The context of learning. In Marton et al. (1984)

Ramsden, P. (1985) *Alternatives to Learning Skills* Paper presented at the 6th Australasian Tertiary Study Skills Conference, Adelaide

Säljö, R. (1979) *Learning in the Learner's Perspective, I – Some Commonsense Conceptions* Reports from the Institute of Education, University of Gothenburg, No. 77

Svensson, L. (1984) Skill in learning. In Marton et al. (1984)

Tabberer, R. (1984) Introducing study skills at 16 – 19 *Educational Research* 26, 1-6

van Rossum, E.J. and Schenk, S.M. (1984) The relationship between learning conception, study strategy and learning outcome *British Journal of Educational Psychology* 54, 73-83

Weinstein, C.E. and Mayer, R.E. (In press) The teaching of learning strategies. In M.C. Wittrock (Ed.) *Handbook of Research on Teaching* (3rd edition) New York: Macmillan

15

Learning Processes and Learning Skills

Paul Ramsden, David Beswick and John Bowden

Recent investigations of student learning in higher education throw into sharp relief the issue of how to encourage meaningful approaches and discourage reproductive ones. How can teachers provide the conditions that will foster students' intentions to understand (deep approaches)? How can teachers devise the strategies that will maximize the probability of students engaging with learning materials at an appropriate level (holistic approaches)? The evidence is clear that surface-atomistic approaches – describing a relation between student and task and characterized by the intention to memorize or reproduce and by distortion of the underlying structure of the task – are easily induced in students (Marton and Säljö 1976) and all too common in higher education (Ramsden 1984; Laurillard 1984). Teaching strategies and assessment conditions that will elicit deep and holistic approaches – ie approaches that enable learning of the kind which teachers in higher education value to take place – are difficult to devise.

Encouraging students to reflect on the process of learning appears to be one possible method of encouraging the desired meaningful approaches to learning. Phenomenographic research into student learning refers to the idea of 'thematization' or awareness of purpose. Säljö (1979) describes adults who have made the activity of learning an 'object of reflection', who can talk about and analyse their processes of learning and their learning strategies, and who realize the value of alternative strategies in different contexts. From an entirely different perspective, cognitive psychologists have argued that individuals' 'metacognitive' abilities can be developed by intervention programmes. These involve training in identification of the learning strategies being used and assessment of the value of particular strategies for achieving goals (Wagner and Sternberg 1984).

It has been maintained that helping students to become metacognitive about their learning, and at the same time teaching them a repertoire of strategies to choose from, will permanently enhance their learning (Biggs 1985). While more traditional study skills courses tend to concentrate on techniques of studying which are popularly supposed to characterize competent learners, more recent 'learning-to-learn' methods emphasize the development of awareness of different learning strategies and the students' competence in selecting appropriate strategies to fit the task in hand. It seems clear that learning skills taught metacognitively need to be integrated into the teaching of subject matter (Biggs 1985) and hence it would appear appropriate that subject teachers should be involved in learning skills programmes.

An Investigation

In an effort to investigate the means by which meaningful approaches to learning might be facilitated some experimental interventions were planned at the University of Melbourne. Members of the Centre for the Study of Higher Education had been working for some time with teaching staff in several departments in a programme aimed at developing the capacity of staff to facilitate the learning skills of students. The participating departments in the work described here were in anatomy, chemistry, history, and psychology, together with the joint faculty first-year programme in engineering. The ways in which students were recruited to participate in special activities varied from one department to another. In engineering, the students who were specially encouraged to participate were those showing signs of failure by the middle of the first year. In other departments a more open invitation was issued.

For the most part the learning skills programme consisted of taking part in small tutorial groups in which problems and approaches to learning were discussed. Members of the project team met with teaching staff to develop the programme. Lecturers were encouraged to identify themes which would be important in their disciplines, but in the event most interventions were advertised in similar ways. Topics like time organization and study management, using text-books or reference materials efficiently, revision techniques, and note-taking were commonly mentioned. However, the sessions did not present a set of 'right' techniques that students should follow, but aimed at encouraging awareness of different methods and stressed the importance of selecting those methods that suited the students and their subject-matter.

Two members of the project team attended most sessions, one an observer and the other someone who would be regarded by teachers as a 'learning skills expert'. In one department, where the sessions were run by the lecturer in charge of the subject, the 'expert' was effectively a second observer for substantial periods. In another, a department where few staff attended the sessions, the team member was the group leader and the 'expert' role was quite explicit. There was one department in which a number of teaching staff attended sessions; the consequence being that a substantial part of the time was spent discussing the way the course was organized, and what was expected of students, with students criticizing aspects of the course and their own character in the natural setting was that, as we intended, most of them focused on skills which were considered important for successful learning in each course.

An inventory of deep-holistic and surface-atomistic approaches to learning was administered both to students who attended the learning skills sessions and to non-attenders near the beginning of the year and again at the end of the academic year. The approach scales consisted of items deriving mainly from the meaning and reproducing orientation scales of the Lancaster Approaches to Studying Inventory (Ramsden and Entwistle 1981; Ramsden 1983). Examples of items used in the present study appear in Table 1. Other information available on the individual students included their academic and social backgrounds, represented by such variables as their performance in the examinations which qualified them for university entrance, the type of schools they had attended, their places of birth and those of their parents, and some individual difference measures in attitudes and motives.

DEEP-HOLISTIC	I try to relate new material I am studying to what I already know on that topic
	I set out to understand thoroughly the meaning of what I am asked to read or study
	I try to work out several different ways of interpreting my findings
SURFACE-ATOMISTIC	I find that I have to read things without having a chance to really understand them
	I concentrate on memorizing a good deal of what we have to learn
	Although I remember facts and details, I find it difficult to fit them together into an overall picture

---

Table 1
Examples of deep and surface items.

In order to obtain insights into the dynamics of any change in students' approaches to learning, intensive interviews were held with a small sample from the departments. The students were asked to describe any changes they had noticed in their learning strategies during the course of the year; the learning skills group were asked whether their approaches had been influenced by their experiences in the sessions. The interviews were semi-structured and followed the form of inquiries into students' approaches to realistic learning tasks previously developed in Sweden and Britain (see Marton, Hounsell and Entwistle 1984).

Three types of analysis were undertaken. First, a simple bivariate analysis was carried out, relating dependent variables in the approaches to learning and in the results of assessments both to the interventions and to the background conditions with which students came to their courses. Secondly, multivariate analyses were conducted, mainly using regression models for the prediction of the dependent variables, with special attention to the effects of the interventions on the residuals in the end of the year variables after differences at the beginning of the year had been accounted for. Thirdly, the qualitative information was examined for an understanding of the processes by which any effects might have been brought about.

We were interested especially in the influence of the sessions on deep-holistic approaches and surface-atomistic approach scores at the end of the students' first year of university study. Within the learning skills group, students would be expected to develop an increased awareness of their own learning processes and intentions, and to become more competent at controlling and monitoring their cognitive processes. The increased meta-learning capability resulting from the interventions should be evident in these students' reports of their general approaches to academic tasks: ie they should score higher on deep-holistic and lower on surface-atomistic than their counterparts who did not attend the sessions.

We were also interested in the possible effect of the sessions on the results of assessments and on students' self-ratings of their academic progress. To these ends it was necessary to discover whether attenders and non-attenders differed from each other in terms of background variables (eg age, sex, subjects studied, country of birth and country of parents' birth, type of school attended, and school attainment) and in terms of approaches to learning in the first term (ie as reported prior to the sessions).

Results and Discussion

To all intents and purposes there was no difference between the learning skills and the non-learning skills students before the sessions took place. Students whose fathers had been born in a non-English speaking country were more likely to enrol, but the attenders and non-attenders did not differ in their school attainment or in their approach scores in the first term.[1]

However, differences between the groups were apparent after the sessions (Figure 1). Deep approach scores decreased in both groups, and there was a statistically significant increase in surface approaches in the learning skills group. Multivariate analyses confirmed this general movement towards increased surface approaches among the learning skills participants. The increase could not be explained by differences between subject areas or differences in background variables.

We found no relationship between participation in the groups and students' first-year performance, either when self-rated or as indicated by grades. Correlations between approaches (at the end of the year) were positively related to performance for both attenders and non-attenders. However, while there was a negative correlation between surface-atomistic approach and grade in the non-learning skills group there was a positive relationship in the learning skills group. Self-rating of progress was a fairly good predictor of actual grade for both groups, but a better one for the learning skills students.

Although there are several plausible interpretations of these results, the most satisfactory explanation for the marked increase in surface approaches and for the observed relationships between grades and approaches in the experimental group seems to be that the programme encouraged students to adopt strategic variability. In other words, they learned to adapt their approaches to the demands of assessments. Although they may have learned to select 'appropriate' strategies, their perception of appropriateness was presumably different from that of their teachers.

Analysis of data from the ten students who volunteered for interview and who had participated in the learning skills programme provides support for

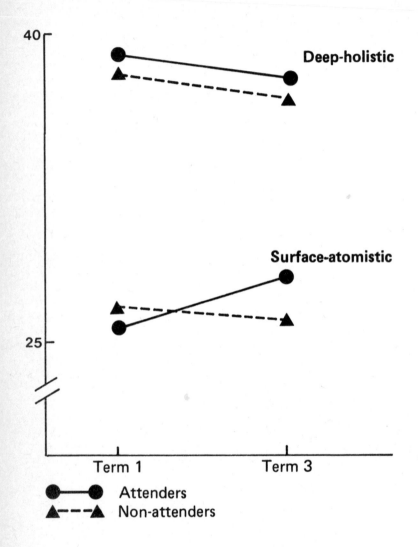

Figure 1
Effects of learning skills attendance on deep-holistic and surface-atomistic approaches to learning.

this interpretation. One student, for example, found that the sessions provided the impetus to deal with an assessment that was perceived to be inappropriate by developing tactics aimed at maximizing success. These involved a focus on techniques aimed not at learning the subject but at impressing the staff; notice how the emphasis is on the assessment context of learning rather than its content:

> I'd say the thing that would get you through [this subject] is not what you know but how good you are at learning. How quickly you adapt to the techniques involved in learning in the lecture environment, in passing exams, in getting assignments in with good marks.... Your whole thing has got to be slick... the sessions gave me a few hints... I suppose there was a stage when I changed around and tried to be not really well known by the students, but by the staff, to try to be known as the guy who intends to get a pass. (Wayne)

Another student recognized that the assessment in his subject to some extent rewarded surface approaches, and he seemed to be saying that the sessions had provided him with useful tips for maintaining the effort to adopt a reproductive strategy:

> I don't think you have to understand, you just have to be able to recite, which is unfortunate... you can spend all your time memorizing things and then you'll go really well but you might not know as much about it.... I used some of the techniques they suggested [in the learning skills groups] and they were excellent... I had a motivation problem to get down and do the work. I just wasn't doing it, being away from school for so long. I was getting the understanding together but wasn't blowing all my hours away doing rote learning. So I thought that maybe if I got motivated to go to that I might be able to put myself into a frame of mind to pick up some hints and some practical advice. (Dennis)

The interview data suggest that the effects of learning skills interventions are only understandable when the students' experience of them in relation to assessment and their preferred approaches to learning are taken into account. The sessions may have reinforced tendencies to surface approaches by their stress (as perceived by students) on time utilization, on techniques for remembering lecture material, and 'techniques involved in learning... to cut down on the understanding and just aim at the marks' (Wayne). The effect is not separate from the students' perceptions of assessment and teaching, for it is against the background of inadequacies in these matters that the learning skills advice has been made use of. Some of the learning skills group appear to have used the experience rationally, taking hints and techniques from the sessions to help them cope with academic demands. Unfortunately it appears that this entirely logical response has led to a result opposite to that intended by the group organizers. If the students have developed metalearning skills, those skills are being mediated through the teaching and assessment context and thereby increasing the incidence of surface approaches.

The interview data offer an explanation why the learning skills students do not display the expected negative correlation between surface approaches and grades. They have no doubt learned to deploy surface approaches more successfully than their non-participant counterparts. As Svensson (1984) points out, atomistic (surface) approaches to learning are tedious and unrewarding methods of study, and it is not surprising that students adopting them complain of constant problems with organizing time. The interviewed students who reported advantages from the programme typically identified their problems as being to do with motivation and time allocation in studying, and remarked that the sessions helped them to overcome these difficulties.

Conclusions

It is clear from the investigation that attendance at learning skills groups increased the reported incidence of surface approaches. Although it might have helped some students to avoid failure, participation was not associated with a better than average level of grades.

These findings are consistent with the theoretical understanding of student learning within the normal context of assessment and teaching (see Marton, Hounsell, and Entwistle 1984). They also reflect the 'arguments from experience' of critics of study skills programmes and suggest that learning skills sessions which might be expected to enhance metalearning run similiar risks of reinforcing rather than weakening minimalist approaches.

It is perhaps a little sad that staff who were genuinely concerned to improve the quality of undergraduate learning appear to have produced effects which, while they might have helped students to reach short-term goals, are certainly not in accordance with the declared academic values of the individuals or of the institution. The special effort made in the learning skills groups appears to have achieved at best some strategic improvement in students' capacities to cope with assessment.

The results reported here suggest that we should be cautious about recommending the more general use of learning skills programmes in the first year of higher education (cf Chapter 14). They also sound a warning against extrapolation of evidence from learning strategies training programmes carried out under experimental or quasi-experimental conditions to the everyday setting of undergraduate learning. Whether based on concepts from cognitive psychology (see Weinstein and Mayer 1984) or on commonsense notions of 'good study habits', such experiments may have limited relevance to the problem of improving student learning because they do not take account of the interaction between students' intentions and the context of learning. Students actively and critically extract from skills programmes what is useful to them; 'what is useful' is a function of their perceptions of the requirements of assessment and teaching. If learning-to-learn programmes are part and parcel of subject teaching, *and* if they take place in a supportive teaching context, they may have value (see Chapter 14)).

Whatever we decide about the future use of interventions designed to improve student learning, it is important to avoid two misconceptions. First, the idea is unsupportable that there are process skills or principles of learning that can be taught to students and then applied irrespective of content and context. Even if we allow that such principles of learning may be identified, attempts to teach them as skills suffer from one fatal flaw. The way in which students learn them cannot be expected to be different from the way in which they learn other subject-matter, and students can only apply them in the context of the learning of subject-matter.

Second, the idea that deficiencies in learning arise from the absence of some quality within a student (which can be added by teaching it to the student) is pedagogically naïve. Everyday teaching wisdom tells us that the educational problem is not that of filling students with knowledge, but of changing the way in which they understand some aspect of a subject. Approaches to learning do not describe a student attribute, but rather a relationship between an individual and a learning task. From this perspective, improving student learning means paying attention to that relationship, and that means improving teaching. Improved teaching does not entail the discovery of general principles for designing learning tasks that will encourage deeper, holistic approaches, but discovery of the forms of misconception held by students and identification of the types of errors in processing they present. Armed with this understanding, teachers have a better chance of eliciting the learning they value.

Acknowledgements

We are grateful for research assistance by Judith Boreham, Craig Lonsdale, and Kate Patrick.

Note

1 For a full analysis and discussion of the results summarized here, see Ramsden, P., Beswick, D.G., and Bowden, J.A. (in press) Effects of learning skills interventions on first year university students' learning *Human Learning*.

References

Biggs, J.B. (1985) *The Role of Metacognition in Enhancing Learning Skills* Paper presented at the Annual Conference of the Australian Association for Research in Education, Hobart

Laurillard, D.M. (1984) Learning from problem-solving. In Marton et al. (1984)

Marton, F. and Säljö, R. (1976) On qualitative differences in learning. II – Outcome as a function of the learner's conception of the task *British Journal of Educational Psychology* 46, 115-127

Marton, F., Hounsell, D.J. and Entwistle, N.J. (Eds) *The Experience of Learning* Edinburgh: Scottish Academic Press

Ramsden, P. (1983) *The Lancaster Approaches to Studying and Course Perceptions Questionnaire: Lecturers' Handbook* Oxford: Educational Methods Unit, Oxford Polytechnic

Ramsden, P. (1984) The context of learning. In Marton et al. (1984)

Ramsden, P. and Entwistle, N.J. (1981) Effects of academic departments on students' approaches to studying *British Journal of Educational Psychology* 51, 368-383

Säljö, R. (1979) *Learning in the Learner's Perspective. I. Some commonsense conceptions* Reports from the Institute of Education, University of Gothenberg, No. 76

Svensson, L. (1984) Skill in learning. In Marton et al. (1984)

Wagner, R.K. and Sternberg, R.J. (1984) Alternative conceptions of intelligence and their implications for education *Review of Educational Research* 54, 179-224

Weinstein, C.E. and Mayer, R.E. (1984) The teaching of learning strategies. In M.C. Wittrock (Ed.) *Handbook of Research on Teaching* (3rd edition) New York: Macmillan

Part 5

Assumptions, Objectives, Applications

16

On Knowing Ourselves as Learners and Researchers

Sarah J. Mann

There are a number of substantive assumptions underlying current research on student learning. I shall address two questions that concern the assumptions that are made about the people whom we investigate, our relationship to them, and ourselves.

The first question is: What view of the nature of human beings and of how they learn do we express through our research practices? The general issue of the models or images of human beings that are inherent in different approaches to research has been explicitly considered by a number of writers (Shotter 1975; Chapman and Jones 1980; Morgan 1983). In the present context the issue bears upon the extent to which it is possible to link together cognitive psychology and educational research in order to illuminate student learning.

The second question is: What role and status do we give ourselves as researchers in our investigations of how students learn? This question focuses upon where we stand as researchers in relation both to *others* as learners and to *ourselves* as learners.

On Knowing Ourselves as Learners

The present collection of papers brings together in one volume examples of research from education and from cognitive psychology, and explores the extent to which the two areas of research together throw light upon the nature of learning in higher education. However, if we do want to deepen our understanding of student learning in this way, then we need to consider the basis on which the two disciplines are founded. That is, we should examine the methodological and epistemological assumptions that underlie the two areas of research, and uncover the researchers' particular and possibly different views about the nature of human beings and how they learn.

Such assumptions necessarily express a particular set of views of how we best find out about the topic under investigation, what it is that we can find out, and how we know that what we find out is valid. In other words, they arise out of the assumed appropriateness of the particular research procedures and theories employed, and express the foundation upon which the resulting data are taken to be valid. More fundamentally, however, how we choose to study people reflects our view of the nature of human beings, and thus of ourselves. In the present context, we are interested in the study of learning in higher education. The approach to research that we adopt expresses certain assumptions about how we may best find out how people learn, and about the validity of the data we collect. These assumptions in turn express a particular image or model of the nature of human beings and of how they learn.

These assumptions are implicit in the choices the researcher makes with regard to the issues and theories to be examined and with regard to the methods and analytical procedures to be employed. Moreover, the language in which the researcher reports the study further expresses these assumptions: the type of language chosen is not simply a vehicle for the report but itself expresses particular views of reality that are usually taken for granted. For instance, the titles of two of the books cited earlier (*Models of Man* and *Images of Man in Psychological Research*) imply a specific view of the nature of human beings: either woman is excluded from the model or else woman is implicit within the image of man.

In exploring the sorts of assumptions about the nature of human beings that are expressed in research, I shall focus in particular on research methods – methods rather than disciplines, because I do not want to suggest that all research in cognitive psychology expresses one view and all research in education expresses another. I belive that individual studies in either field will tend to express, through the range of different methods that they use, particular views of the nature of human beings and of how they learn. Moreover, any one study may itself express a contradictory combination of views.

The different research methods used to find out about how people learn (for example, open-ended interviews, structured interviews, questionnaires, reaction-time experiments) all express through their design in theory and through their creation in practice particular views of the best ways of finding out about human learning. These appear to lie along a continuum from 'asking people' to 'testing people within tightly controlled structures'. (I shall deliberately present a stark picture of the two ends of the continuum in order to sharpen the distinction. However, it is of course often the case in practice that different methods at different points on the continuum will be used.)

asking ——————————————————— testing

Each end of the continuum expresses a particular conception of the nature of human beings that serves to ensure the validity of the research method. (For example, within one study students may be asked to complete a 'test' and then be interviewed on how and why they carried it out. We need to ask what purpose the particular method serves. Is testing being used in order to find out about some hypothetical unknown as it is revealed through the test results, or is it being used in order to understand – by asking – students' experiences and actions when tested?)

On the one hand, if I use students' descriptions of how they learn in order to understand how they learn, then for my data to be valid I need to assume that human beings are purposeful and active communicators living in a social world, who can take control of and responsibility for their own learning. I have to assume that they are or can become aware of their learning experiences, and that they can share with me their actions and the meanings they give to their actions, as they relate to learning. Moreover, I have to assume that we – the researcher and the students – can reflect upon our past and current learning and can communicate with each other by means of language in such a way that we attain full understanding of the students' experience.

On the other hand, if I use data that I have obtained by testing people under certain controlled conditions in order to understand how people learn, then for my data to be valid I need to assume that people are passive and controllable beings existing in a deterministic world. I have to assume that they do not bring with them knowledge and past experiences, purposes, or expectations which might influence the effect upon their learning of the independent variable that I am seeking to research. Furthermore, I have to stand apart from my subjects and render them object rather than subject in my own experience. I have to assume either that I am somehow super-human, or else that they are not strictly human at all: if I assume otherwise, my data will be contaminated by them and rendered invalid.

Mair (1970) expressed this separation of researchers from their subjects:

> We note that, as a rule, the experimenter makes use of people to help him answer questions which he, not they, raise more frequently than ever.... He makes use of some form of deception, misinforming subjects about what they are doing or about what this indicates about themselves; often he takes little care or exercises little responsibility, concerning the effects which stressful experimental tasks or conditions have on subjects, other than as regards his interest in the experiment, in short or long term; seldom does he give subjects much opportunity to express their concerns or ideas relating to their experimental experience; seldom does he engage in repeated encounters with subjects, mostly preferring single or few meetings with naïve subjects. (p.159)

Similarly, Morgan (1983) has described how a research perspective's favoured methodology expresses the particular assumptions about the nature of the object of study and the most appropriate means for conducting the research:

> The image of the phenomenon to be investigated provides the basis for detailed scientific research concerned to examine, and perhaps operationalize and measure, the extent to which detailed aspects of the image characterize the phenomenon. The image generates specific concepts and methods of study through which knowledge of the phenomenon can be obtained. In effect, methodologies are the puzzle-solving devices that bridge the gap between the image of a phenomenon and the phenomenon itself. Methodologies link the researcher to the situation being studied in terms of rules, procedures, and general protocol that operationalize the network of assumptions embodied in the researcher's paradigm and favored epistemological stance. (p.21)

When we draw upon findings and theories from different individual studies, particularly when these are themselves grounded in different fields of study and working within different paradigms, we need, in order to understand how students or others learn, to be clear about the models of human beings and of human learning which they implicitly express. Otherwise, we run the risk of relating theories, methods, and findings which are grounded upon differing assumptions. That is, we may be in danger of merging findings from studies whose implicit views of learners may be largely contradictory.

Moreover. if we are interested in understanding how students learn in order to develop more effective educational practice, it is important for us to consider the assumptions on which both research findings and educational practice are based. Assumptions about learning which are implicit in different research approaches may both inform and arise out of assumptions about learning which constitute the foundation of particular educational practices – and vice versa. For example, the view of teaching as the transmission of knowledge may rest on the assumption that knowledge is the equivalent of a body of facts and that learning is the internalization of such facts. Equally, a research approach which assumed learning to be the internalization of a body of facts might try to uncover and understand students' learning processes by analysing recall protocols from their reading of texts in terms of the facts expressed in those texts.

We are left with a conundrum: how do we best find out about learning if whatever research method is adopted presupposes a particular view of learning? How then can we evaluate research findings about learning in order to inform good educational practice?

On Knowing Ourselves as Researchers

An examination of my second question may offer a tentative way forward: what role and status do we give ourselves as researchers in our study of how students learn?

Overwhelmingly, research on learning in general and on student learning in particular talks about learners as if they were other than the researcher. This is especially perplexing in the investigation of student learning where one can be entirely sure that the researchers and theorists concerned have all been students themselves. Moreover, although these researchers may no longer be enrolled in formal courses of study, they are by the nature of their work engaged in a process of finding out, of discovering, of learning, of coming to know. Learning is surely fundamental to the researchers' work. And of course researchers are human beings too.

Instead of rendering ourselves – as researchers and as teachers – other than and separate from the students with whom we are working, should we not reflect upon ourselves as former students and, most importantly, as past, current, and continuing learners, so that when we research into and teach students we are also researching into and teaching ourselves? As Mair (1970) observed:

> Everything the psychologist does as a scientist is part of his capacities and skills as a human being and is therefore by definition part of the subject matter which, as a psychologist, he claims to study. While psychologists as scientists no doubt have a lot to teach themselves and other people,

psychologists as people have a lot more to teach themselves and others who study people, because they are and will always be the subject matter which by their disciplines they seek to understand a little further. (p.169)

In day-to-day life we appear to judge the truth of something according to whether it matches our feelings, confirms and can be accommodated within our beliefs and assumptions, and is of practical use. We need to ask ourselves whether in fact as researchers we use similar criteria in order to validate how and what we find out, even though we may espouse other, more objective criteria. Unless we begin to include ourselves amongst the researched and to examine our own underlying assumptions – attitudes, values, and beliefs – about the nature of ourselves in the world and about how we learn within the world, we cannot know how we as people and we as researchers interrelate in our research. We risk missing potentially rich and vivid pictures of how we learn and of how we can improve on how we uncover how we learn.

Concluding Remarks

I end by summarizing my concerns through six questions which I believe we need to address if we are to locate ourselves as researchers in relation to our subject and to our methodology:

1 What do I – the researcher – bring to the research situation in terms of knowledge and past experiences, attitudes, values, and beliefs?
2 How do these personal contributions affect how I find out something and what I find out?
3 What can this tell me about how I – and others – learn?
4 What views do I implicitly express through my research approach about the people I am researching and about how they learn?
5 Is this a view I want to express: does it complement my values, attitudes, and beliefs, and my own view of myself as a human being and as a learner?
6 What views are expressed by the theory and research in which I ground my work: do these views conflict with my attitudes, values, beliefs, and conceptions of myself as a human being and as a learner?

Such questions do not of course let us off the hook; they force us to confront our own particular conception of the nature of human beings and of how they learn, and thus to question our own work for the hidden assumptions it contains. Through this reflection on ourselves and our research we may arrive at a richer picture of ourselves as learners and of how we may best find out about how other people learn.

References

Chapman, A.J. and Jones, D.M. (Eds) (1980) *Models of Man* Leicester: The British Psychological Society
Mair, J.M.M. (1970) Psychologists are human too. In D. Bannister (Ed.) *Perspectives in Personal Construct Theory* 157-184. London: Academic Press

Morgan, G. (Ed.) (1983) *Beyond Method: Strategies for social research* London: Sage Publications

Shotter, J. (1975) *Images of Man in Psychological Research* London: Methuen

17

The Impermeable Membrane

Desmond Ryan

When will academic teaching incorporate student learning research? The issues raised in this paper are general issues, relevant to the theme of the psychology of student learning – but in fact of more relevance to the researchers than to the research, since what follows is really a meta-paper, not scholarly or scientific, but practical; not focused on the conclusions of scientists and scholars, but on their practice. It is a plea for an altered emphasis.

My point of entry into the problem area is as follows. While it is possible that I am over-generalizing from limited experience, I have found that lecturers, both in universities and in the public sector, do not share my enthusiasm for research on student learning. In general, it is a useful body of knowledge, the only field of knowledge which could provide a grounding of theory and principles to what is after all their principal activity. Nevertheless, lecturers find it difficult to assimilate. Hence, despite their veneration for theory and a rational approach in their discipline, they remain atheoretical and intuitive in their teaching.

Since the learning researchers have established beyond doubt that the consequence of this intuitive approach is a large amount of unsatisfactory learning by students, should not their next research objective be to explore the processes of teaching? For, as we have been shown all too well by the research that has led up to this book, the learning world of students is not an autonomous world. It is a world dominated by the lecturers, to an extent they themselves do not appreciate. The road to improved student learning passes through their domain. Inasmuch as this book has a practical thrust, lecturers are implicitly the objects of it. The obstacles to turning them into willing subjects in the improvement process are what I shall be exploring.

Whilst it is true that since the 1960s the 'study of teaching has become accepted not exceptional', the claim that 'our knowledge of lecturers, and the part they play in teaching has grown substantially, [whereas] students have remained shadowy and insubstantial figures' (Hounsell 1984, p.189) is in my view still somewhat premature.[1] By, for example, a close attention to the contextual dimension of learning, we now know *why* students adopt the learning strategies that they do, ie what it is about the academic tasks and expectations, largely mediated to them by their lecturers, which leads them to adopt deep or surface approaches, etc. But where is the Perry or the Marton of the lecturers? Yes, we know *what* they do; and the wave of prescriptive tomes on what they *should* do looks set to reach similar proportions to the old 'How to study' guides –

which, given what we know from the hard-nosed phenomenography about how much effect those have, should give us pause. But if we are to bring about real improvements in student learning by ensuring that students are better taught, we shall first have to understand *why* higher education teachers teach in the way they do.

Since it is the duty of those whose sins cannot be brought to account to throw the first taxonomic essay into the intellectual murk, I shall pose two questions. The second I shall leave on the table for those who are better qualified to answer than I am. Answering the first is my way of indicating the kinds of area I think the learning researchers should next look at.

Question A: Is it something about the work of practising teachers which makes them indifferent or even hostile to the conclusions of research on student learning?

Question B: Is it something about research on student learning which makes it difficult to disseminate its results among practising teachers?

My answer to Question A will have three strands:

i   Pointing to important consequences of the fact that lecturers define themselves as subject specialists;
ii   Sketching briefly how they are constrained by being the inheritors of a folk-lore of practice;
iii   Pointing out how confining are the expectations the higher educational system has of the lecturers themselves in its allocation of tasks.

The piece as a whole is not an attack on academics, though I point out some areas where they could do better what they aspire to do well, ie teach. Nor is it a panegyric, though I believe their dedication to the truth is an important ideal, worthy to be matched against didactic effectiveness where students are intelligent and motivated. It is really a plea for a greater all round self-awareness, to enable the academic vocation to survive in educational institutions, where it is now most endangered.

Lecturers are Subject Specialists

When we ask higher education lecturers, even the greater part of secondary school teachers, what they do, the answers are almost inevitably of the kind 'I teach metallurgy/French/psychology.' The discipline or subject is what commands their loyalty – even as against their institution. Correspondingly, success in the discipline is what confirms their identity, gives reputation and reward; and, although it is less than fifty years since research became a contractual obligation of university teachers in the UK, success means success in research – in some science faculties, to confess an interest in educational concerns is to indicate that one no longer has what it takes to keep up with the research frontier. Success in the discipline through research even drives the work ambitions of a growing population of teachers in public sector institutions, albeit they were founded not to do research but to be teaching institutions.

Typically, lecturers are dominated, even deformed, by their discipline and its ethos. Under today's conditions of scarcity each subject culture, far from being one branch on the great tree of knowledge, is more like a separate species of plant, struggling each against all for light, space and nutrients, in all but total indifference to the fate of others – *pereat mundus, fiat physics*. Each subject culture will have its own vocabulary, methodology – even, according to Becher (1983), its own epistemology:

> ... the essential tasks of those seeking to advance understanding in any ... intellectual domain will be determined in large part by the characteristic epistemology of that domain – and hence ... the disciplinary cultures of academics will be conditioned in their turn by the nature of the knowledge which they pursue.

This diversity is not just characteristic of the major groupings of disciplines mentioned by Becher – the pure sciences, the humanities, the technologies and the social sciences – but holds also within the groups.

> At first sight the human sciences – at least to anyone who has played however small a part in their development – are striking not for their unity, which is difficult to formulate and to promote, but for their long-standing, confirmed, fundamental, indeed almost *structural* diversity. They are first and foremost narrowly themselves, putting themselves forward as so many different countries, so many languages, and less justifiably, so many competing race-tracks, each with its own rules, its own scholarly enclosures, its commonplaces comprehensible only to itself. (Braudel 1980 p.55)

This pronounced differentiation of the disciplines among themselves is true not only for lecturers but also for students. Students in the UK can still (in July 1985) self-select themselves into disciplines. A random dip into research on students reveals that, at student level, disciplines can differ significantly: on the social and political beliefs of their students, irrespective of ability (SSRC funded research on why more able students do not choose to go into industry, carried out at Bath University by Cotgrove and Weinreich-Haste, reported in *The Times Higher Education Supplement* 24 December 1982); on the distribution of degree results, where 'degree candidates in one subject are ten or more times as likely to get a first as in others' ('Measuring by degrees on the performeter' *The Times Higher Education Supplement* 26 July 1985); even on the characteristics of graduate students' wives and the propensity of their marriages to break down – 'Divorce seems to be a concomitant of intellectual turbulence ... while stable marriages are a concomitant of life within a discipline that is enjoying a state of relative calm' (Hudson 1983, p.7).

A discipline usually has a limited number of topics at the forefront of research at any time. This does not mean that the majority of practitioners are working on the same topic (though it is true in some scientific sub-fields) but that only a small number of topics attract the interest of more than a few researchers. These are the stock problems which are the focus of conferences or the subject of disputes in the journals; at any moment they mark the 'growth poles' of the discipline; they are typically the point of entry for research students, and they attract a disproportionate amount of grants.

Correspondingly there is a limited number of centres of leadership in each discipline at any one time. Those in the field know where these are, who is working there and what they are working on, even what exact target they are trying to achieve. These centres construct, occasionally transform, the agenda for the subject, originate the concepts, place their young graduates in vacancies throughout the field. Sometimes this leadership is the consequence of certain outstanding individuals, and may move on, or pass away with them; sometimes it results from a coming together of two or more talents who collectively 'gel' or 'spark'.

To insiders, therefore, this limitation of centres of leadership and topics for concentration means that disciplines are highly structured social institutions, for all that they seem to be an anarchic wilderness to outsiders, and to beginners. Each discipline also has its history, whether presented as a chronicle of great names conversing across centuries, a shelf of great books, a list of experiments which changed its direction, a sequence of paradigms. Older disciplines lean to the names and their cardinal texts; younger disciplines, often secessions from older intellectual territories, mark their rise by the issues and controversies which have led to their present independence. Invariably, the edges of disciplines are well policed; work on the margins has difficulty in getting a hearing, and the inter-disciplinary individual or institution lives under the fear of all genetic 'sports', mass attack by 'normal' scientists[2] or scholars.

When lecturers look at a class, such is their highly differentiated world view. This knowledge, these very particular perspectives through knowledge, make up the 'subsidiary awareness' (Polanyi 1963) of those who work in any academic field. However subsidiary, the awareness conditions their teaching strategies, conditions their feelings about what content (ie whose achievement) is to be planned, how it is to be sequenced and given emphasis, to what apotheosis or denouement it should lead, at what point their own work should enter the picture.

When typical[3] lecturers lecture, even carelessly and for the umpteenth time, it is an existential act. They create a world and claim a place in it. They privilege their claim by the order they give to the world and the care they take to establish their descent from heroes of old. If they have published they will have critics to refute and competitors to discredit; the subject as a whole will have to be so contextualized that their contribution makes sense, their existence is justified. This world is more than competitive, it is violent and treacherous. An academic career is like a medieval journey, its goal a mystery, the unstraight way leading through dark woods and up steep slopes, past gaily patterned leopards and truculent knights clad all in black; relieved only by the occasional fair, joust or solemn liturgy. Even the most eminent (Lewis 1966, p.33) have nightmares that a single mistake will destroy their careers. As in other spheres of life fuelled more by obscure desire than by rational will, past potency is no guarantee of future, one can easily lose one's 'standing', become intellectually flaccid, a limp(ing) presence, good only for committees.

Academics do not teach students, they teach their subject. In this world, students are not the 'subjects' of a purposive process; they either participate, or they are the audience. They are not the 'clients' of a practising professional or 'consumers' of a commercial service; they are the onlookers at a public re-enactment of hours, days of private struggle in study, library or laboratory. They are the reason for this enactment, but they do not cause it to happen in the way it does. Lecturers are primarily subject specialists, not teachers of students, nor members of a profession, keen to update their 'professional skills' by 'staff development' courses. Knowledge is their working material – securing it, clarifying it, integrating it, sharing it, destroying it. Skill with knowledge got them the job, not skill with students; the prize for supreme skill with knowledge is to be dispensed from teaching any but the students they choose, to be able to get on with their 'own work'.

As teachers, the typical academics' 'crime' is that they treat students as though they were academics too. That is to say, as though they were as interested in the subject as the lecturers are, as though minor shifts in a corner of the cosmos of knowledge should be major events in their lives, as though for them too the tastiest treat were knowledge in the raw, chunks of it, to cut their teeth on.

> The dialogue between pupil and teacher need not be fundamentally different from that between scholar and scholar. Its avowed end is not the same: it is the initiation of another into a universal activity, not the discovery of truth. But this can be done only by treating the dialogue as if its end were the discovery of truth. (Phillips Griffiths 1965, p.196)

While such treatment has the not inconsiderable virtues of being liberating and unpatronizing, it is perhaps not educationally sound for those who will never again, if they can help it, meet knowledge in the raw – those who are now, with the emergence of universities as the principal mechanism of social mobility, perhaps in the majority. Whence the 'paradox of academia': passionate but bad teaching makes minds grow towards the truth, while good teaching can dulcify sharp minds into polite unintelligence. What by rights should sink into the mud instead rises towards the light, while the well taught remain no more and no less than that.

In a curious way, academics have been the midwives of modernity and yet remain themselves pre-modern figures, the last of the wild men, feeding on dreams, preaching respect for truth and passionately committed to their own ideas, continually worsted by the natural desire of the reason to be unreasonable, lovers of scholarship who can hate other scholars.

> If a man will comprehend the richness and variety of the universe, and inspire his mind with a due measure of wonder and of awe, he must contemplate the human intellect not only on its heights of genius but in its abysses of ineptitude; and it might be fruitlessly debated to the end of time whether Richard Bentley or Elias Stoeber was the more marvellous work of the Creator: Elias Stoeber, whose reprint of Bentley's text, with a commentary intended to confute it, saw the light in 1767 at Strasburg, a city still famous for its geese. (A.E. Housman, quoted Nuttall 1986, p.11)

The uses to which knowledge is put depend strongly on the receptivity of the potential users (Husen and Kogan 1984, p.64). In so far as a higher education teacher is typically academic and dominated by his discipline, and also to the extent that he is a member of an institution where the characteristic outlook is appropriate to competitive academicism, his receptivity to student learning research is likely to be low, should he encounter it. This may change when the last vestiges of medieval values are extirpated, when the university is finally 'domesticated' for senior members as it has been for junior, when they acknowledge

> the eclipse of the splendid barbarity which has marked the long military-monastic tradition of English higher education; all the discomfort and dirt that has been properly a part of it. And now there are girls at Balliol, and central heating – and students are bathed in eternal pastoral care. (Musgrove 1978, p.402)

Lecturers Inherit a Folk-Lore of Practice

The practising teacher, let us say, exists totally immersed in an intellectual medium. This intellectual medium is at the same time cognitive and emotional, scientific and primitive. It is also historical, a complex culture evolving over time. The processes whereby new recruits are socialized into the culture, these too serve to keep research on student learning peripheral to the work of teaching.

An academic discipline is a cultural system. Each has its own symbols, rituals, languages and roles. It has a material base: terminal, test-tube, text, tribe. It has its approved methods; and its recognized short-cuts. As with any other culture, the process of becoming an academic is one of 'socialization'. Teaching members of the culture are socialized, not trained; training does *not* give membership of an academic culture, and in fact there is an inverse relationship between academic status and the taking of training courses to 'qualify' for teaching work.

Academics come to their role as if to an inheritance. This they are prepared for by living in the relevant cultural world, as the young master by living on the estate, the young magnate by passing through the departments of the family firm. As teachers, they are therefore the creatures of an oral tradition. As future scholar or scientist they are scrupulously trained: no care is not taken which will make their work more rigorous, articulated and compelling. Languages must be mastered; with all relevant methods they must be entirely familiar; the context must be portrayed in all relevent detail; the preceding literature surveyed and key points isolated. As trainee scholar or scientist, rational methods, self-criticism and attention to detail are constantly harped on. But teaching is just something they drift into or have thrust upon them, perhaps with a few tips from an old hand.

Teaching is one of a pair: the preparation for and the passage into administration is of an exactly similar kind:

> Academic decisions are on the whole made by academic men: the University Grants Committee and the Research Councils consist predominantly of scientists and scholars; even the members of the Committee of Vice-Chancellors and Principals were scholars once upon a

time; and all British universities see to it that their internal affairs are run by academics. Yet all over the country these groups of scholars who would not make a decision about the shape of a leaf or the derivation of a word or the author of a manuscript without painstakingly assembling the evidence, make decisions about admissions policy, size of universities, staff-student ratios, content of courses, and similar issues, based on dubious assumptions, scrappy data and mere hunch. (Ashby 1963, p.6)

Higher education teaching and administration, therefore, resemble the lore of the school playground or the street, cultural forms just picked up through group belonging. This contrasts with academic content which is the counterpart of nursery rhymes and parlour games, dutifully taught, as an aspect of the adult role, by parents and their accomplices.

> While a nursery rhyme passes from a mother or other adult to the small child on her knee, the school rhyme circulates simply from child to child, usually outside the home, and beyond the influence of the family circle. (Opie 1959, p.1)

Without being too fanciful, one could liken the careful nursery rhyme coaching by the mother to the disciplined thesis guidance by what the Germans call the 'doctor-father', the supervisor; and the child's recitation before their nursery/primary school teachers and classmates to the departmental graduate-faculty seminars – both occasions where the carefully prepared content goes on public display, the moment of truth. Just as the adults – parents or teachers – are dismissive about 'Mister Fatty Belly, how is your wife?' (Opie 1959, p.1), so senior academics – so scrupulous about accuracy of results, logical coherence in argument – are entirely casual about teaching, pushing graduates into tutorial fellowships ('just a line on the CV, to show you've done some') as if the actual work involved was no different from their vacation job selling ice cream. It should be no surprise that graduates, of whatever age, are in their teaching as unselfconscious, as unaffected by the sophisticated world of occupational research, as the ice cream salesman.

How easily we criticize this blindness! How oblivious academics are to the absurdity of the figure they cut in the modern world, the world where 'efficiency 'n' effectiveness' are 'ongoing' and where the 'bottom line' has the discernment once attributed to the ducking-stool. And yet ... is it anachronism? Or is it logically related to the work?

'Methods attack their objects only from without. Academics are not anti-method. They use methods, even to an extreme degree, to attack their object – ignorance' (Ashby 1974, p.83). It is their own ignorance that they attack from without, assault with methods. But when it comes to communicating the results of their work, they see their problems from within. They live within a world, self-constructed to a greater or lesser extent, and teaching means initiating newcomers into that world, sharing its meanings. They know what it is that they want to share; when they teach someone who really wants to share it, the greatest gift they can pass on is their methods for attacking ignorance and constructing meanings, organizing successful raids on the unknown or the erroneous. They teach, so to speak, the scholar's woodcraft, in the only place where it can be taught, where the examples are to hand and where what the woodcraft is needed for is powerfully present to the mind of the student. The absurd figure, from *their* point of view is that of the student who wishes to learn woodcraft, perhaps to the highest level, but has no motive to enter the woods, be it for hunting or hiding, or classifying species, or mapping ecosystems, or simply to be 'transported and ravished by the green trees', – to become 'most ourselves' by being 'swept clean out of ourselves in wonder and delight' (Reeves 1978, p.6).

To insist that they should be 'trained' to teach such students on recognized educational principles is, they would say, to compound a category mistake with the absurdity, for it requires them to focus on the communication of what is already known rather than on how to make productive raids on what is not. This displaces a vital part of their own educational message – *how* scholars and scientists approach their work – and gives absorbing and redeploying academic content a wholly disproportionate place in the purposive activities of students. Students' minds, quite properly, frequently fall short on the mastering of content for which they have no real projected use. The circle of absurdity is then closed by proposing that they should be taught 'study skills', the content-free arabesques of mental culture, a general skill appropriate to a world spurred into even more rapid change by technology, but equally a skill which has nothing to do with how scholars become scholars (Gibbs 1981), or with how anybody at all learns how to distinguish the true from the generally accepted.

Lecturers are Constrained by the System

Higher education teachers, I have maintained, are strongly conditioned in their work by their identity as subject specialists, and by the manner in which they are socialized into that identity. A third, also powerful, source of constraint on how they teach lies in the educational system as it impinges on them, and this in two ways:

i   how it allocates tasks;
ii how it conditions students' expectations.

I have discussed this at length elsewhere (Ryan 1984) so I shall somewhat compress what follows.

'The principal ingredient of a role is the role expectation'. Practising teachers in higher education are expected:

to communicate knowledge and develop skills and understanding...
necessary for the qualifying exam...
with the allocated materials...
in the allocated accomodation...
as required by those to whom they are accountable...
who themselves have to deliver on other factors.

The teaching task is therefore subject to a series of constraints, to wit, successively: curriculum, assessment, resources, environment, organization, and so on. Because of the segmentation of the academic 'profession' (Bucher and Strauss 1963), the impact of these constraints is *highly variable*, between sectors, subjects and institutions, over time. At one extreme lies the paramedical lecturer on a qualifying but non-degree course in a nineteenth-century annexe of a college of technology with an authoritarian head of department and a non-supportive local authority – at the other lies (lay?) Howard Kirk (Bradbury 1975). If the qualifying body states that the curriculum for the Part I Exam will have this much anatomy, that much physiology, plus physics, biology, chemistry, psychology and sociology *and* no contact with patients, it comes as no surprise to hear the lecturers say that in Year I there is only one teaching method: 'Pound it in'.

Fired with reforming zeal, educational developers and learning researchers sometimes talk as though lecturers were entirely free agents; if they chose, they could do better. My (perhaps anomalous) research and development experience in the public sector has led me to conclude that teachers there are as constrained by the practical limits of time, space, curriculum and politics as university teachers are by their fear of losing intellectual face before students or colleagues. Neither group chooses to teach badly. But good teaching becomes a secondary consideration. First they must come up to scratch on all the tasks where their poor performance will not be compensated for by extra effort from students.

Lecturers' strategies are, therefore, coping strategies. Rational strategies to maximize learning outcomes are ruled out by the number and shifting quality of the constraints through which lecturers have to pick their way. The explicit hierarchy of course objectives gets crowded out by the mass of secondary objectives lurking in 'subsidiary awareness', especially in today's politically turbulent environments. Coping strategies don't maximize, they 'satisfice'; they are 'ploys' which solve the greatest number of problems at once. But they solve the teachers' problems, not those of the students.

Whereas rational maximizing strategists ask the question 'What am I trying to achieve?', coping strategists ask 'What am I going to do?' 'What am I going to do?' is 'gut' planning. Since I am isolated in an inward-looking academic tribe without access to the works of learning science in our vernacular, my answer is another question: 'What is everybody else doing?' Since I am dominated by content, the answer is a chunk of content: 'We'd better do intra-cellular chemistry next – that always comes up'.

Teachers do not act on the basis of informed scientific knowledge; rather they select their courses of action by referring to established norms and precedents for ways of acting that have come to constitute acceptable practice. (Van Manen 1977, p.219)

This, then, is the key question: what is *in* the teacher's mind, and weighing *on* it, as he or she puts together a teaching strategy, long- or short-term? Very little in their education, or in their socialization, or in their circumstances as role-performers, presses them to do anything other than to ask 'What am I going to do?' In the main what is sought is 'valid' rather than 'effective' curriculum, what is acceptable in the circumstances.

Most of us, most of the time, do the best we can in the circumstances. This means we try to think ahead, imagine in advance the effects on ourselves and other people of what we propose to do, and then do it. The manner in which we apply anything we know in what we do is not usually very clearly defined or in the focus of our consciousness. What we know informs our desires and fears and beliefs and intentions, and it is, roughly speaking, out of such unspecified and unanalysed beliefs and intentions that we act – most of the time. (Britton 1973, p.11)

This observation of Britton's seems no less apposite for teachers in universities and colleges than it is for those in primary schools. The learning researchers have done an excellent collective job in revealing, in irrefutable detail, the consequences for students of what academics as teachers do. But it is the *circumstances* in which they do what they do that we continue to take it for granted that we understand. I am not sure that we do: some hard-nosed phenomenography could present us with some quite surprising findings.

Generally speaking, then, lecturers' response to their allocated tasks is to pick their way through their constraints with coping strategies, to develop what will be accepted as valid curriculum. For this reason, too, their receptivity to the methodological prescriptions implicit in the work of the learning researchers, or explicit in the proselytizing of staff development enthusiasts, would be likely to be low.

The Ambiguities of Our Own Practice

There was a time when poor learning or poor academic performance by a student was accepted as straightforward evidence of intellectual mediocrity. Learning research has since revealed the complexity of the learning process, and shown how learning strategies are students' attempts to adapt to academic demands as they perceive them.

The time has now come when poor student learning is attributed to bad management of the learning environment by academic staff; this in its turn is accepted as straightforward evidence of the professional mediocrity of staff. I have here tried to question that over-simplification and, by analogy with what we have understood from the research on student learning, to suggest that staff teaching strategies are their attempts to adapt to pressures as *they* perceive them – academic, cultural and environmental. Staff may be mediocre managers of their students' learning environments – but it is not because they are mediocre professionals. Other priorities supervene.

I have tried also to make clear my belief that the academic has a valid claim for the value of his work, in its ideal form; and the educationist for his work, in its ideal form. I do not stand on one side or the other: the pursuit of truth and the education of the young I see as terminal values, between which there is no rational way of adjudicating. The absurdity in this dual task is that there are sides at all.

As my concluding plea for more research on academics, let me attempt to be convincing about the power of the 'other priorities' by detailing my own experience at the conference which gave rise to this book. This was a joint activity between two learned societies, differing considerably in their range of membership, extent of common knowledge and focus of commitment, but both keen to promote interdisciplinary give and take. The form of the conference was absolutely right – for a scientific conference. But with this form, the purpose of the conference – interdisciplinary give and take – was unachievable. The methods of presentation, the level of presentation, plus the architectual environment and the work load, pushed me at least into surface-level processing with a vengeance. (Only when these proceedings are published will I know what I have learned there!) In other words, conference organizing fell under the curse of teaching, to see its potential to provide opportunities for high-grade exploratory learning in a supportive environment sacrificed to the tyranny of academic respectability and to an unreflective response to the unscrutinized expectations communicated by sociotechnological work settings (Westbury 1973; 1978). Here, too, academic, cultural and environmental constraints distorted 'What are we trying to achieve?' into 'What are we going to do?' When the chips are down and our careers are on the line, we are all dominated by content. Our theories of the learning process are no more influential over our conference practice than they are for teachers in class. As learning researchers, we do not differ from the academics whose management skills we criticize: the prescriptions of 'proper' procedure have also pre-empted *our* practical mission.

Which brings me back to where I began. Since it seems to be the case that situational constraints – academic, cultural, environmental – triumph inevitably over our best intentions and turn out to be the real determinants of our practices, I renew my plea for more research on those which affect the work of academics. Teaching should not be the only activity of teachers to be subjected, in its turn, to this process: conferences, publication, administration, academic politics, these are all activities whose patterns of pressures form the context in which that so complex behaviour, teaching, has to take place. Neglecting them, we will not secure valid knowledge of why teachers teach in the way that they do by (however close) an acquaintance with the literature on student learning. And failing *that* valid knowledge, dustbin logic will continue to accuse teachers of mediocre professionalism in the management of the learning environments of their students.

While there is a certain natural justice in the students' lack of motivation or intelligence as an explanation of learning failure being replaced by the teacher's poor professionalism, the times are not such that we can smile. And while learning researchers can justifiably claim that academics have not been 'scientifically rational' about their teaching; and educational developers that they have failed to prioritize objectives and apply techniques in a 'professionally informed' approach; when politicians and their journalists join the chorus of condemnation, we face the danger of a general collusion to turn 'the lazy lecturer' into a folk-devil whose function is not only to protect us all from the effort involved in trying to understand the systematic complexities of higher education, but also to discredit the academic vocation. Grandiloquent though it may sound, behind the academic stands truth itself. As we enter an age of scarcity and ugly choices mount, we should worry more about it.[4]

Notes

1 '... what is singularly lacking is a study of the university teaching profession which provides a comprehensive description of what staff in a particular university actually do, why they do it and how students and others respond to them' (Startup 1979, p.vii); 'There have been very few investigations of ... the "sociopsychological environment" of academics' (Powell et al. 1983, p.298).

2 'The great insight of Thomas Kuhn's *Structure of Scientific Revolutions* has nothing to do with scientific revolutions (he leaves these a mystery), but is rather his picture of scientific practice ("normal science") as a closed system, deeply conformist, as entrenched as the law or the church. Scientists like it that way; they will try every trick, such as anomaly labelling, to cling to the theories ("paradigms") they've got' (Roy Porter *The Times Higher Education Supplement* 5 November 1982).

3 For reasons which will become clear in a moment, and in a simple statistical sense, women academics cannot yet be considered 'typical', at least not in the UK.

4 This chapter follows the argument as given at the conference. The final section is an extension into an argument, or some remarks made extempore, as a result of reflecting on Professor Perry's contribution the day before. I am grateful to Marjorie Reeves and Tony Nuttall for a correction in emphasis, and Bernard Longden for general stimulus and support.

References

Ashby, E. (1963) Introduction: decision-making in the academic world. In *The Sociological Review: Monograph No.7* (Sociological Studies in British University Education)

Ashby, E. (1974) The academic profession. In *Adapting Universities to a Technological Society* San Francisco: Jossey-Bass

Becher, T. (1983) Public faces, private lives *The Times Higher Education Supplement* 9 December

Bradbury, M. (1975) *The History Man* London: Secker and Warburg

Braudel, F. (1980) Unity and diversity in the human sciences. In *On History* Translated by Sarah Matthews. London: Weidenfield and Nicolson

Britton, J. (1973) Preface to Rosen, C. and H. *The Language of Primary School Children* Harmondsworth: Penguin Education

Bucher, R. and Strauss, A.L. (1961) Professions in process *American Journal of Sociology* 66, 325-34

Gibbs, G. (1981) *Teaching Students to Learn: A student-centred approach* Milton Keynes: Open University Press

Hounsell, D. (1984) Understanding teaching and teaching for understanding. In Marton et al. (1984)

Hudson, L. (1983) *The Great Miscegenation – or the joyous union of the imagination and the machine* London: SIAD – Maurice Hille Award

Husen, T. and Kogan, M. (Eds) (1984) *Educational Research and Policy – How do they relate?* Oxford: Pergamon Press

Lewis, C.S. (1966) *A Grief Observed* London: Faber

Marton, F., Hounsell, D. and Entwistle, N. (Eds) (1984) *The Experience of Learning* Edinburgh: Scottish Academic Press

Musgrove, F. (1978) The domesticated university *New Universities Quarterly* Summer

Nuttall, A.D. (1986, forthcoming) Scholarship and morality *Higher Education Newsletter* 11 (June)

Opie, I. and P. (1959) *The Lore and Language of Schoolchildren* Oxford: Clarendon Press

Phillips Griffiths, A. (1965) A deduction of universities. In R.D. Archambault (Ed.) *Philosophical Analysis and Education* London: Routledge and Kegan Paul

Polanyi, M. (1963) *The Study of Man* Chicago: University of Chicago Press

Powell, J.P., Barrett, B. and Shanker, V. (1983) How academics view their work *Higher Education* 12 (3) 297-313

Reeves, M. (1978) Knowledge for what? *Higher Education Group Newsletter* November

Ryan, D.P. (1984) *Development and Constraint: Innovations in teaching methods and staff development in the Scottish Central Institutions* Glasgow: The Queen's College

Startup, R. (1979) *The University Teacher and his World* Farnborough: Saxon House

Van Manen, M. (1977) Linking ways of knowing with ways of being practical *Curriculum Inquiry* 6 (3) 205-28

Westbury, I. (1973) Conventional classrooms, 'open' classrooms and the technology of teaching *Journal of Curriculum Studies* 5 (2) 99-121

Westbury, I. (1978) Research into classroom processes: A review of ten years work *Journal of Curriculum Studies* 10 (4) 283-308

18

The Different Forms of Learning in Psychology and Education

Diana Laurillard

I want to argue that there are fundamental differences in the forms of learning addressed by cognitive psychologists and educationalists. The argument focuses on two aspects: the nature of the phenomena described, and the nature of the environments being learned.

The phenomena explained by a psychological theory of learning are the successes of human cognition. The mechanisms posited are designed to account for how learning takes place, where the content of the learning is the physical and social world around us. The phenomena investigated in research on student learning, on the other hand, usually concern failure to learn. The content of the learning that is supposed to take place is a different kind of world: the world of other peoples' ideas. To encapsulate the contrast: a psychological learning theory has to account for why everyone learns to tie their shoe-laces; an educational learning theory is concerned with why almost no-one learns to solve the Schroedinger Equation.

If we ask the question 'Why do people fail to learn X?', psychologists and educationalists are likely to give different kinds of answers. The assumption behind the theme of this book is that the psychologist's answer will be useful to the educationalist. I want to argue that it is not, but that the educationalist can, nonetheless, make use of psychological learning theories. The argument goes like this:

Why do people fail to learn X?
Psychological theories, especially information processing theories, tell us they fail to learn because they are not applying the necessary mechanisms, or not applying them appropriately.

Can we transfer those explanations directly to explain why students fail to learn?

The answer is no, because the content, the world of academic ideas, is an 'unnatural' environment.

The learner has immediate and elaborated access to the 'natural' environment of the real world and has evolved the cognitive capabilities appropriate to learning such an environment.

But access to the 'unnatural' environment of the world of academic ideas is extremely impoverished, by comparison, and the same cognitive capabilities do not work as well.

In education, students fail to learn, at least partly, because the environment does not afford learning.

The remedy implicit in this account is, therefore, not to put on study skill courses, but to enrich students' means of access to the unnatural world of academic ideas.

Therefore: we need the theories of cognitive psychology to tell us how an environment affords learning. We can then use this to construct the means of access that will turn an unnatural environment into one that affords learning.

Since the argument, which I shall now expand, rests on the idea of *affordance*, I want to discuss that first.

Affordance and Learning

What does it mean to say an environment *affords* learning? The natural environment affords the perception of itself by being immediately accessible to the observer. The theory of 'affordances', described by Gibson, is a way of accounting for the success of human cognition in learning about its natural environment. An 'affordance' is what the observer directly apprehends: '...what we perceive when we look at objects are their affordances, not their qualities' (Gibson 1979, p.134). An affordance is a collection of properties 'taken with reference to the observer' (ibid, p.143). Thus we apprehend 'graspability' first, and only later come to learn that this is composed of 'texture', 'size relative to the size of my hand', 'distance from me', 'form', 'substance', etc. The idea of affordance is not unlike the earlier ideas of 'demand character' (Koffka 1924), and 'valence' (Lewin 1936), which also recognized the importance of the meaning to the observer in the perception of an object. But there is a crucial difference, pointed out by Gibson: the earlier concepts located these peculiar relativistic properties in the mind of the observer, making them 'phenomenal' objects, since they clearly were not physical. Gibson makes the bolder assertion that an affordance is neither physical nor phenomenal, 'neither an objective property nor a subjective property; or it is both if you like.... It is equally a fact of the environment and a fact of behaviour' (ibid, p.129). As long as there are no strict dualists among us, this is a reasonable conclusion.

It is also philosophically respectable, being mirrored, for example, in Merleau-Ponty's argument against the dualism of psychology (pre-1963): 'What is artificial in the alternatives of psychology can be seen from the point of view which we have adopted. After the psychology-as-a-science-of-the-facts-of-consciousness has come the psychology-without-consciousness of Watson.... It is not seen that, from the moment behaviour is considered "in its unity" and in its human meaning, one is no longer dealing with a material reality nor, moreover, with a mental reality, but with a significative whole or a structure which properly belongs neither to the external world nor to internal life' (Merleau-Ponty 1963, p.182). The idea of 'affordance' resolves the 'artificial alternatives'. Thus, the idea of affordance is in sympathy with current preferences in student learning for a phenomenological perspective.

The idea is also in sympathy with other psychological theories of learning which describe the process of learning as a number of mechanisms, both conscious and non-conscious, which operate on our perceptions, and direct the form of interaction we have within the world, to enable us to build new, and progressively effective behaviours. These include mechanisms and procedures, such as repeated practice, feedback systems, hypothesis-testing, trial-and-error, analogical reasoning, etc. What has characterized many of the mechanisms posited is a kind of 'automaticity', ie there is an acknowledgement of the symbiotic nature of the relationship between the human brain and the world, in the sense that the idea of affordance describes, which means that we cannot help but perceive an afforded percept, and we cannot help but learn an afforded behaviour.

One example is Schank's account of dynamic memory: learning takes place *automatically*, as expectations created by past experience, ie scripts, fail in new situations, and dynamically alter memory. These modifications are produced by the 'reminding' experience, together with the explanation of the failure. The modifications count as learning, and will generate new behaviour in the next situation encountered (Schank 1982).

A second example is the attempt to define learning in terms of production systems, where 'production rules' provide the mechanism that connects 'declarative' knowledge – what you know already, whatever is stored in long-term memory – with behaviour. A production rule is an 'IF... THEN... ELSE...' statement. Because production rules can take the validation of other rules as their argument, this simple mechanism can provide extremely complex structures capable of giving an account of how a new behaviour could be built up in response to a new stimulus, given a particular set of declarative knowledge (Anderson 1983). Again, the idea of automaticity underlies the account, as the process of learning 'runs', rather as a computer program runs, and failures are bugs, which could be, for example, the absence of a rule, or a faulty rule.

The automaticity that characterizes many theories of learning in cognitive psychology is important because it is an acknowledgement that (i) the environment affords the original percepts, and perception remains unproblematic in these accounts, and (ii) the environment also affords the learning of more complex constructs and behaviours. Automaticity is the adjunct of affordance.

If we accept that in psychology we are talking about an environment that affords learning, then it becomes clear that transfer between psychology and education will be difficult, because in education we have an *un*natural environment that does *not* afford learning. That is the point I want to argue now.

Natural and Unnatural Environments

What are the key differences between natural and unnatural environments? By 'natural environment' I mean the physical and social world around us. It is the environment that human beings typically learn to manipulate. The 'unnatural environment' I am concerned with here is the world of academic ideas. As educationalists, we want to know why people learn or fail to learn physics, history, sociology.

The natural and the unnatural environment are distinguished by the fact that the former provides knowledge of the world, the latter provides knowledge of descriptions of the world. It is the difference between perceptual knowledge (of the physical world) and what I choose to call 'preceptual' knowledge (of the theoretical world). ('Preceptive' = 'mandatory; didactic; instructive', *Shorter Oxford English Dictionary*.) It is the knowledge of *pre*cepts that gives us so much trouble, and is what concerns educationalists. What makes them difficult is that they are not afforded to us in the way that *per*cepts are.

The mechanisms of learning established by psychology are developed to describe the functioning of an organism that has a 'symbiotic' relationship with its environment – that is in its appropriate ecological niche, to use Gibson's metaphor. Cognitive psychologists elaborate the details of how the process of learning can work and how it does work. But they take for granted the existence of the 'affordances' that make this possible. It is the affordances of the environment that are problematic for the educationalist. The learning of precepts is not equivalent to the learning of percepts.

It might, of course, be argued that learning precepts is rather like learning concepts and, certainly, cognitive psychology has made a considerable contribution to our understanding of conceptual learning. But again, this has usually related to those concepts afforded by the physical environment, such as 'tact', 'hypocrisy', and so on. The mechanisms of concept learning have been studied in relation to, for example, attributional concepts which can be learned through instances and non-instances of the concept. But the mechanisms that are appropriate for learning 'red circle' must be quite different from those needed to master the concept 'molecule'. An attributional concept like 'red circle' can be learned from a domain of objects that include only red things, blue things, circular things and square things, because the domain can be partitioned into instances and non-instances of the concept, and the positive instances adequately describe the concept. But we cannot do the same thing for 'molecule'. It is not a concept that is adequately described in terms of its attributions. Its logical structure is more complex.

Thus the results of studies of concept learning cannot be transferred to education because (a) attributional concepts are too simplistic for that research to be relevant, and (b) more complex concepts, such as conservation, are in any case afforded by the environment. An individual only has to interact with the environment for sufficient time in order to learn the concept. It is therefore unlikely that the results of conceptual learning will transfer easily to preceptual learning.

A further aspect of cognitive psychology that should be relevant to education is the work on text processing. But how relevant is it? Much of this work has focused either on short texts – on sentences and paragraphs – or on simple texts, with a descriptive or narrative structure. There are no analytic methods for studying the processing of texts the length and complexity of a chapter in an academic textbook. Undoubtedly, the strategies we use for processing sentences play a part in the way we process chapters, but the complexity of the processing at the macro-level is too great to gain much from the micro-level descriptions. The linear structure of narratives, and even hierarchic propositional structures, used for example by Meyer (1975), are far less complex than the rambling and untidy structures that underlie most academic texts. Unravelling those is likely to require a qualitatively different kind of cognitive processing. So again, text processing is unlikely to transfer directly to the learning of precepts.

Learning precepts is different from learning either percepts or concepts because our means of access to them are so limited. We cannot experience structuralism in the same way as we experience good table manners. We cannot experience molecules in the same way as we experience dogs. Because we have to rely on the artificial structuring of our experience of precepts, via academic texts for example, it is unlikely that the mechanisms we use in the natural environment will transfer directly to this unnatural environment. Thus our means of access to precepts becomes critical to our success in learning them.

The Means of Access to Academic Knowledge

Examples drawn from recent research in student learning demonstrate two ways in which preceptual and perceptual learning are different: the structure of the unnatural environment does not afford learning of preceptual knowledge; and the affordances that are provided afford the learning of things other than preceptual knowledge because our cognitive capabilities have been developed to deal with the affordances of the natural world, and they do not transfer to the unnatural world.

The unnatural environment I am referring to is the variety of educational media through which we gain access to preceptual knowledge. Lectures, text, problem-solving, essay-writing, laboratory practicals – are all ways in which we come to know the precepts of the academic world. Of course, the way that an academic text is structured hardly provides a tranparent means of access to the precepts it is describing, and this causes many students to misinterpret what it is saying.

One common difficulty has been identified by Ference Marton and Roger Säljö. This is the inability to perceive the 'figure-ground' structure in a text. Many academic texts have this form, where the figure-ground refers to the principle-example, the main argument-evidence, the generalization-instance. There have been several replicated studies of students learning from such texts and these show that within any group some students will report the text as being about the principle, eg, scientific method; others report the same text as being about the content of the example, eg the discovery of the causes of childbed fever in the 19th century (Marton and Wenestam 1979).

The same pattern has also been found in the context of a different medium, namely a television programme. When students were asked to summarize an educational television programme that had the main argument-evidence format, some of them described the main argument, namely that childrens' television is culturally determined – but others described it in terms of the evidence that was put forward, namely that Sesame Street is about working-class street-life, whereas Play School is about middle-class home-life (Laurillard 1983).

The figure-ground structure is certainly something that affords perception. It would be surprising if someone were unable to recognize the figure and the ground in a painting like the Mona Lisa. However, it is not particularly surprising that students have difficulty with the text described above. In the first case, the principle takes up the title plus 5 per cent of the text, the remainder being a description of the example. In the second case, the statement of the main argument takes up about 5 per cent of screen time, the remainder being used for programme extracts providing the evidence for the claim. Leonardo da Vinci had the sense to give the Mona Lisa more than 5 per cent of the canvas. She would still have been figural even if he had not, but, as the above educational examples show, it does not help perception of structure to make what is figural so insignificant relative to what is ground.

Academic texts often obscure the precepts they are describing, in such a way that it becomes surprising that students ever learn anything. They do learn things by using strategies specifically developed to overcome the deficiencies of the environment. Marton has described one of these strategies as 'deep-level processing'. It refers to a collection of activities such as 'looking for the main point', 'comparing one part of the text with another', 'looking for the structure', etc. And this is what the student has to do just to be able to see what the text is actually about – the equivalent of perceiving. This is not the same as learning, as being able to remember and apply and develop the precepts found in the text. Deep-level processing is what the student needs to do just to see what is there. It is not done by every student all the time. It is a strategy developed, presumably in the same way as our everyday cognitive capabilities, to be suited to the demands both of the environment and of the student's own interests and values. Students actually want to learn their subject, at least some of the time, and sometimes manage to find the intellectual apparatus necessary for doing this in the face of even the most obscurantist text. The problem for students is that so many academic texts do obscure their structure. In other words, the unnatural environment fails to afford learning, by making even the initial apprehension of the precepts difficult.

A second failure is in providing only very poor means of access to the manipulation of those precepts. Learning through problem-solving is one example (Laurillard 1984). Students *should* find that their normal problem-solving strategies, transferred from the natural environment, should be some help. But the 'unnatural' problems of the theoretical world are not usually appropriately set up. Students are not given the kind of problem that would allow them to operate on the environment as they would expect to.

For example, in learning about digital process control, students have to learn the language (assembler), the system analysis of the mechanism to be programmed (eg traffic light control), and the procedure for expressing this as a computer program. The problem they are faced with, if solved on a computer, is manipulable; it is amenable to trial-and-error, or hypothesis-testing; they could repeat the problem with various different conditions; they could get feedback; ... in fact the problem is exactly analogous to what every five-year-old learns to do at school when they start giving instructions to each other on how to play a game. It is not a task that is intellectually very demanding.

But what happens in the unnatural environment of a university course? The problem is not solved on the computer. It is set as a pen and paper task. The language is learned by look-up. The mechanism is modelled on paper. Feedback is obtained, not directly from the model, nor from its interpretation in a domain, but from the tutor. And, reasonably enough, the students reconstruct an entirely different problem, ie the one afforded by this situation. The problem is no longer one on microelectronics. Their strategies of 'working backwards', 'relating this problem to another familiar one', 'hypothesis testing', 'checking back', etc. are all used, ie transferred from their learning about natural environments, but they cannot be deployed to a problem about microelectronics, because it has not been set up that way. It is not microelectronics that is providing the feedback, it is the tutor. So the problem they define for themselves is the problem of getting full marks from this tutor. And that has been properly set up. They can work backwards from the kind of solution they know the tutor likes ('box diagrams'), they can use knowledge of similiar problems ('look up the one that was marked last week'), check back ('how does my answer compare with the one we did in class'), and so on. This is the problem the environment affords. And it has very little to do with microelectronics.

Thus the structures of the environments we offer students often do not afford learning of the precepts we want to convey.

The point is illustrated further by some of the research on students reading academic texts. Students' reports of their reading of a chapter reveal quite alarmingly inappropriate strategies, their main focus being to memorize key words and phrases, with little attempt to integrate the information with previous information, or to discover the structure of the argument. Research studies of this kind have been replicated in several different academic contexts: in different countries, with different age groups, different subject matter, etc., and show that the phenomenon of 'surface-level processing' is widespread. It is alarming because it is not a good academic approach to learning a subject. But is it really so inappropriate? From the students' point of view, they have to be able to refer to the right experiments in a psychology paper, quote the right formulae in a physics paper, work in the right events in a history paper. For most students, the inclusion of a quantity of facts is a better guarantee of a good mark than relying on the quality of an argument.

Some of the above studies have found that students' adoption of surface-level processing depends on the context within which they are doing the reading (see Marton et al. 1984). By investigating the same students' behaviour over a number of normal academic tasks, it was possible to show that students used surface-level processing when they perceived that that was what the situation, namely the exam or essay, demanded. When they knew they could not get away with the mere regurgitation, or when they were motivated by interest in the subject itself, they penetrated further into what the text was about.

It is clear that academics have long recognized the need to attach artificial devices to the academic learning process in order to encourage learning to take place. The educational system has an elaborate array of rewards in the form of exam results, and feedback in the form of marked exercises. The necessary mechanisms for learning have been duly adopted as psychologists discover what they are. But the transfer to the academic environment has not preserved the internal relations between content and feedback. The rewards and the knowledge of results do not come from what is being learned, as they do in a natural environment. They come from something external to the content, namely a tutor. Wanting to get a good mark for the physics test does nothing in itself to help the student to understand the physics, except, perhaps, that it directs them to look at the physics book rather than go to the movies.

The consequence of this is that the content being learned as a product of those mechanisms is how to pass exams, how to operate a computer, how to present answers for the marker, how to make a good impression on the tutor, etc. The successful learners are the 'cue-seekers' and the 'cue-conscious' (Miller and Parlett 1974) – the ones who pick up the cues on how to pass exams. And that would be acceptable if learning how to pass exams implied that they had learned the subject. Unfortunately, passing an exam often has little to do with having a real grasp of the subject. Noel Entwistle's studies, for example, show that 'A' level is a poor predictor of university results (Entwistle 1974). More recently, Dahlgren's investigations show that students who have obtained good exam results still cannot answer adequately the most basic question in their subject if it is different in style from those they have studied for (Dahlgren and Marton 1978). Students who have been studying economics for three years, and have passed the final exam, cannot answer a question like 'Why does a bun cost 12p?'. The question is different from those they studied for the exam, and students learn what the environment affords. It affords the learning of how to pass exams, and that is not the same as learning the subject.

How is it that some students do manage to learn some physics, history and sociology occasionally? I have argued that what they are offered by the academic profession does not help them. And in so far as it affords anything, it affords the learning of something else entirely. In order to go beyond what the situation offers, students have to adopt a strategy that is capable of penetrating the surface of the text, ot the lecture, or the TV programme. Such a strategy has been discerned in student learning behaviour, and has been given the now familiar name 'deep-level processing'. It has been established that the adoption of this strategy relates to an intention to understand the material, and relates empirically to better summaries of the text concerned. Nonetheless, surface-level processing has the character of *automaticity* that, *if the environment were properly structured*, would lead to learning of the content. Deep-level processing is a deliberate attempt to destructure the environment as given, in order to penetrate the obscured meaning.

It may be that there is no analogue of deep-level processing in the learning of a natural environment. The meaning of a percept is given in the perception of it. There is no sense in which the perceiver has to go beyond what is afforded to what is hidden. This is what deep-level processing allows the student to do. In the natural environment, the learner's goals and values tend to coincide anyway with the content of learning afforded by the environment: everyone finds the sensation of balancing pleasing, and the social rewards of imitation exciting, so everyone learns to walk and talk. But this aspect of learning does not transfer to the academic environment: in preceptual learning, the learner's goals must *not* be personal, their values must *not* be governed by an immediate emotional response to their experience. In order to apprehend the precept at all, the learner must ignore this immediate response, and adjust their goals to coincide with an attention to what the author's goals are, what the author is trying to communicate. Many of the students who summarized the scientific method text as being about the cause of childbed fever described that as being the only point of interest the text had for them. The format of the text, as I suggested, certainly afforded the learning of this precept in a way that it did not afford the learning of the form of scientific method. And for these students, their immediate emotional response coincided with that secondary aspect. So that is what they learned. In order to learn what the text was *actually* about, it was *necessary* for them to adopt deep-level processing.

Summary

Where does this lead? To a recognition that learning precepts is fundamentally different from learning percepts; that therefore the mechanisms of learning that are derived from the learning of percepts, namely the content of a natural environment, do not transfer directly to the learning of precepts, namely the content of an academic environment; that students do exhibit the various mechanisms of learning posited by cognitive psychology, but applied to a poorly structured environment they result in poor learning, unless overridden by special strategies; that artificial mechanisms fail because they do not preserve the relations between content and feedback that exist in the natural environment from which they were transferred.

There are two remedies implicit in this account. One is to teach all students deep-level processing – which incidentally only gets them as far as apprehending the correct precepts, not learning them. The other is to reconstruct the academic environments we control so that they do afford learning. For this, we need help from psychology.

Our problem is that at present cognitive psychology produces generalized, not content-specific principles and theories of learning. The teacher needs help in reinterpreting these for specific content. They are usually derived from particular instances, which necessarily concern the learning of some particular content, but when they are generalized, the particular content is screened out. It would be better, from the educationalist's point of view, if some trace of the content were left there in the formulation of the principle, to make it possible to see what part it plays. A general principle that describes, for example, the importance of active manipulation, or of relating new knowledge to existing knowledge is no help because it does not clarify the logic of the relationship between the cognitive activity and the content to be learned. We need cognitive psychology to tell us, in a content-specific way, how a natural environment affords learning. Then, perhaps, we can construct the means of access that will turn an unnatural environment into one that affords learning.

References

Anderson, J.R. (1983) *The Architecture of Cognition* Harvard University Press

Dahlgren, L.O. and Marton, F. (1978) Students' conceptions of subject matter: An aspect of learning and teaching in higher education *Studies in Higher Education* 3, 25-35

Entwistle, N.J. (1974) Aptitude tests for higher education? *British Journal of Educational Psychology* 44 (1) 92-96

Gibson, J.J. (1979) *The Ecological Approach to Visual Perception* Houghton Mifflin

Koffka, K. (1924) *The Growth of the Mind* Routledge and Kegan Paul

Laurillard, D.M. (1983) *Some Phenomena of Learning from Television* AVMRG Report, Open University

Laurillard, D.M. (1984) Learning from problem-solving. In Marton et al. (1984)

Lewin, K. (1936) *The Principles of Topological Psychology* McGraw-Hill

Marton, F. (1976) On non-verbatim learning II. The erosion effect of a task-induced learning algorithm *Scandinavian Journal of Psychology* 17, 41-48

Marton, F., Hounsell, D. and Entwistle, N. (1984) *The Experience of Learning* Edinburgh: Scottish Academic Press

Marton, F. and Wenestam, C-G. (1979) Qualitative differences in the understanding and retention of the main point in some texts based on the principle-example structure. In M.M. Gruneberg, P.E. Morris and R.N. Sykes (Eds) *Practical Aspects of Memory* Academic Press

Merleau-Ponty, M. (1983) *The Structure of Behaviour* Beacon Press: Boston

Meyer, B.J.F. (1975) *The Organization of Prose and its Effects on Memory* Amsterdam: North-Holland

Miller C.M.L. and Parlett, M. (1974) *Up to the Mark. A study of the examination game* Guildford: SRHE

Schank, R.C. (1982) *Dynamic Memory* Cambridge University Press

19

'A Word is Worth a Thousand Pictures'

Michael W. Eysenck and David Warren Piper

The central issue of this book is the relationship between cognitive psychology and educational research and theory. As various contributors have
indicated, cognitive psychology has so far failed to have a major impact on
theory and research in higher education. At first glance, this is a puzzling
state of affairs. One of the main concerns of congitive psychology is with the
processes and skills involved in learning, memory, and problem solving, all of
which are of crucial significance in the education situation. It is true, of
course, that there is nothing like complete overlap between the interests of
cognitive psychologists and educational researchers. Educational researchers
investigate a wide range of factors that influence academic achievement,
including the teaching styles of the lecturing staff, the interests, motivations,
and goals of the student learner, and more general social and cultural
influences, whereas the focus of most cognitive psychologists is on a much
narrower set of variables that are directly implicated in the learning process.
Nevertheless, cognitive psychologists and educational researchers have a
number of mutual interests, and the failure of these to stimulate fruitful
interaction requires explanation.

Possible explanations are dealt with in the sections that follow. A review of
Diana Laurillard's attempt (Chapter. 18) to account for the schism is
followed by some alternative explanations of our own. Potential ways in
which educational research and practice might benefit from cognitive
psychology are then examined, and in the final section the analysis of student
learning is placed in the broader context of the educational system as a
whole.

Laurillard's Analysis

Natural vs. Unnatural Environments

Diana Laurillard argues that cognitive psychologists investigate learning of
the physical and social world (described as the 'natural environment',
whereas student learning deals with the world of academic ideas (referred to
as the 'unnatural environment'). Laurillard expresses the distinction

between the natural and unnatural environments in the following way: 'The natural and the unnatural environment are distinguished by the fact that the former provides knowledge of the world, the latter provides knowledge of descriptions of the world' (pp.200-201).

It is initially disconcerting to discover that cognitive psychologists investigate learning and memory in the natural environment, since one of the commonest criticisms of cognitive psychology relates to the extreme artificiality of most laboratory research. According to Neisser (1982):

> The psychologists who have spent a century studying esoteric forms of memory in the laboratory are not really uninterested in its more ordinary manifestations.... Their preference for artificial tasks has a rational basis: one can control variables and manipulate conditions more easily in the lab than in natural settings. (p. 12)

Part of the apparently wide gulf between the views of Laurillard and Neisser (1982) may be due to the different meanings that each attaches to the term 'natural'. Nevertheless, on almost any definition it seems incongruous to us to describe as a natural learning environment the sequential presention of 20 or 30 unrelated words at a rate of one per second.

There are other difficulties with the destinction between natural and unnatural environments. For instance, by lumping 'walking' and 'talking' together in the 'natural world', symbolic representation is included. The line therefore has to be drawn elsewhere to separate the academic from the natural world.

The starting point for Laurillard's distinction is J. J. Gibson's Theory of Affordance: the natural environment affords original perceptions and also affords the learning of more complex structures. But the learning of more complex structures does conceivably involve the automatic and unconscious application of *abstract* rules or concepts. So, the unconscious and automatic employment of implicit abstraction has to be seen as a 'natural' response to Laurillard's 'natural' world; yet she also argues that when academics seek to make implicit abstraction explicit, they contribute to an artificial environment. One could argue that making the implicit explicit introduces it to the experienced world, that is, into the natural domain, albeit in symbolical form. This would be compatible with other parts of Laurillard's argument where symbolic representation, whether language or red circles, are admitted to the natural environment.

Academics, argues Laurillard, deal in precepts, which differ from percepts and concepts in that they offer no 'affordance'. Concepts such as 'dog' and 'cat' and even 'conservation' are, she writes, experienced; whereas 'molecule' and 'structuralism' cannot be experienced. The problems of experiencing 'doggyness' are legion; Wittgenstein's example was 'game', which defies definition but nonetheless is a commonly held concept. Choosing 'molecule' as an example of a precept which cannot be experienced seems to overlook the degree to which people, when they imagine such entities, call upon what they have experienced so as to give such abstractions substance. Ping pong balls and gravity are dragooned into service to explain the molecule, much as images of man, in the name of God, are employed to encompass the inconceivable. And, while to Laurillard structuralism cannot be experienced like table manners, others might argue that that is precisely the way in which it is experienced: both being a protocol for going about a ritual task.

The efficacy of Laurillard's suggestion that natural mechanisms of mankind allow people to learn through perception, but not preception, is thrown into doubt. It is further unclear why the unnatural environment of academia should consist of lectures, texts, and *laboratory practicals* (p.202, our italics). We would argue that a laboratory experiment is often explicitly designed to provide a direct experience of the natural world, certainly a highly selected portion of the natural world, patently under controlled conditions, but nonetheless a natural phenomenon unmediated by language or symbolism.

What is Laurillard's unnatural environment then? It is not the man-made environment because a table affords the percept that it will support an object and hurt if walked into, just as well as a natural rock will. It is not the world of symbolism, nor yet the implicit made explicit. Is it then when experience is selected and controlled as in the laboratory experiment? That conclusion does not seem to forward Laurillard's discourse. One is led to conclude that there is no clear division between the natural and unnatural environments.

If, instead, the line is drawn between interactive and non-interactive communication, Laurillard's argument is sustained.

Perception and the Real World

Bishop Berkeley haunts the interstices of the stepping stones of Laurillard's argument. The logical impossibility of mankind consciously experiencing any environment except through percepts is not acknowledged. And so the power of culture to provide those abstractions by which we shape our experience of the world around us is missed. 'It would be surprising if someone were unable to recognize the figure and the ground in a painting like the Mona Lisa', says Laurillard. For us, the surprise is that they do. Even accepting a Gestaltist belief in an inherent tendency to organize the visual field into figure and ground, it still takes experience, dare one say learn-ing, to perceive the real world in such artifice as painting. (And further training to perceive the configuration of pigments that creates the illusion.) Central to any culture are those abstractions passed on in symbolic form from one generation to the next which fashion the world of experience. The mathematics of the scientist enable students in the laboratory to interpret, see, perceive, put significance to what they observe. The model of a text (principle – example, main argument – evidence, generalization — instance) is the organizer which allows the student to perceive the principle as being both distinct from the rest of the text and of primary significance to the educational purpose of the reading exercise. In the realm of perception there is no distinction between natural and unnatural worlds; and there is no difference between the natural and the academic environments, one affording experience and the other not. Social perception in the cave is the same as in the common room. And such is the lesson of psychology, and, what is more, that branch of psychology to which J. J. Gibson has made a significant contribution.

Abstraction and Extrinsic Goals

There is a form of artificiality common in contrived education which Laurillard discusses (pp.203-5). Teachers do devise artificial learning experiences and provide artificial rewards and punishments. However, a distinction might be made here. When a student is learning to use a computer by sitting at a keyboard, the educational goal is intrinsic to the *activity*; the same goal is extrinsic to the activity of sitting in a lecture room and being told how to use the keyboard. That is rather different from the case which Laurillard cites, where the reward being offered, such as passing an examination, is extrinsic to the learning *goal*. All too easily, as Laurillard points out, these artificial devices for rewarding learning reinforce trivial activity, leading students to seek success in terms of an artificially created reward system which may overshadow, mask, and sometimes exclude the kind of learning which is accorded a greater value, even by those teachers whose contrivances undermine it. But Laurillard takes a further step, and sees these failures in education as an inevitable evil of constructing an unnatural environment. Rather, such failures might be seen as the inexpert use of the very facilities which allow mankind to build a civilization through successive generations. For it is the very use of artificial learning activities, to which the educational aims must be extrinsic, that has allowed mankind to short-circuit the necessity of each generation learning the way of the world afresh. The adoption of artificial rewards for activity to which goals are extrinsic is, therefore, not the key issue. The reward of irrelevant and trivial activity is.

By using language and symbolism we are able to give learners direct access to concepts, generalizations, theory so that it is unnecessary for them to be experienced firsthand. In Laurillard's example, the firsthand experience of circular and square things, red and blue things is not necessary in conceiving the idea of a 'red circle' if it may be described in other terms. Furthermore, it is at least questionable whether encountering the shapes and colours unmediated by language would be sufficient experience to ensure the formation of those particular concepts; it is not clear that circles and redness are such self-evident categories that they would universally be alighted upon and accorded significance without them being related to language or to some universal utility. Such abstractions or generalizations are potent precisely because they provide access to negotiating the natural environment; indeed, their potency is dependent upon the extent to which they provide access to the environment through the mediation of perception. J. K. Galbraith, at the beginning of a television series on economics, reviewed the impressive array of devices the studio had made available to help him: pictures, charts, animated sequences, models, games and actors who through mime and plays would illustrate economic principles at work. 'And if all that fails,' he confided, 'I can always explain it to you; after all a word is worth a thousand pictures.'

So teaching the abstract is a very economic way of helping people learn about the natural environment. It is a precious means to a universal end, and education becomes purposeless when the means gets separated from the end. Then academic learning becomes a pejorative term because it denotes an empty ritual. An example would be engineering students being set to learn the relations between the molecular structure of polymers and their physical properties, but the practical significance of this classification for simplifying the hunt for appropriate materials for machine parts being overlooked — or, rather, taken for granted.

Such 'academicization' of a subject, rendering it entirely into the abstract, does seem to conjure up an unreal world; although to call it an academic environment which students are invited to inhabit perhaps attributes to it a pervasiveness greater than it has (except perhaps for the mad). But even this academic dreamland can be negotiated without recourse to deep-level processing, provided the academics will talk to the students. Only if the academic discourse is immutable, the text linear, the programme unbranching, is that peculiar adaptation to impoverished communication required.

Success and Failure

Laurillard suggests that the main concern of cognitive psychologists is to explain the successes of human cognition, whereas that of educationists is usually to account for failures to learn. We doubt the assumption about cognitive psychologists. A striking counter-example is the very extensive research on the Wason selection task (see Eysenck 1984), a task on which the failures greatly exceed the successes; indeed, only four or five per cent of university students solve the problem correctly with the standard version of the task. And Bartlett (1932) put forward a very influential theory of memory which laid particular emphasis on the systematic errors and distortions that frequently characterize long-term memory. In research, we believe, the very mechanisms of cognition are explored by testing where they fail. In the same way that failures in logic (à la Wason) give insight into the normal processes of thought, so does the study of illusion facilitate an understanding of normal visual perception.

We would propose alternatives to Laurillard's explanation of the profound differences that exist between cognitive psychologists and educational researchers.

Alternative Analyses

Origins and Scale of Research

Two major differences between the concerns of psychologists and of educationalists relate to scale and purpose. The cognitive psychologists' primary focus is the building of a coherent and elegant theory. Questions are raised when rival theoretical explanations exist for what is observed, or when what is observed is not explicable in the current theory. The scale of the resultant investigation is minute; for example, the order in which subjects turn over a series of cards designed to reveal a principle of classification, or how a sentence is processed, or how precisely stated problems are solved. For the educationalist questions are raised when professional practice fails. The problems do not arise from unsatisfactory theory, but from unsatisfactory practice. The scale is large: why students fail courses, don't understand books, get dispirited by educational regimes inflicted upon them, or fail to perceive that a problem exists. The relationship of theory to practice differs in these two circumstances, and has been explored elsewhere (eg Travers 1962; Nesbit and Broadfoot 1980; Warren Piper 1981).

Processes and Reductionism

Differences in the scale and origins of research are by no means the only salient differences between cognitive psychologists and educationists. Many cognitive psychologists (but relatively few educationists) are especially interested in identifying the processes and mechanisms that combine to produce task performance. A prime example comes in research on the Sternberg task, in which subjects have to decide as rapidly as possible whether a probe item matches any of a small number of items that have just been memorized. Despite the fact that subjects usually respond to the probe in less than one second, Sternberg (1969) argued that reaction time is affected by the times taken to complete each of four separate processing stages: encoding the probe; serial comparison of the probe against each of the memorized items; response decision; and response selection and evocation. This attention to the fine grain of cognitive processing is in marked contrast to the concerns of educational researchers, who tend to be more interested in the end product of a learning experience than in the intervening processes.

From this perspective, the crucial issue is whether the identification of processes or mechanisms by cognitive psychologists can be of use to educational researchers. There is some plausibility in the reductionist notion that research at a molecular level can provide explanations at a more molar level (eg, physiological findings may clarify our understanding of psychological phenomena). However, reductionism typically provides very limited explanations. One may go further, and argue that in many cases a molecular account is simply irrelevant to phenomena at a molar level. For example, carpenters and physicists may both have a detailed understanding of wood, but the physicist's knowledge of the atomic structure of wood is of essentially no relevance to the carpenter.

It is entirely possible that the relationship between cognitive psychology and educational research is not as fruitless as that between the physicist and the carpenter. Nevertheless, there is little evidence as yet that the dissection of small-scale tasks into their constituent processing stages has anything very much to offer educationists. However, an increasing number of cognitive psychologists are pursuing research interests that do seem of potential relevance to educational practice, and some of these success stories will be discussed below.

Potential Relevance of Cognitive Psychology

Common Language

Cognitive psychology provides the potential for a common language for describing both the subject matter of academic courses and the processes of learning. Behaviourist psychology could never do that because it deliberately eschewed, or at least postponed, consideration of the intervening mental processes that connect stimulus with response, seeking first to establish empirical correlations. Thus, the emphasis was on the conditions under which learning takes place and the measures of learning were those most easily quantified. Typically, a Behaviourist psychologist asked 'how much is remembered?' rather than 'what are the qualities of what is remembered?' So, when applied to education, Behaviourism has led to theories of instruction rather than theories of learning: learning is better when feedback is given, rewards and punishment discriminate desirable from undesirable behaviours, and so forth. Although this can lead to a taxonomy of types of learning, it is a category system couched in terms quite other than those required to analyse subject matter. By contrast, cognitive models describe types of knowledge and so can be used to analyse subject matter. A physics syllabus can be parsed in accordance with Perry's scheme. Exam questions can be tested to check whether they 'remind' students of something they have learned. The task of recalling knowledge, of seeing a particular as an instance of a general category, can be separated from the original act of conception. Cognitive psychology leads directly to a language of epistemology and so does the analysis of an academic discipline.

Learning and Memory

Not surprisingly, much research on student learning has focused on the relative effectiveness of different learning strategies. This general approach has been followed in a number of the studies reported in this book, and it clearly is a sensible approach. The usual experimental procedure is to instruct one group of students in the use of one learning strategy, and a different group of students in some other learning strategy. After both groups have been given an equal opportunity to acquire the learning material, some form of test or examination is given to ascertain which learning strategy is more effective.

This method of comparing two learning strategies suffers from clear limitations as far as cognitive psychology is concerned. A learner's ability to remember what has been learned depends not only on the processes occurring at the time of learning, but also on the information that is provided at the time of retrieval (Tulving 1983). Thus, it is entirely possible that one learning strategy could appear more effective if one form of retention test were used, whereas the other learning strategy might triumph with a different retention test. Consider, for example, the task of learning six new concepts (eg, 'Crinch: To make someone angry by performing an inappropriate act'). Nitsch (1977) investigated two different learning approaches on this task. After all of the subjects had been given all of the concepts and their definitions, they were asked to identify examples of each concept. For half of the subjects (the same-context subjects) all of the examples for each concept related to a particular context, whereas for the remaining subjects (the varied-order subjects) a number of different contexts were used with each concept.

Which approach produced better learning? If learning is appropriately measured by the ability to name the concepts when presented with examples of them, then the same-context subjects learned much better than the varied-context subjects. However, on a subsequent transfer test with examples based on completely new contexts, the varied-context subjects identified the concept correctly more often than the same-context subjects (84 per cent versus 67 per cent respectively). Thus, it cannot be argued that different measures of learning will produce the same basic findings. The level of remembering depends critically on the relevance of what has been learned to the kind of memory test that is used.

In sum, the finding that the conditions of learning often interact with conditions of testing in determining memory performance is an important one that has relevance for much research into student learning. If it is ignored, there is a grave danger of erroneous conclusions being drawn from inadequate data.

Motivation and Emotion

One of the most important differences between research in cognitive psychology and in student learning is in the emphasis placed on motivational and emotional factors. While educationalists disagree among themselves on many issues, they would probably nearly all subscribe to the view that effective student learning requires appropriate motivational and emotional states. Powerful evidence of the importance of motivation in everyday learning has been marshalled by Howe (Chapter 12). In contrast, cognitive psychologists rarely consider motivational or emotional factors at all, a fact which one of us (Eysenck 1984) has recently bemoaned. Cognitive psychologists typically attempt to ensure that their subjects are well motivated and reasonably unemotional, and their failure to manipulate motivational and emotional states means that they do not know whether cognitive performance is affected by motivation and emotion.

However, recent evidence from the laboratory within the motivational-emotional area seems of real relevance for education. One starting point has been Gray's (1973) hypothesis that introverts are especially susceptible to negative reinforcement and punishment, whereas extraverts are particularly affected by reward. This hypothesis has received reasonable support from laboratory studies, and McCord and Wakefield (1981) decided to test it in a classroom setting over a period of eight weeks. They established by means of observation the consistent individual differences among teachers in their use of praise and punishment in the classroom, and obtained a highly significant interaction between the effects of the teacher's teaching strategy and of student personality upon academic achievement. Extraverts learned best when taught by a teacher who provided mostly praise and other forms of positive reinforcement, whereas introverts learned best when taught by a teacher who provided a fair amount of punishment. The great magnitude of these effects demonstrates beyond peradventure the need to consider motivational factors in predicting academic achievement. The findings also indicate that an adequate understanding of the effects of motivational factors on learning requires consideration of individual differences in personality.

Deci (1975) has proposed a theoretical approach to motivation which is based on laboratory research, but which is of relevance to student learning, arguing that one should distinguish between extrinsic and intrinsic motivation. Extrinsic motivation involves the use of external rewards (eg praise, money), whereas intrinsic motivation involves no apparent reward other than the performance of a given task with the associated internal feelings of competence and self-determination. Some educationalists seem to assume that one of the aims of effective teaching is to increase the motivation of the learner by seeking to maximize extrinsic and intrinsic motivation independently, on the assumption that both motivational factors simply summate to determine the overall level of motivation. However, Deci argues persuasively that matters are more complex than that. Intrinsic and extrinsic motivation are not independent of each other, and increasing extrinsic motivation (eg, by offering a financial incentive) can actually lead to reduced intrinsic motivation, as Perry (1981) has noted. According to Deci, intrinsically motivated behaviour is regarded by the individual as self-determined. The provision of external rewards often alters the perceived locus of causality, making the people concerned feel that they are motivated solely by the external rewards and not by internal factors. In other words, the individual feels like a 'pawn' being controlled by external agencies, and these feelings of being manipulated dissipate intrinsic motivation.

The experimental evidence (reviewed by Eysenck 1984) broadly supports Deci's theoretical position, but has added a further complexity. While it is perfectly true that external rewards and incentives frequently reduce intrinsic motivation, there are a number of exceptions. Feelings of competence are an important aspect of intrinsic motivation, and external rewards which serve to strengthen feelings of competence can actually lead to enhanced intrinsic motivation.

One of the limitations of the approach adopted by Deci (1975) is that he paid relatively little attention to the possibility that the effects of motivation on performance might depend importantly on the nature of the task being performed. Hockey (1983) pioneered the approach of attempting to provide a sketch-map of the performance consequences of incentive manipulations, an approach that was taken further by Eysenck (1984). Incentives typically increase attentional selectivity, increase the capacity of short-term storage, increase distractability, increase performance speed but decrease accuracy, and have no effect on long-term memory or the efficiency of retrieval. From this sketch-map one can predict reasonably well the effects of incentive on any given task. Performance will be improved if the task primarily demands short-term storage and speed of processing, but will be impaired if the task requires extreme accuracy or involves conditions of distraction.

In sum, laboratory-based research into motivational and emotional phenomena has identified a number of important principles that could well be applied to the task of improving the efficiency of student learning. In the case of individual differences in susceptibility to reward and to punishment, the translation from the laboratory to the classroom has already occurred, and the similarity of the findings obtained in the two settings is dramatic.

The Broad Perspective

Why is it quite reasonable for academics, within their own legitimate terms, to proceed with no recourse to educational theory or the professional training of a teacher? The answer is elegantly expounded by Desmond Ryan (Chapter

17) and illustrated by Paul Ramsden and his colleagues (Chapter 15). If all subjects have their own epistemology then it is only too easy for lecturers to dismiss the claims of educationists as being unsoundly based. So the findings of educational research are seen either as obvious, if they coincide with the individual's own experience, or wrong, if they do not. This commonly leads to a curious and contradictory argument being advanced. The way in which the student has to learn about, say, physics or engineering, it is claimed, is peculiar to the subject, because the criteria by which good evidence is distinguished from bad and truth from falsehood is the very basis of the discipline. It is accepted that such is the case for all subjects. All, that is, except the one which refuses to stay in its own discrete territory. When education brings its methods of analysis and applies its criteria of rigour to investigating how physics or engineering is taught, then it is asked to justify itself, not against its own paradigms of veracity, but rather against those of the subject matter being taught. And many times one hears lecturers claiming that students must learn their particular subject in a way unique to that subject whilst also insisting that they themselves will only entertain learning about education if it abandons its internal rationality in favour of that with which the lecturer is most familiar from his own subject. Of course, some will acknowledge the ultimate dream of Science to reduce everything to that one all-encompassing principle – but not yet, Dear Lord, not yet; until then You (or the Blissfulness of Ignorance) are sufficient.

Are we seeking to be one step nearer that Ultimate Unity when we wish to integrate the theories of the cognitive psychologist and those of the educationist? If we are, is that a good idea? Well, yes and no. Yes, when we act as theory builders (academics); no, when we try to offer help to the practitioner. Provided, that is, that we regard the practitioner as the professional rather than the craftsman. For the craftsman has to learn what to do and is judged by the way he does it, the end result following inevitably from correctly undertaken procedures: doing the job in the right way leads to the right results. The professional, by contrast, has to deal with the unforeseeable, where his actions do not inevitably have the same effect (as, for example, when we teach). He draws, therefore, on theory to inform his actions in novel situations. Thus professional training his three elements: theory, operative skills and evaluation. The purpose of the theory is precisely that discussed earlier in this chapter: to help people form perceptions about matters so complex (eg, why a student is failing to learn) that without the theory their understanding would remain inchoate. Now, the job of the trainer of professionals is to help them with the Here and Now. The larger the number of theories and the greater their diversity, the more varied can be the ways in which the practitioner can interpret events. Such variety is important because until that great and glorious day when the secret of the universe is unlocked within one all-encompassing principle, each of our theories, those partial models of reality, reveals *one* truth, but not The Truth. So, a theory which gives an insight into Jack's difficulties of learning, and is sufficiently accurate for remedial action to be effective, may totally fail to explain Jill's problems. Thus it is that failure is the rule in teaching and that professionalism resides in having another theory to try when the first is found wanting. What the practical teacher needs is more theories, not fewer. Because Marton and Entwistle (eg, Marton et al. 1984) deliberately pick up their threads from Wertheimer does not mean that the Behaviourist theories are to be ignored. Found wanting, yes: just as the Gestaltists were found wanting by the Behaviourists.

Calling on incompatible theories does not denote weakness of spirit or lack of clear thought (although both these things can lead to such an end). Rather, it is thinking at or above Perry's (1981) Position 5 (see Chapter 1), where truth is seen as contextual and relativistic. Theories, our view of the world, are man-made; they are a product of human brains.

Even though competing theories can in themselves be clear and coherent, we should not seek to ban ambiguity altogether; we should also learn to relish it. Relish, that is, not that form of ambiguity which comes from muddled thinking and irresolution, but the kind that captures the many facets of a truth and which allows us to delight in complexity. Even in science we should delight in irony as one of the highest forms of expression and having nothing whatsoever to do with sarcasm. Through a rich multiplicity of understanding, both Art and Science can reinvigorate the familiar by changing the mind of the perceiver and thus the perception. The natural environment changes when we do. Why else does history exist?

Yes, let us have more interaction between psychologists and educationalists, let us bring them into one discourse and when we act as academics let us seek to reconcile contradictory theories by replacing both; but, as practitioners and lovers of mystery, let us enjoy the different epistemologies, indeed call in more, such as those inherent in, say, literary criticism.

Literary criticism is indeed a prime candidate, a point which Desmond Ryan makes (Chapter 17): psychology might be regarded as the basic of the social sciences and textual criticism has moved into its sphere. Cognitive psychology is as reductionist as one can be in psychology; after that, it becomes biochemistry and physics. So cognitive psychology is the epicentre of all our work; those of us in education should not lose touch with it, and if we are not psychologists now, we had best set about becoming so.

It was argued above that cognitive psychology might one day provide a common language for describing the content of academic courses and the processes of learning. If matters progressed so that psychological and educational theory were combined, would this amalgamated theory become a means to academic teachers' ends? And if it did, would they see it as such? Would the relevance of such a theory to teachers' legitimate ends be so plain that they would avidly learn it and incorporate it into their world view and their view of the subject? The answer to all three questions must be 'no'. For though an all-embracing theory may well improve their ability to teach, such increased capacity will remain only a potential unless their opportunity and incentive to teach are also attended to. All three are necessary ingredients of change. Ability alone does not change practice (unless the joy of its exercise is so great in comparison with all other motives that all barriers are swept aside, all opportunities taken).

Finally, let us consider the wider context in which students learn and we teach. The educational system serves many purposes for many people. The actual learning of course material may form a very small part of the benefits students derive from involvement in the system. Similarly, helping students to learn better may be an even smaller element in the satisfaction a staff member gains from joining the collegium.

Students may take a subject, not because they want to study and understand it, but because they want to *have* studied it and be able to apply it. They may be at college to please their parents, or because the tide of events carried them there, or because the alternative may seem worse or they wanted three years without responsibility, or because they needed to get away from home, or because they wanted to be respected or simply noticed by their teachers. Learning more effectively is not going to improve any of those goals, and as reasons for being in the educational system, they may outweigh the wish to learn.

Staff join universities and polytechnics for a myriad of reasons other than the joy of teaching: the research, the exercise of power, freedom to control their own time, the status, their inadequacy of coping elsewhere, the fear of leaving when they graduate; all may play their part. Even the joys of teaching might reside in the respect or admiration awarded by disciples. Becoming good at teaching or understanding how others learn may add little to the well-being of the teachers.

Thus, improving learning may make an infinitesimal difference to the overall benefit to either students or staff.

Other matters are political and ephemeral. Even commonplace assumptions like the primacy of 'the course' are products of our time. When students went to university to 'read a subject', it was not to follow a pre-set course. The question of their efficiency in learning a set syllabus simply did not arise. Nowadays our thinking about education is so dominated by 'the course' that the need for it is taken absolutely for granted, and uncritically we adopt progress through it as an unquestionable measure of success.

In our view, research in higher education and research in cognitive psychology, in progress and developing, is indeed of mutual concern and advantage. However, interaction between the two on the subject of student learning, as exemplified by the discovery that some students learn things by heart so as not to fail their exams, while others look for significance and want to succeed in their own terms, is still, in the whole brew of higher education, as yet rather small beer.

References

Bartlett, F.C. (1932) *Remembering: A Study in Experimental and Social Psychology* Cambridge: Cambridge University Press

Deci, E.L. (1975) *Intrinsic Motivation* London: Plenum

Eysenck, M.W. (1984) *A Handbook of Cognitive Psychology* London: Erlbaum

Gray, J.A. (1973) Causal theories of personality and how to test them. In J. R. Royce (Ed.) *Multivariate Analysis of Psychological Theory* New York: Academic Press

Hockey, R. (1983) Current issues and new directions. In R. Hockey (Ed.) *Stress and Fatigue in Human Performance* Chichester: Wiley

Marton, F., Hounsell, D. and Entwistle, N. J. (1984) *The Experience of Learning* Edinburgh: Scottish Academic Press

McCord, R. R. and Wakefield, J. A. (1981) Arithmetic achievement as a function of introversion-extraversion and teacher-presented reward and punishment *Personality and Individual Differences* 2, 145-152

Neisser, U. (1982) Memory: What are the important questions? In U. Neisser (Ed.) *Memory Observed: Remembering in Natural Contexts* San Francisco: Freeman

Nesbit, J. and Broadfoot, P. (1980) *The Impact of Research on Policy and Practice in Education* Aberdeen: Aberdeen University Press

Nitsch, K.E. (1977) *Structuring Decontextualized Forms of Knowledge* Unpublished PhD thesis, Vanderbilt University, Nashville, Tennessee

Perry, W.G., Jr. (1981) Cognitive and ethical growth: The making of meaning. In Chickering, A.W. and Associates *The Modern American College: Responding to the New Realities of Diverse Students and a Changing Society* 76-116. San Francisco : Jossey-Bass

Sternberg, S. (1969) The discovery of processing stages: Extensions to Donders' method *Acta Psychologica* 30, 276-315

Travers, R.M.W. (1962) A study of the relationship of psychological research to educational practice. In R. Glaser (Ed.) *Training, Research, and Education* Chichester: Wiley

Tulving, E. (1983) *Elements of Episodic Memory* Oxford: Oxford University Press

Warren Piper, D. J. (1981) The application of theory in higher education. In R. Oxtoby (Ed.) *Higher Education at the Cross Roads* Guildford: SRHE

Author Index

Subject Index

The Society for Research into Higher Education

The Society exists both to encourage and co-ordinate research into all aspects of higher education, including academic, organizational and policy issues; and also to provide a forum for debate, verbal and printed. Through its activities it draws attention to the significance of research into, and development in, higher education and the needs of scholars in this field. (It is not concerned with research generally, except, for instance, as a subject of study.)

The Society's income derives from subscriptions, book sales, conferences and specific grants. It is wholly independent. Its corporate members are institutions of higher education, research institutions and professional, industrial, and governmental bodies. Its individual members include teachers and researchers, administrators and students. Members are found in all parts of the world and the Society regards its international work as amongst its most important activities.

The Society discusses and comments on policy, organizes conferences and encourages research. Under the imprint SRHE and Open University Press, it is a specialist publisher of research, having some 40 titles in print. It also publishes Studies in Higher Education (three times a year), which is mainly concerned with academic issues, Higher Education Quarterly (formerly Universities Quarterly), mainly concered with policy issues, Research into Higher Education Abstracts (three times a year), International Newsletter (twice a year), the Bulletin (six times a year); and, jointly with the committee for Research into Teacher Education (CRITE), Evaluation Newsletter (twice a year).

The Society's committees, study groups and branches are run by members (with help from a small staff at Guildford), and aim to provide a forum for discussion. The groups at present include a Teacher Education Study Group, a Staff Development Group, a Women in Higher Education Group and a Continuing Education Group; these may have their own organization, subscriptions or publications (e.g. the Staff Development Newsletter). The Governing Council, elected by members, comments on current issues; and discusses policies with leading figures, notably at its evening Forums. The Society organizes seminars on current research for officials of the Department of Education and Science and other ministries, and an Anglo-American series on standards. It is in touch with bodies in the UK such as the NAB, CVCP, UGC, CNAA and the British Council; and with sister bodies overseas. Its current research projects include one on the relationship between entry qualifications and degree results directed by Professor W.D. Furneaux (Brunel) and one on 'Questions of Quality', directed by Professor G.C. Moodie (York). A project on the evaluation of the research standing of university departments is in preparation. The Society's conferences are often held jointly. Annual Conferences have considered 'Professional Education' (1984) and 'Continuing Education' (1985, with Goldsmiths' College), 'Standards and Criteria in Higher Education' (1986, with Bulmersche CHE), 'Restructuring' (1987, with the City of Brimingham Polytechnic) and 'Academic Freedom' (1988, with the University of Surrey). Other conferences have considered the DES Green Paper (1985, with the Times Higher Education Supplement), and The First-Year Experience (1986 & 7 with the University of South Carolina and Newcastle Polytechnic). For some of the Society's conferences, special studies are commissioned in advance, as 'Precedings'.

Members receive free of charge the Society's Abstracts annual conference Proceedings (or 'Precedings'), Bulletin and International Newsletter and may buy SRHE and Open University Press, books, and Higher Educational Quarterly at booksellers' discount. Corporate members also receive the Society's journal, Studies in Higher Education, free (to individuals at a heavy discount). Corporate members also obtain Evaluation Newsletter and certain other journals at a discount, including the NFER Register of Educational Research. There is a substantial discount to members, and to staff of corporate members, on annual and some other conference fees.

Further information	SRHE, at the University, Guildford, 6U2 5XH, U.K. (0483)–39003,
Catalogue	SRHE & OPEN UNIVERSITY PRESS 12 Cofferidge Close Stoney Stratford, Milton Keynes MK11 1BY (0908) 666744